Publish Your Nonfiction Book is a useful, accessible, and timely resource that provides excellent guidance and insider advice for prospective authors. Perhaps most importantly, it demystifies the often mazelike publishing process, making it possible for writers with talent and ambition to get their work into print.

> —Jason Prince, Vice President, Publisher, Sterling Publishing

Publish Your Nonfiction Book is practical, straight-forward, helpful, and tells the truth about publishing! This is the perfect guide to go from dream to reality on your publishing journey. Highly recommended.

> —Joel Fotinos, Publisher, Tarcher/Penguin

If getting published is your plan, take note of a few things: Mere talent isn't enough. Neither is tenacity. You need tools. In this insiders' guide, Martin and Flacco open up their specialty kit of wrenches, calipers, and pneumatic nail guns. You'll find all you need here to get started with building your literary career.

> —Joel Miller, Vice President of Editorial & Acquisitions, Thomas Nelson

Martin and Flacco's book is your insider's guide to getting published in the turbulent world of a book business in transition. It's filled with good tips and techniques, but, best of all, it never minimizes the hard work, discipline, and perseverance that it takes to be a good writer.

> —Alan Rinzler, Executive Editor, Jossey-Bass/John Wiley & Sons

Having been in book publishing for almost forty years, I've always been surprised at the dearth of thoughtful, insightful, and informative books on the integral things a writer needs to know about publishing a nonfiction book. Well, now I've found what I think is the best book of its kind, and one that can make a tremendous difference in the lives of writers and writers-to-be. In _Publish Your Nonfiction Book_, Martin and Flacco use their years of experience and their insiders' understanding to provide an easy-to-follow path to building a successful career in a volatile and competitive marketplace. It will become an invaluable classic on any writer's bookshelf.

> —Roger Cooper, Vice President, Publisher, Vanguard Press

When I see a submission from Sharlene Martin and Martin Literary Management, I sit at attention. From pitch to proposal to finished project, Sharlene always hits the mark. She and Anthony, both at the top of their game, consistently deliver commercial, well-positioned, riveting work. So whether you are just getting started or facing your hundredth rejection, this book will help you experience the inside track and professional wisdom that can take you one step closer to publishing success.

—Michele Matrisciani, Editorial Director, HCI Books

For every aspiring writer—even for authors with a book under their belt—*Publish Your Nonfiction Book* will prove an essential guide through the entire publishing process. Sharlene Martin and Anthony Flacco cover all the bases—sizing up today's media landscape; how to write and submit the best queries; and dissecting book proposals that publishers have acquired. I have published many books on books, and this is one of the most useful handbooks I've ever seen. I will recommend it to all my authors.

—Philip Turner, Philip Turner Book Productions

Anyone who has ever dreamed of writing a book must read this one first. A rare blend of publishing wisdom and psychotherapeutic sensitivity, it leads you through today's realities without bursting your bubble. It's as essential as a dictionary for everyone, from the wanna-be writer to the best-selling author!

—Carole Lieberman, M.D., Media Psychiatrist and Best-Selling Author

Publish Your Nonfiction Book is sure to become essential reading for aspiring writers. Clear, concise, and well written, the book's enjoyable step-by-step approach is as accessible as it is appealing. Martin and Flacco have written a useful reference for newcomers to the world of publishing.

—Airie Stuart, Senior Vice President, Publisher, Palgrave MacMillan

Sharlene Martin and Anthony Flacco have used their considerable experience as a successful literary agent and widely published writer, respectively, to demystify the publishing process for nonfiction books in a way that any writer will find to be informative and enlightening. *Publish Your Nonfiction Book* clearly explains the process unlike any other book that I know about. I'll be recommending it to writers that I work with.

—William Shinker, President, Publisher, Gotham and Avery Books

PUBLISH YOUR NONFICTION BOOK

STRATEGIES FOR LEARNING
THE INDUSTRY, SELLING
YOUR BOOK, AND BUILDING
A SUCCESSFUL CAREER

W

WRITER'S DIGEST BOOKS

www.writersdigest.com
Cincinnati, Ohio

SHARLENE MARTIN AND **ANTHONY FLACCO**

For more resources for writers, visit www.writersdigest.com/books.

To receive a free weekly e-mail newsletter delivering tips and updates about writing and about Writer's Digest products, register directly at http://newsletters.fwmedia.com.

13 12 11 10 09   5 4 3 2 1

Distributed in Canada by Fraser Direct, 100 Armstrong Avenue, Georgetown, Ontario, Canada L7G 5S4, Tel: (905) 877-4411. Distributed in the U.K. and Europe by David & Charles, Brunel House, Newton Abbot, Devon, TQ12 4PU, England, Tel: (+44) 1626-323200, Fax: (+44) 1626-323319, E-mail: postmaster@ davidandcharles.co.uk. Distributed in Australia by Capricorn Link, P.O. Box 704, Windsor, NSW 2756 Australia, Tel: (02) 4577-3555.

Library of Congress Cataloging-in-Publication Data

Martin, Sharlene.

 Publish your nonfiction book : strategies for learning the industry, selling your book, and building a successful career / Sharlene Martin and Anthony Flacco.

    p. cm. *4259 2716 3/10*
Includes index.

ISBN 978-1-58297-578-8 (pbk. : alk. paper)

1. Authorship--Marketing. 2. Authors and publishers. 3. Book proposals. 4. Queries (Authorship) I. Flacco, Anthony. II. Title.

PN161.M376 2009

070.5'2--dc22   2009021653

Designed by Claudean Wheeler

Production coordinated by Mark Griffin

DEDICATION

Sharlene Martin

This book is dedicated to my mother, Ruth Levin, who always made me believe I could be as successful in life as I ever wanted to be. I am inspired daily by her memory and am grateful to have had such a role model.

I also dedicate this to my partner, in all senses of the word, Anthony Flacco, whose support has been unwavering for over sixteen years—both personally and professionally.

And, to my children, Jill and Scott, who have made the gift of motherhood the most rewarding life experience of all.

Anthony Flacco

My family, my partner, and my C.O.D.L.s (cats-of-doglike-loyalty) are my foundation, and I am grateful for them. But I dedicate this book to every one of you who lose sleep at night because you are burning with something that you have to say, and you are convinced that you can write a book that matters. The world needs to hear from you, whether it knows it or not.

ACKNOWLEDGMENTS

We would like to thank Lisa Wysocky for her assistance with the manuscript. She is a trusted editorial eye, a great writing client, and a true friend. We also thank Hannah Im, our intern from the University of Washington. She was invaluable in helping to proof and evaluate this manuscript and has a great future in publishing.

To our family of friends at Writer's Digest: editor Kelly Nickell, along with Jane Friedman, Chuck Sambuchino, and Greg Hatfield—thanks for your belief and faith in our message. We'll say it again here: No one comes out of the womb a published author—someone always gives you that first chance. Special thanks from Sharlene to Writer's Digest for giving her that chance through their magazine and with this book.

Several clients of Martin Literary Management graciously allowed their words and stories to be part of the case studies of this book: Lisa Wysocky, Brad Cohen, Dr. Stan Kapuchinski, Suzanne Hansen, Amanda Lamb, Jeffrey

Ford, Janet Horn, Robin Miller, Ron Saxen, Keith and Brooke Desserich, and Jennifer Taggert.

We also thank Richard Curtis of Richard Curtis Associates. Sharlene loves telling the story of how he "saved" her from her first auction. He is a generous man with a knowledge of this industry that is unparalleled, and we're both grateful for the "jump-start."

Special acknowledgments to The Mouthinator, Justin Loeber, who has become a dear friend whose wisdom is truly appreciated.

We'd also like to thank the following for their contributions to the research: Justin Loeber, president of Mouth Public Relations; Michael Fragnito, vice president and editorial director of Sterling Publishing Co.; Heidi Krupp-Lisiten, CEO and founder of Krupp Kommunications (K2); Peter Lynch, Editorial Manager—Trade, Sourcebooks, Inc.; Christina Katz, author of *Get Known Before the Book Deal*; Michaela Hamilton, editor in chief of Citadel Press, and executive editor at Kensington Publishing Corp.; Neville L. Johnson, media attorney; Ian Kleinert of Objective Entertainment; Marji Ross, president and publisher of Regnery Publishing, Inc.; Kimberley Cameron, president of Reece HalseyNorth/Paris/New York; Adam Chromy, literary manager and founder of Artists and Artisans, Inc.; Scott Hoffman at Folio Literary Management, LLC; Jamie Brenner, agent with Artists and Artisans, Inc; John Willig, president of and literary agent at LiteraryServicesInc.com; Lisa Kaufman, marketing director and senior editor at PublicAffairs; Gene Taft of GT/PR LLC; Jane Wesman of Jane Wesman Public Relations, Inc.; Lynn Goldberg, CEO of GoldbergMcDuffie Communications; Jill Danzig, president of Danzig Communications; Marika Flatt, founder of PR by the Book; Mary Gleysteen, events coordinator, Eagle Harbor Book Company; and Kate Siegel Bandos, founder and chief publicist at KSB Promotions.

And to all the publishers, editors, publicists, and writers that we work with day in and day out: heartfelt thanks for your trust and support.

ABOUT THE AUTHORS

Sharlene Martin

Sharlene Martin is the founder of Martin Literary Management, a West Coast nonfiction literary management company. A rapidly growing list of sales to most major publishers and to a host of independent publishers of specialized genre books demonstrates her remarkable rise in the publishing industry. Her agency's motto is "Considerate literary management for the twenty-first century," and she brings those words to life every day with her clients and colleagues in the publishing industry. She is a staunch advocate for great emerging writers and, as such, serves as a member of the advisory board for the Writing Certificate Program at the University of Washington in Seattle. For more, see www.MartinLiteraryManagement.com.

Anthony Flacco

This is Anthony Flacco's sixth book as a writer of fiction and nonfiction, with a list of publishers such as Bantam/Dell Books, St. Martin's Press, Ballantine Books at Random House, and Sterling Publications. He has also written articles on a variety of subjects for such diverse places as *Reader's Digest, Stars and Stripes*, and numerous literary websites and blogs. He serves as an editorial consultant for Martin Literary Management. His freelance work as a ghostwriter and story editor has brought novice writers of numerous books through the writing process to final publication. Additionally, he is an experienced public speaker who frequently gives seminars on writing. For more, see www.AnthonyFlacco.com.

TABLE OF CONTENTS

INTRODUCTION

The purpose of this book is to demystify today's mainstream publication process for determined nonfiction writers who intend to sell their work and become published authors. Writing for publication is a complex endeavor, but the process is less daunting when you understand the way that it works and you can visualize how your endeavors will fit into the picture. This book is directed to you and to your literary ambition. It will give you the necessary knowledge and tools to achieve your goal.

It is not difficult to understand the publication process once you learn how it works; the rest of the journey is a continual series of challenges that will require great personal effort and will test the strength of your resolve. Nevertheless, most published authors consider the end goal to be well worth the time and energy that they have invested to get there.

Simply put: How badly do you want it?

Everything that you have heard about the thundering stampede of unsolicited manuscripts that leap across the transoms of agents, managers, and editors throughout the literary business is true. Still, that vast herd is constantly being thinned by many of the writers themselves. They allow their courage to become daunted by the level of persistence required to write something true and see it through to publication, or they buckle under the strain of presenting their work so that it is seriously considered. Their willingness to give in to failure leaves more room for you to find success as a published author.

To make sure you are equipped for facing this journey, we have provided you with the road map—inside information on the literary market. The tools explained here are designed specifically to enable you to

- develop an approach to your work that is smarter and more effective than a large portion of the competition;
- understand how the current state of the publishing industry affects you;
- learn why you should build your platform to become an expert in your area of nonfiction—and how to do it;
- learn the requirements of various nonfiction categories and be certain that your approach is the most commercially rewarding;
- progress successfully through all the stages of building a book proposal or manuscript;
- learn how to write a winning query letter and then select the appropriate literary representatives to receive it; and
- make savvy and well-informed moves throughout the sale, editing, publication, and promotion of your work.

We refer to today's ideal author as being a "considerate writer," one who carefully considers the structure and function of the literary market, including the question of how his or her work will fit in there. Considerate writers are mindful of the position of those who receive their calls, letters, e-mails, and submissions, so that they always express an exemplary standard. Considerate writers are determined to sharpen their skills and improve their game precisely because they have carefully considered the market in which they seek to prevail. That is the path offered to you in this book.

The majority of your competitors will not present themselves or their work properly. This can be to your benefit, of course. Many would-be writers fall for the empty promise that the book-writing biz is a great career for those who want to make big money fast, but you as a serious writer understand that it takes a lot of dedicated effort to make you and your work stand out in the best possible way. You simply must leave your competition behind. You will put yourself ahead of the pack when you combine the strength of your desire with the principles in this book.

The first step is having a clear understanding of today's publishing industry. Knowing what happens, who does what, and why it is done will help you to make informed decisions. Think of your nonfiction book project as your wholly owned and operated small business within the publishing industry. Using this mindset, you will out-research and out-perform your competition so that editors will be eager to sign you and your book.

The methods we discuss are based upon the publishing successes of others. We will point out mistakes that many writers make so that you can maneuver around them. We will also discuss the pros and cons of seeking publication through the various mainstream, small press, and self-publishing or print-on-demand outlets. In the bigger picture, this book also offers solutions to common problems in the writing life, along with specific ways to maintain individual discipline and a positive outlook.

HOW TO USE THIS BOOK: THE THREE-TIME READ

The First Read

First you want to know if this book offers useful information and a system you want to follow. You'll likely skim through the entire book first, whether you are ready to put the specific steps to work yet or not. You may not even have read this introduction your first time through. This is a perfectly legitimate way for you to get acquainted with this book. We hope you will notice that this book is dedicated to escorting you along your journey to publication, and that, while the topic of self-publishing is covered, our specific purpose is to *secure mainstream publication for writers of commercial nonfiction books.*

The Second Read

This time you will read more carefully and give more thought to detail. This second reading should take place as soon as you decide the time is right to begin the publication process in earnest. Slow down enough to absorb the specifics. This way, once your process has begun, you will remain certain of your overall direction even when you work at the most minute level of detail. That will be vital to your forward momentum.

The Third Read

This is your working read. Start reading when you decide it's time to utilize the production aspect of this book and begin generating tangible results. This time, commence with that section of the book that corresponds to where you are in the process—whether you are just getting started or you have a proposal or manuscript ready to go, and work the process step-by-step from that point on.

No matter where your point of entry is for the third reading, begin by *re-reading chapter 1.* That chapter serves as an attitude adjustment to help you focus your mental game. In publishing, losing at the mental game frequently means that a writer's determination falls victim to frustration, to the point of despairing of ever achieving one's goal. But we are here to support you along that journey, all the way through to its successful conclusion.

HOW TO SURF THE TIDAL WAVE IN TODAY'S NONFICTION BOOK MARKET

The path to mainstream publication demands more than a great leap of faith from you. Positive thinking is necessary for motivation, but it alone cannot bring you to success in the publishing industry. Let us repeat that note: *It is not enough merely to have faith in yourself.*

The vital ingredient will be your own determination to see your work in print from a mainstream publisher. No aspiring writer can trust in raw talent alone when it comes to doing competitive work and presenting it in the best way. For one thing, the glut of competition is huge. Consider the vast annual numbers in the publishing world. Bowker, the exclusive United States ISBN agency, and the recipient of the most dependable title and publisher information available, reports that in 2008, there were 275,232 new titles and editions published by some 86,000 publishers, 75 percent of which were nonfiction titles. Additionally, another 285,394 print-on-demand titles were produced in 2008, making the total number of new or revised book titles in excess of 550,000.

You can run with that pack and you can push through to the lead. If you do, it will be your refusal to accept failure that sustains your determination until you emerge as a published nonfiction author.

CONSIDER THIS ...

Countless prospective book authors have felt the pain of persistent rejection. So if it has happened to you, at least know that you are not alone. It only feels personal; it really is not. The mega-bestseller *Chicken Soup for the Soul* by Jack Canfield and Mark Victor Hansen reportedly was rejected 140 times. In case you skimmed over that last sentence, it bears repeating: The authors received 140 rejections before the book found a publisher.

A host of other highly successful books have collected piles of rejection letters before they found their place on bookshelves. There is something to be said for drive and perseverance, but this wave of rejection overwhelms many prospective authors, causing them to give up. Writers who experience a series of rejections often lack the knowledge that would have protected them from that discouraging experience. In many cases, they *sent in their submissions much too soon* because they felt anxious for a positive result.

Your preparation will be in place before you ever send out a query or proposal. Knowing the process, knowing the market, and knowing your work, you can make sure that your project is truly ready before it goes out the door. Once your book project enters the marketplace, the quality of your preparation will be tested. No longer safely hidden so only you and your trusted friends can read it, your work will be exposed to the scrutiny of highly critical strangers. These people are charged with the task of making sure their company's time and money are not wasted on books that are unlikely to sell. However, if your work is genuinely ready, the response will be positive.

There is a caveat, however: Even the smartest and most qualified people make mistakes. This may happen to you. Sometimes an editor and publisher slip and buy a book that fails to find an audience and is derided by reviewers. Sometimes a mistake goes in the opposite direction and causes the publisher to fail to recognize the value of a proposed book. Logically, mistakes can be made by others anywhere in the handling of your material. The mistake may even be that of failing to acknowledge you at all.

However—and this is a powerful however—as long as you have properly held up your end of the bargain by the way you handle both your work and your marketing process, be assured that their reaction is only a subjective response. Nothing else. The sad reality is that when the glut of manuscripts on the desks of agents and editors meets the filter of their individual and professional preferences, the writer's deck often comes pre-stacked.

There is real power available to you in that knowledge, however. It changes the way you think about things by depersonalizing inevitable frustrations. Those changes in thinking will help to keep your energy moving in positive and productive directions.

PSYCHOLOGICAL PREPARATION

There is an important bit of psychological preparation that you can do to protect yourself from the blow of rejection. Most industry professionals will be considerate professionals in responding to your work, but every business has its victims, and while the world of books is frequently more civil and considerate than other segments of the business world, there are still those who will make a victim of you if they can.

It exists on both sides of the intake desk, and you may be certain of that. The same individual who is less than attentive to you is being slighted and ignored by others, since the social disease of disrespect has spread through civilization like a virulent strain of flu. Your job is to stop the circulation of the virus with you. You do not do this by sheer willpower and self-control, or else the bottled-up resentments and angers that you must humanly feel in reaction to such treatment will turn against you with one or more of the many stress ailments that strike us.

Rather, you do it with knowledge and the power that the knowledge imparts to process their behavior toward you through your understanding of the book business in general and your appreciation of the wonderful payoff that comes your way at the end of the path, where you transform those minor obstacles into the steps that you climb to reach your goal.

The most dangerous victimizers in the publishing world are not the crooked ones. Such people seldom operate for long before the grapevine gets their number, and the Internet has plenty of websites, discussion forums, and blogs that diligently point them out. Instead, the worst victimizers are the ones who operate on the emotional level, those who burst your bubble and shatter your dreams. The most difficult aspect of this grim little factoid is that many do their damage with no particular ill will toward you at all.

Often, agents or editors only have to ignore your carefully written query letter to inflict pain on you. Or worse, they might just send back a snide dismissal of your query, a real snark-in-a-box smack over the head.

Or perhaps they might accept the query letter and request your material, but then reject your pages with a form response that leaves you feeling as if your work was never actually read.

Or worse yet, they could read your query and then go ahead and request your material, but … never … respond … at … all. (Insert long silence here.)

Or far worse that *that*, they might read the query, request the work, take forever to respond, and then send back a completely anonymous rejection slip that leaves you once again wondering if your pages really were evaluated.

Or hey, as long as we're sliding down the razor blade banister, how about when the query is accepted and the material is read in a timely fashion, but *then* a cruelly painful critique comes back? This happens, perhaps, when the recipient of your manuscript has just had their worst day in years, or perhaps because they had an unhappy childhood. Whatever the cause, you will hate it, we all hate it, and it is true that only a little of such treatment is enough to set any hopeful writer's pajamas on fire.

PROTECTING YOURSELF WITH PATIENCE

But that is not going to happen to *you*, dear considerate author. Even if many—or most—of your query letters are ignored, you can protect yourself from despairing of your goals with the knowledge that the time it takes to acknowledge you as a writer, especially when an agent passes on your work, is a large and constant task. And yet since agents work on commission, their time is far better spent reading their existing clients' work and representing it. This is why you have to detach yourself emotionally from the process and play it like the game of strategy that it is. It ain't you, baby. Patience is a specific chip in this game, and the power it gives you will manifest in the results that you achieve.

You cannot obtain patience simply by gritting your teeth and swallowing your concerns, or restraining the panicked phone calls and neurotic e-mails. Rather, you learn to understand that while it is unfortunate that not all interaction in the literary marketplace can be infused with civility, this says nothing at all *about you*. Curt or ignored queries are not a comment on your worth as a writer, or a reflection upon you as a person. They are not a statement of anything more than the reality of how agents and editors must allocate their time within this intensely competitive business.

You can protect yourself by acknowledging that you, too, would have to budget your time if you worked in that field. This leads to a freeing bit of wisdom, which is that you do not win this one by pacing the floor at night and suffering through a two A.M. review of your soul. You win by staying busy with the task at hand, which is the continuous attention to your platform (see chapter 3). Instead of giving in to uncertainty, consume your time with the activities we lay out for you, which will enhance your platform and your writing career.

And to any hapless writers (the kind who lack your determination and commitment) who happen to open this book to this section and find themselves shocked by a little hardcore reality, we say: sure—a note to you from the agent or editor would be nice. You, Hapless Writer, have worked hard. Is a little appreciation too much to ask? A sincere letter? A creative comment or two? Perhaps an analysis of the work's strengths and weaknesses? Suggestions as to which other agents might want to represent this work? The private phone numbers of the top publishers in the biz? A check to compensate you for allowing the agent to read your stuff?

A DOSE OF REALITY

Picture this, oh Hapless Writer: an invitation to a fabulous lunch at Tavern on the Green in Central Park, a weekend ensconced at the agent's guest house in the Hamptons, the use of their Mercedes, the run of the ranch. Plus, after every meal: anything you desire for dessert, *whether or not* you clean your plate! The agent reconsiders! You are represented! The book sells for megabucks! *The New York Times* swoons! Oprah is calling!

Hapless Writer's phone: Ring, ring!

Hapless Writer: "Hello, Oprah?"

Voice on the phone: "Uh, no. This is not Oprah."

Hapless Writer: "But Oprah is supposed to be calling! It says so right there in the above paragraph! Read it yourself!"

Voice on the phone: "Yeah, sorry, but this is Reality calling."

Hapless Writer: "Reality? How many times do I have to tell you—stop bothering me!

Reality: "Can't. Not in my job description. Now please drop the pointless fantasy and step to one side of the nearest door frame. Place both hands on the frame at about chest height. That's good. Now arch your back. Right, bend it backward, there. Good. Then snap your forehead in a sharp forward motion and into the wood. Ready? Here we go: And *one!* And *two!* And *three!* Now hang up and continue reading."

Of course, while such treatment may be necessary to address the naivety of our Hapless Writer, none of that will be necessary with you, because the moral of the story is that empty fantasies are unnecessary when you do it like you mean it. In this instance, doing it like you mean it consists of giving yourself helpful reminders as often as necessary about the nature of the literary business and the impersonal way that it sometimes operates. The affirmations will keep you on course while protecting you from despair and the wasted energy of useless frustration.

You are likely to find that one of your first psychological hurdles arrives with those disturbing statistics about the number of writers who are trying to secure a mainstream publisher, vs. the declining state of reading in our bite-sized, Web-surfing era. There is truth in the numbers. Every literary representative receives hundreds of queries each month, or even each week. All of it represents countless thousands of aspiring writers, out there waiting for a reply.

Do you recall the famous footage of the Asian tsunami rolling over the beach and swooping in over the town? To an agent sitting down at his or her desk, the flow of incoming queries and manuscript submissions looks about the same.

HOT TIP!

There *is no* "tidal wave" of quality efforts. The logjam comes from work that is poorly done and unready for the market, and that fact is *your* ace in the hole.

PUTTING THIS HOT TIP TO WORK

Yes, Virginia, the terrible truth of the literary business is that a large number of the manuscripts and book proposals that clog the acquisition system are not very good. Many of them are half-hearted, half-done efforts from people who are motivated more by reasons of ego or economics than an acceptance of the amount of energy required to write a piece of work that is worthy of a stranger's time and money.

When you put this information to work, part of the benefit comes from reminding you to keep your commitment to do carefully considered work, beginning with your creation of *a compelling platform*. Your platform is made up of your unique experiences and credentials that, combined, give you national exposure and make you the "only" person who can write and market your book. (More on your platform in chapter 3.) This also remains true while you move on to the:

- book proposal (see chapter 5). Yes, even if your manuscript is finished, you should accompany it with an abbreviated book proposal that includes your platform, comparables, and marketing plan;

- initial query letter (explained in chapters 7, 8 and 9). Success arrives after a sustained commitment to the ongoing process of

    contract negotiations and sale;

    in-house editing;

    legal vetting of your work, when necessary; and

- publicizing the finished book upon its release. This is absolutely necessary if you intend to sell copies beyond your personal circle of family and friends. It is the topic of publicity that brings us to our next area of concern: media skills.

MEDIA SKILLS

Is there anyone out there who still needs to be convinced that media skills are essential to every writer? The dilemma for many writers is that many are reticent by nature, often among the last to feel the urge to dance around in a spotlight. Nevertheless in our media driven society, it is incumbent upon *you* to regard each of the various forms of media appearances as a part of your working tool kit. You must put in as much private rehearsal time as necessary—preferably with the assistance of an experienced book publicist—to polish your public persona and to become smooth and fluent with your promotional language. This promotional language is what you will use to communicate your book's ideas in media-friendly sound bites. The practice time that you invest at this point is especially important, whether or not you are the life of every party and are comfortable at the center of public attention. It is important because even if you are a naturally gregarious person it still takes time and effort to polish those skills into the best possible billboard for you and for your book.

Heidi Krupp-Lisiten, CEO and founder of Krupp Kommunications (K2), was the publicist for one of the best-selling books and brands of all time, *The South Beach Diet*. She credits the willingness of the author, Dr. Arthur Agatston, to polish his skills and follow their lead as a primary reason for the book's success.

"Dr. Agatston was a true partner," she said, "passionate, flexible, and always available for media. He had a program that worked and he trusted K2 as his partner to help him get on the airwaves, position his message, as well as manage any and all media inquiries for three years."

You will learn much more about gaining great media skills in chapters 3 and 16. For now, stay the course.

STAYING THE COURSE

The number of writers who are attempting to garner a book contract is high, while the National Endowment for the Arts reports that in 2008 only 50.2 percent of the population read more than one novel, short story, poem, or play in the previous twelve months. Thus it is not only the writing of the book that is important, but the vital process of hooking the readers.

CHAPTER 2

THE MANY FORMS OF
NONFICTION

The first step in creating a nonfiction book that will find a publisher—the right publisher—is to determine exactly *what* the completed book is intended to be and *how* it will deliver its message. Can you visualize your completed book, down to the minute details?

The nonfiction book writer who lacks clarity of purpose and method will unintentionally blend multiple nonfiction forms. The result is likely to have a patchy feel, with setups that fail to pay off and with swings of narrative focus. Whether or not your readers analyze it in those terms, they will recognize that the material does not work. We call these efforts hybrids, and they are tough to sell in the publishing world. Why? Because books sold in bookstores and online or shelved in libraries are all sorted by subjects. And if your book blends two or more subjects—or worse yet, two or more genres—*where does the bookstore place you? Can your potential readers find the book?* If your readers can't find you, they can't buy you.

THE TWELVE MAIN TYPES OF NONFICTION BOOKS

This chapter outlines the most common types of nonfiction books, with a number of sub-forms branching from them. Each category has its own characteristics and brings its own challenges for the writer in structuring the concept, writing the book, marketing it to the book industry, and promoting the published book.

First determine where your proposal or manuscript falls within the categories. This will affect the way your work is constructed and presented, right down to your initial query letter.

1. PRESCRIPTIVE (INSTRUCTIVE)

This category includes the classic how-to books and can encompass any subject—repeat, *any subject*. Essentially, the fundamental message of these books is that the author knows how to do something (fix a car, write a book, counsel relationships) and has the experience and background support that they claim. In this category, the strength of a writer's platform (see chapter 3) is crucial. The implied question of every nonfiction writer, especially the writer of a how-to book, is always the same: "*Who are you* to write about this topic?"

 HOT TIP!

Successful prescriptive books constantly reinforce the message that the writer's expertise is both real and substantive.

As we said, prescriptive books cover just about every topic; here are some of the most common subsets.

Advice/Relationships

Books offering advice of life and relationships are in the how-to category because they attempt to impart knowledge or wisdom, and offer suggestions for achieving desirable states of self-esteem or for establishing gratifying personal relationships. These books are often strongly positive in nature, and focused entirely on increasing a reader's personal or relationship awareness. *Love Smart: Find the One You Want—Fix the One You Got* by Dr. Phil McGraw and *The Proper Care & Feeding of Husbands* by Dr. Laura Schlessinger are well-known prescriptive relationship books that have become bestsellers—helped by being hyped on Dr. Phil's daily television show and to Dr. Laura's massive radio audience.

There are piles of dating books out there in the vein of *He's Just Not That Into You: The No-Excuses Truth to Understanding Guys* by Greg Behrendt and Liz Tuccillo, former writers of HBO's *Sex and the City*. Many dating books are written by fresh new writers who bring their own twist to the page.

Every once in a while a powerful inspirational book comes along, such as *The Last Lecture* by Randy Pausch with Jeffrey Zaslow. The idea of a "last lecture" is traditional for departing professors at Carnegie Mellon University. When it came time for Randy Pausch to give his, he left his live audience stunned in their seats. The video of that lecture became an overnight success story on the Internet and led to a $6.7 million book deal with Hyperion.

Some advice books can be much darker in style and tone, with the intent to instruct or warn on a serious topic, such as Gavin de Becker's *The Gift of Fear*, which instructs on recognizing hidden clues to the existence of sociopaths and protecting against criminal attack. There is a strong need for a credible platform with these books. The audiences who are enthusiastic over these books are likely to have already heard plenty of opinions on the topic, so foremost in their minds will be the question of how much stock they should put in what you say.

Scholastic Textbooks

There is a perennial need for freshly written and updated textbooks. The books in this category are all of classroom quality. They may address any topic, but each book will conscientiously balance the overview of the topic against factual details and methodology. Most important of all, a book such as this will be aimed directly at the age or education level of the intended reader. Unless the book is directed at the collegiate or postgraduate reader, its language and syntax will be appropriately scaled and might be accompanied by extensive artwork. Nevertheless, the book will deliver all of the pertinent information on the topic, regardless of the reader's presumed abilities or limitations.

An author's platform here will almost always have a strong educational and career basis. A good example is *A People's History of the United States: 1492 to Present* by Howard Zinn, an historian, playwright, and social activist. Occasionally, a "guest book" is accepted in a scholarly field based upon an author's extraordinary professional accomplishments in some related field. In either case, platform comes before anything else, regardless of how strong the writing may be.

All textbooks are subjected to countless hours of scrutiny by equally countless sets of eyes. These books are complex to research and intricate to construct, so they are seldom written in full prior to approaching a publisher. Therefore, while a good proposal can garner a scholastic book contract, that proposal will have to reflect the same quality of structural clarity and depth of detail that will be expected in the finished book. No writer should go near this type of book unless prepared to undergo the most stringent peer review.

2. LIFESTYLE BOOKS

Lifestyle books cover those things that we do in our day-to-day lives, such as cooking, parenting, traveling, etc. It is a popular category with book buyers, but the competition can be fierce. An author's platform is very important throughout this entire category, so again, it's not enough to have a book about a better way of living. Authors here must present themselves as a complete package, bringing a built-in audience along with them.

Cooking

Foodies take heart! Cookbooks continue to be a staple of the publishing world, but the intense competition from culinary magazines and foodie websites has set the bar high when it comes to persuading the public to shell out money for cookbooks. As with most topics in this day and age, information on cooking is now easily obtained cheaply or for free.

Today's cookbooks must be fresh and original, and do much more than offer a mix of great recipes. Each proposed dish must be clearly described and include food preparation photos and finished dish photos that are attractive and well composed. Successful cookbooks are likely to include interesting cultural facts about the origin of the cooking style used and even descriptions of the regions where the ingredients are obtained.

Plus, today's cookbook authors are expected to demonstrate expertise in recipe conception, ingredient selection, food preparation, food photography, basic farming and harvesting methods, and a wide range of cultural awareness. This will all be combined with an engaging narrative style that encourages the reader to accompany the author on an adventure in the kitchen.

Potential sales of these books are also highly driven by platforms, so be sure to develop yours before going down this road. Try blogging or writing feature articles for cooking magazines such as *Bon Appetit* or *Gourmet*. Teach culinary arts (even if it is in your home). The point is to get your foot in the door. Perhaps the journey will take you to the life of a media personality such as Rachael Ray, Emeril Lagasse, or Anthony Bourdain, or to that of a well-known restaurateur like Rocco DiSpirito. Consider the Skinny Bitch books.

HOT TIP!

The Food Network has turned many a talented chef into a media mogul.

Diet

Diet books frequently break out and sell millions of copies. No one can say for certain which diet will catch the public's fancy and which will be ignored, but this category of book remains lucrative because hope springs eternal.

It should also be noted that the diet genre is not limited to books that prescribe any particular diet. To illustrate, Michael Pollan's book *In Defense of Food: An Eater's Manifesto* goes as far away as eighteenth-century Britain to discuss the writings of Edmond Burke, the British statesman widely considered the father of the modern conservative movement. The unlikely comparison is made applicable when Pollan analyzes the political, social, and personal health consequences of the modern Western diet. He even links the disparate sensibilities of liberals and conservatives with conclusions that the righteous Mr. Burke surely would have condoned: Stick as close as possible to the land, avoid processed "frankenfoods," and base your diet—whatever variations you want to employ—essentially on plant life. Thus the sentiments of an early conservative turn out to be those that any tree-hugger could embrace today.

The driving factor for most books that propose specific diets or nutritional plans is that modern society instills in many people a state of perpetual discontent over their weight. Anyone who has been self-conscious about their weight is certain to have tried slimming down by one method or another, but the majority slide backward and will eventually try again. Therefore, the readers of diet books are ready for the diet plan that will finally do the magic. Are you the one with the answer they seek?

Many of the popular diet books present experiments or studies that are intended to back up the diet being offered. When the diet's credibility is thus established, the diet itself is laid out and mixed with reinforcements about its projected effectiveness. Again, what a diet book is selling most of all is hope. The diet books that succeed are ones that ignite the readers' hopes that this diet is going to be the one that works—at last.

You on a Diet: The Owner's Manual for Waist Management by Michael F. Roizen and Mehmet C. Oz, and *The Best Life Diet* by Bob Greene are a couple of diet books that soared to the top of the best-seller list with huge help from the authors' position in Oprah Winfrey's inner circle of experts. They are your competitors if you are in this field, so get busy on your testimonial page and keep building your platform as the next diet guru.

Health and Health Science

The term "health science" here refers to science expressed at the pop culture level. A book may take a general approach to offering health tips, or it can venture into the scientific range and rely heavily on accepted experiments and case studies. In either case, the writer is addressing an audience who comes to the book already primed to understand or improve their health. Clearly, your health book is unlikely to be the first they have read. Therefore, the wise health writer keeps a clear picture of the potential readership in mind; these readers are motivated toward healthier living and are already educated on the topic to some degree. They have no need of condescension or excessive simplicity. In most cases, what they want is to see the sum total of the fine details and to be assured of their accuracy.

An example of a self-published health book that met enormous publishing success is Kevin Trudeau's *Natural Cures "They" Don't Want You to Know About*. Of course, his infomercials that seemed to run nonstop around the clock helped make this book soar to success.

Travel

Travel writing has evolved into a far more diverse and colorful genre than its traditional image suggests. Few (if any) travel writers can expect to compete in today's marketplace unless they write with observational depth and cultural awareness in addition to a strong appreciation for local varieties of food. Travel writers tend to include observations about the languages, customs, taboos, and personal desires of the local population. Amazing scenery does not cut it anymore. The savvy travel writer today is also a skilled photographer who saves on the cost of hiring a sidekick and personally does the photo work.

A variation of the travel book is the travel biography, popularized in the United States during the last century by John Steinbeck's *Travels With Charley*, and successfully employed by many authors since. Here, a writer uses the premise of travel as a metaphor for personal change. Both the journey and the destination are related directly to the personal evolution or enlightenment of the writer. Food writers and religious writers are also crowding into the category by mixing stories and photos of their journeys with elongated essays of the gourmand or the devotee. This is one category where it is still possible, even if difficult, for a writer without a great platform to find a publisher, provided the travel topic is unique and fresh, and the narrative skills are of outstanding quality. An acceptable way to build a platform in this field is to start your own travel blog. It can become as elaborate as you choose for little to no cost; it's an excellent way to demonstrate to a potential publisher that you have the knowledge, taste, imagination, and communication skills to garner a book audience.

When it is time to test the market, you must come out with a polished book proposal or manuscript, meaning a piece of work with absolutely no flaws in presentation that offers insights from your travels that a reader will want to embrace. *Eat, Pray, Love* by Elizabeth Gilbert is a perfect example of a breakout spiritual travel book that has flown off the shelves onto the best-seller list.

Parenting

The shelves for this category are packed to the rafters with entries, yet a good parenting book is always in demand. Like food and relationship books, parenting books enjoy a constant reader appetite for information, inspiration, and even entertainment.

Platform is very important with parenting advice, even though a case can be made that any experienced and conscientious parent can speak with some degree of authority on the topic. The need for a strong platform comes into play precisely because this is a field riddled with opinion. Parents who passionately believe in their approach to the job differ greatly from one to another, as anyone who has ever attended a PTA meeting can confirm. Therefore, if the author's views and opinions around the issues of child rearing are not backed up by considerable recognized expertise, even the best writers leave themselves stranded in a corner. Your methods may have produced a wonderful child or a family full of them, but readers want to know which accredited program you attended, what your professional experience is within the field, and how you came to the conclusions that you offer, all of this *in addition* to your own anecdotal evidence of having raised children well.

If you are determined to write in this category and do not yet have a compelling platform, begin by getting involved with established parenting organizations. If you are a joiner, work your way up within their ranks.

There is plenty of motivation for putting in the time and work. A cottage industry was born out of the Dr. Spock parenting books of the 1950s, and many parenting experts have cashed in on this subject since then. *What to Expect the First Year* by Heidi Murkoff and *Healthy Sleep Habits, Happy Child* by Marc Weissbluth are two of the many popular books on parenting. There will always be children who are in need of good parenting methods and parents who are in need of finding them. Maybe your book will be added to this list.

 HOT TIP!

The shortest route to success for the new parenting author is to build your platform.

---

3. BIOGRAPHY

Biographies can be either contemporary, about a celebrity or political figure, or historical.

They will be either authorized or unauthorized. If you are writing an authorized biography, you are working with the *written* permission of the figure you are writing about, and this kind of arrangement requires the help of an intellectual property attorney to properly put it into motion.

Unauthorized biographies are much trickier, especially if the person you choose to write about is still living. Be very certain that your sources are accurate and that you get all your facts straight. Inaccuracy can lead to lawsuits, and publishers are cautious about printing anything that has not been vetted and verified. Andrew Morton's unauthorized biography of Tom Cruise was such a risky undertaking that although it was published in the United States, it was never published in Britain, where privacy laws are much more stringent.

Contemporary Biography

Since these books concern living or recently deceased subjects, *story rights* are paramount. Without them, the civil liability overwhelms the value of the story. Even if the subject is a recognized public person, he or his heirs still have the right to sue for any inaccuracy that has damaged them in some way. Because of this, it is important to obtain signed permission from the subject, or if that person is recently deceased, from the closest next of kin.

Even with proper permission, this is a legally dicey field. The writer of any contemporary biography must be aware of the legal potential behind every word, on top of all other considerations behind writing the book well. Christopher Ciccone wrote an unauthorized biography about his sister Madonna. In spite of his provable point of knowledge as her brother, the book was spiked in the U.K. over fears of litigation.

Historical Biography

The use of personalities from any bygone era easily identifies a book as a historical biography. Additionally, a figure who lived at some point during the writer's own lifetime can still be considered the subject of a historical biography if the general feel of the events and circumstances that surrounded the figure during life have significantly changed. It is the level of change—not the number of years—that determines whether a book is historical in nature. The subject may be esoteric, such as *Power of a Woman: Memoirs of a Turbulent Life: Eleanor of Aquitaine* by Robert Fripp, or more familiar to the general reading public, such as transsexuals in *Becoming a Woman: A Biography of Christine Jorgensen* by Richard F. Docter, or it may be vague or mystical in nature, such as *Biography of Satan: A Historical Exposition of the Devil and His Fiery Dominions* by Kersey Graves.

In our litigious society, the safest true-life subjects (and all of their associates) are long since departed, but in certain rare instances, particularly in politics and show business, it is possible to find oneself writing about an era that has passed, but having a long-lived figure who was present for your story and who still lives today. Here the publicly documented record will usually protect you, as long as you are not tempted to venture into tabloid mentality of ugliness-equals-truth. In any case, it is always wise to take care that nothing gets published that could be characterized as hurtful to any surviving family members.

Truman by David McCullough provides excellent commentary on the life of a more recent historical personage, published at a time when some of those present for the story were still living.

Autobiography or Memoir

These two terms are often used interchangeably, except that an *autobiography* is a self-dictated history, and often promotional in nature. *Memoir* is the term used to indicate that a book contains a deeper self-revelatory component rather than a mere recital of deeds and accomplishments.

The most commonly attempted category for new nonfiction writers is the personal memoir. Many writers take literal instruction from the adage, "write what you know." It seems logical to assume that you are who you know best, but you may not be removed enough from your own story to be able to formulate it into a compelling memoir. The question is: How do you convince strangers that your thoughts, feelings, and experiences are so much more worthwhile than their own that they should pay you to learn about them?

Jeannette Walls's touching memoir *The Glass Castle* struck a solid chord with the reading public and spent many months on the bestseller lists. The power of good writing brought fresh energy to an established form.

4. SPORTS

Sports biographies are built on the same logic as general biographies. Refer to the general biography section above for information about them and handle sports profiles accordingly. Subcategories include sports stats, sports psychology, sports metaphors, and sports photography. Sports books tend to have long shelf lives. It seems if you are a fan, you are a fan for life.

The combination sports biography/psychology book *The John Wooden Pyramid of Success* by Neville L. Johnson has enjoyed great sales, as have books like *The Yankee Years* by Joe Torre and Tom Verducci, and *Quiet Strength* by Tony Dungy and Nathan Whitaker.

Platform, as always, is critical here. You must be a winning player or coach, a broadcaster with national name recognition, a photographer for major league teams, or otherwise involved in sports on a national or international scale.

5. HUMAN NATURE (ANALYTICAL)

This is the category for books written by psychologists and sociologists who use their training, background, and personal talents to feature and explain various aspects of human behavior. This category also can include some small measure of qualified punditry if the writer's platform is very strong.

Personality Analysis

The name of this category makes it seem more academic than it really is. Good books in this category can find a considerable readership, and pop up on a frequent basis. Dr. Martha Stout wrote *The Sociopath Next Door* by mixing an informed psychological take on individuals who appear to lack any conscience with a cautionary tale for everyone who is living and working among them. Given the statistical studies that she cites regarding the number of unfeeling manipulators in general society, that puts every one of us in the zone of risk.

History

Some writers choose to make their points about the current state of human relations by casting their eyes backward in time. It can be instructive for us to measure ourselves, or our behavior, against ancestral values. The contrast between then and now may illustrate ways modern society has made progress, including gains in humanitarian concerns, civic equality, employment customs, a population's way of governing itself, education, or military conduct. Although it is true that a good platform is needed to secure a decent publishing contract, in this category the platform may have numerous variations.

A writer might come from a strong academic background: a professorship with visible credentials and an Internet following. Another writer might approach the history of human nature by tracing religious trends through time. This writer will have solid clerical credentials, a large church following, and a major online presence along with a busy schedule of speaking engagements.

HOT TIP!

A real love of research is essential for the history writer. So is the ability to annotate quotes and resources.

In this category, some writers choose to comment on human behavior by tracing the history of humanity's way of governing itself, analyzing what gains have been made over time (say, abolishing state-supported slavery), or writing about things that have been lost to modern culture (such as personal privacy). Doris Kearns Goodwin's *Team of Rivals: The Political Genius of Abraham Lincoln* is a fine example.

Politics

The best political writing goes beyond any author's personal dogma and attunes readers to new ways of looking at life and people through the political prism. This does not mean that a good political book will not have an agenda. To the contrary, most do. However, unless the book is done with penetrating insights that demonstrate a willingness to look at an argument from various angles, the author will only succeed in preaching to the choir.

The point of view that the author holds becomes the book's thematic statement, but if it is skillfully written with a balanced tone and a fair hand, a political book can transcend the expected audience of ditto-heads. It can actually succeed in persuading a reader to adopt (or at least consider) a new point of view.

In the best political writing, persuasion is achieved with nuance and perception rather than bombast and contempt for dissenting views. Rarely, some media personality will break through with a sneering lecture to the ignorant, but new writers will have to shoot for a more universal take. It helps to have a strong credentialed background from which to espouse wisdom, in addition to being media savvy and able to hold your own in debates against Bill O'Reilly, Glenn Beck, the women of *The View*, or any other politically oriented talk show that books authors for appearances. Ann Coulter's books espouse the views of a conservative political pundit, while Arianna Huffington's books are examples of the left side of politics. Both authors write with sufficient intelligence, style, and charm to occasionally win readers from across the aisle.

Current Events

Writing within the current events category is a close cousin to political writing, but as a rule, such books focus on commentary and observation instead of critical analysis and persuasion. The current events writer will tread closely to the pop culture category; the separation comes from pop culture's fixation on passing fads and fashions as opposed to the current events writer's concern with events or trends that reflect larger conditions in society. Thomas L. Friedman's *The World Is Flat* demonstrates how it is done.

6. TRUE CRIME

True crime books are among the most narrative in their form. This category is an authentic storyteller's domain, offering its writers the same challenges and opportunities as those found in writing the most gripping novels of mystery and suspense, but all within the thorny framework of the facts of the case. The writing of a true crime book must employ the storyteller's art of adding new elements of interest on every page, no matter how compelling the underlying crime story might be (the part that is ready-made by the events themselves). To accomplish a compelling read, the writer must create engaging characters for both the protagonist and the antagonist, as well as for the supporting players. Crime stories already provide the who and the how of what was done, so it is only by getting into the minds of the players that a writer can offer the why of it all. Everyone wants to understand why unusual or shocking things occur.

The more your readers understand your characters' ways of thinking and behaving, the more engaged in the book they will become. Most true crime readers are the kind of people who are so disturbed by the evil among us that they gain relief from seeing it made understandable in a narrative story. That is your job, because the news media have already beaten you to the information; your purpose as a compelling crime writer is to bring the "why" to the table.

A good example of historical true crime is *The Devil in the White City* by Erik Larson, while a solid example of contemporary true crime is *The Innocent Man: Murder and Injustice in a Small Town* by John Grisham. *In Cold Blood* by Truman Capote is another good example of a great backlist (perennial seller) true crime book.

Remember that true crime is a category that is normally written by skilled crime writers who make a living hopping from one murder to another, many of them under multiple book deals for a specific publisher. It is rare to just stumble over a great true crime story. True crime is a competitive genre that will demand your best efforts, which must begin with your determination to pursue the right story and secure the rights from the principal player or players.

7. POP CULTURE

This category covers all topics of current art, style, and fashion as reflected in the commercial media—or in the blogosphere, if sufficient numbers of people are involved. Blogs have so saturated the Internet that the point of view, the take, even the gimmick of a pop culture book must be especially clever to compete with written material that is available on the Internet for free. Some writers get around this by using websites or blogs as the database for their books, gaining the added value of a built-in fan base without using mainstream media to create it.

A Hard Day's Write: The Stories Behind Every Beatles Song by Steve Turner is an excellent pop culture sample. This is one area in which you don't necessarily have to have a national platform to succeed, but you do have to have an inordinate amount of knowledge about your subject or be the go-to expert.

8. REFERENCE

A reference book is a compilation of targeted information that usually pertains to a specific subject, in which the information is presented so it can be quickly and easily found. Reference works, such as encyclopedias, are usually referred to for detailed pieces of information rather than read through from front to back. The writing style in reference books is informative; authors typically avoid use of the first person and instead emphasize facts. Indexes are often provided, and many reference books are updated regularly, and in many cases, annually. Books in this category are often sold to libraries, students, and scholars, rather than to the mainstream buying public. Those who do buy, however, often return for the updated versions, so it is fairly easy to create a small but loyal base of book buyers for reference books if the book is targeted and specific enough. *Literary Market Place* is a well-known reference source for the book industry.

Hard Science

These books usually remain within the academic world, with rare exceptions of weighty books that happen to catch public fancy. Stephen Hawking's book, *A Brief History of Time*, surprised everyone with strong sales to a wide audience despite its scholarly concern with astrophysics. It is a rare phenomenon. By and large, these books are narrowly focused to a specific audience. They are seldom written out of financial concerns. They can, however, significantly advance the scholarly status of their authors with their demonstrations of intellect and knowledge.

Scholarly Works

These books often come from university presses and are not intended for commercial status. Here is a category where the tiny profit margin may justify turning instead to self-publishing. Today's scholar enjoys a greater level of freedom from the stringent restrictions of commercial publishing. Such books are seldom designed to break out in the marketplace, so self-publishing can guarantee that determined scholarly writers get published, provided that the manuscript is subjected to credible peer review and careful editing. This can be important to academic status, since self-published scholarly writers may attain a readership as big as they might have gained from a major publisher. The challenge for either situation is public awareness of your book, especially when your target audience is small and specific.

Occasionally some of these books do cross over and achieve some commercial success, such as *The Black Swan: The Impact of the Highly Improbable* by Nassim Nicholas Taleb.

9. RELIGION

This category deals with religious *nonfiction*. That may seem obvious, but it can be complicated by the different religious views of different audience groups. Here, it is harder to define fact and fiction. The religious market nevertheless draws a sharp line between what is false and what is real *to each audience group* without regard to the writer's personal view. If a writer's religious viewpoint steps away from that of the readers, the work will be regarded as *fiction*. That vital fact must never be forgotten when writing in this category.

Scriptural Analysis

Many devoted writers feel a strong desire to share their particular understanding of scripture. This is not a good genre for the emerging writer. Issues of platform will overwhelm all but the most publicly recognized and qualified individuals. It helps if you are a leader of a large, nationally recognized church, or a professor of religious studies or theology at a top university. When we consider that the Bible ranks as the highest-selling book of all time, the value of addressing people's hunger for spiritual understanding is plain to see. Every religious or spiritual concept is valid here.

Spiritual/Inspirational

The many facets of spiritual orientation belong in this category, which is also called "mind, body, spirit." Self-help books that guide readers to better understanding of their own thought processes fall under the "mind" subcategory and include books such as *The Secret* by Rhonda Byrne and *Chicken Soup for the Soul* by Jack Canfield and Mark Victor Hansen. These books focus on finding inner peace through gentle forms of attitude adjustment and mental self-control. The "body" subcategory includes books on yoga, massage, and diet, for the purpose of raising consciousness. Books centered on "spirit" include works that address the human being as a spiritual entity who exists above and beyond physical life. John Edward, Sylvia Browne, Deepak Chopra, and Wayne Dyer are all well-known authors in this genre.

10. COLLECTED SHORT WORKS

Article-length pieces of nonfiction that share a unifying theme are occasionally grouped into a single book of collected works. Examples include a group of writers who have all done articles on the writing process, or a group of chefs who have each written articles on cooking, or a group of athletes who write individual tales of physical endeavor. The collection is usually that of a number of authors, but if a given author has an established name, say a celebrity journalist or a celebrity political writer (a celebrity anything, really), all of the work in a collection may be from one source.

Unless you want to compile and edit such a book on your own, there is really no way to write for a collection unless invited to participate. Instead, the lesson to take away from this category is the value of writing and publishing articles *in addition to or in lieu of* writing full books.

HOT TIP!

Any article that you publish can be picked up later for a collection (with your permission).

New writers will sometimes find publishing an article easier than securing a contract for a book. So if you need to fatten up your platform, get published by online magazines, newspapers, or blogs. Most such outlets are always on the lookout for another talented contributor. Publications usually have a schedule with topics outlined sometimes two years in advance. Some pay for your work, some do not, but everything you write and publish will serve to build your platform.

A search engine can guide you through the Internet to a number of publications that address your area of expertise. Read what they are already publishing. Note the length, style, and tone of their articles. Look at the range of styles of the writers they publish. This will give you a clear idea of how far you can push your own work in style and tone while still presenting the editors with something they can use. If you have no immediate prospect for publishing a full-length work, consider turning to nonfiction articles as your way of doing what writers do—write—and to increase your market presence. Editors cannot include you in their books of collected works unless they know you are out there.

Check out *The Norton Reader: An Anthology of Nonfiction* edited by Linda H. Peterson and John C. Brereton.

11. HUMOR

There is a reason that good comic writers are paid so well. Comic writing is easy to read, fun to laugh at, and extremely difficult to execute. Anyone who lacks an extraordinary level of comic talent quickly discovers this upon attempting to "write funny." It is an elusive goal because it *seems* as if anyone with a decent sense of humor ought to be able to do it. After all, you know what you find humorous and what you don't. So why should it be any more difficult to determine which of your own thoughts and observations are funny?

Since nothing is going to stop you from writing in this category if you are absolutely determined, at least consider this: The key lies in the balance between subjectivity and objectivity. The true comic writer is able to balance the schizophrenic task of subjectively responding to an idea in a humorous way while also remaining reasonably objective about how his humor will be perceived by others. This is a challenge for anyone. That is why you can find even the most famous and successful comic narrative writers using open mic nights at comedy clubs to verbally test material.

A surprising number of humor writers try to shortcut the process by preparing their manuscript, and then attaching a letter full of hyperbole about how funny their work is. It is strange that otherwise intelligent people adopt the belief that they can convince an agent, editor, publishing house, and readership of their comic skills simply by describing their own work with superlatives.

If you have a humorous approach to a book, be certain to test market it to as wide a range of friends, co-workers, and acquaintances as you can. Work with your book club or writing group. Cultivate the opinions of smart people who like to laugh and who are honest enough to let you know when you are missing the mark, but also generous enough to give positive feedback when you get it right!

For an example of a humorous narrative, consider *Smotherhood* by Amanda Lamb.

12. ILLUSTRATED ART

This category includes coffee table books, as well as training books for the novice and advanced books for the experienced visual artist. The advent of illustration and animation software, digital photography, and online visual editing capabilities has opened the illustrated art field wider than ever before. What was once the province of graphic illustrators, comic artists, sketch artists, and painters is now a field wide open to anyone with a powerful computer and a few good composing and editing programs.

The basic challenge remains the same: How well can you put your imagination to work in creating illustrations that will captivate a readership? Today's market is complicated by the fact that many people have access to the tools that will produce illustrated art, so some readers may value art less if they think they can produce it themselves. Whether they can or not is still a matter of talent, but the aspiring author wanting to publish in this category has the additional hurdle to clear in the form of public perception of the value of art. Toward that end, consider *The Complete Idiot's Guide to Altered Art Illustrated* by Allyson Bright Meyer.

This does not mean that you should not go forward with your plans if your strong desire is to produce such a book. Tackle your illustrated art book project with more care and passion, and that will show in the finished product.

IF THE SHOE FITS …

Which of these categories fits you and your book project? Now that you understand the pros and cons of each category, keep the requirements of your category in mind while you read all about building your platform in the next chapter.

CHAPTER 3

THE PLATFORM
DANCE

The word *platform* has become part of the nonfiction lexicon. As a writer, your platform consists of those unique experiences and credentials that combine to demonstrate how you are the most qualified person to write and market your book. The platform is one of the most important components to the success of your proposal; it is a primary marker that agents and editors will use when evaluating a book's chances for commercial success.

The building of your platform is where the process of creating your book actually begins. If you find inspiration before you build a platform of credibility, that does not necessarily close down opportunity to you. It does, however, force you to play catch-up with your competition. Your platform is definitely the place to begin doing that.

Therefore, if you have already begun work on the book—and even if you have finished it—your wisest course of action is to stop everything else that you are doing and tend to your platform. *This is not a detour.* Rather, this is the best way to streamline your process.

"Platform is essential," said Peter Lynch, editorial manager for trade books at Sourcebooks, Inc., "and it is one of the first things I review in the proposal. Lack of a strong platform will make it almost impossible to proceed. In all cases, the better platform a first-time author can offer, the more likely it is that their proposal will be chosen for publication.

The author's track record is such an important part of purchase decisions made by the stores, that for a first-time author (who of course doesn't yet have a track record), the platform is the next best information we can provide to convey confidence that this book will generate more attention than competing books."

Today's publishing business casts its authors in the same way that Hollywood studios cast their actors, as the main selling point. Your platform is who you are for the purposes of bringing credibility to your book and being able to market it. It is the sum total of your education, professional experience, marketing experience, and overall media savvy.

According to Christina Katz, author of *Get Known Before the Book Deal*, your platform consists of "all the ways you are visible and appealing to your future, potential, or actual readership."

The good news here is that no matter who you are, there is a great deal you can do to produce an effective professional image within your book's area of concern.

THE TWENTY-FIRST CENTURY PLATFORM

In a sense, a writer's platform is as important as it is today because of the proliferation of electronic media throughout every level of society. The main reason you are obligated to tend to your public image is because it is available in so many more places than ever before, especially on the Internet, and all writers are tasked with the job of making themselves heard.

Some writers are fortunate enough to have a platform built in. A psychologist writes about human behavior, as in *Real Life: Preparing for the 7 Most Challenging Days of Your Life* by Dr. Phil McGraw. A former police officer writes a true crime thriller, as in *The Onion Field* by Joseph Wambaugh. Then there is *State of Fear* by Michael Crichton, in which a medical doctor uses his scientific knowledge to challenge current theories on global warming.

Most publishers want the author's platform to be as precisely spot-on as these examples. In addition to all these credentials, they also want you to have a track record of strong past book sales.

If you are not operating at the level that Peter Lynch describes, you can still build a case for your own credibility by demonstrating:

- the number of hits you get monthly on your website

- how many articles you've published (and where)

- how often you give lectures where you can sell books in the back of the room

- personal contacts you have (or can develop) to promote your book

- any media coverage, such as a recent television appearance (it would be oh-so-nice if you had your own talk show—preferably a network or nationally syndicated talk show with top ratings)

The challenge for you is that publishers can, and do, get those things. Consider the financial benefit of such built-in publicity and it becomes obvious that your platform challenge is real. The only rational and success-oriented response is to meet that challenge head-on.

"I am constantly amazed when authors or agents send me proposals with no platform information," said Michaela Hamilton, editor in chief of Citadel Press at Kensington Publishing Corp. "We can't seriously consider a new project without that important piece of the picture. Platforms may take various forms. Some authors are celebrities, so we know we can get media attention for them—provided they are willing to commit their time when the book published, and provided they have something juicy to say. Other authors are experts with strong credentials. With them we need to take a different tack; they may not make the morning TV shows, but we can expect them to receive attention from others in their fields. For new authors, contacts for quotes are essential. If the author isn't a 'name,' we need some serious names to endorse the book early in the process, so their blurbs can appear on the cover. In addition, we expect a new nonfiction author to have or create a website and build up an Internet presence. We are looking for authors who are able to take a very proactive role in promoting their books."

This is why the most important preparation you can make in your publishing process is to begin *building your platform in advance* of submitting your book manuscript or proposal. If you start when sending queries and proposals, you are already too late; those who have tended to their preparation will simply outpace you. Live interviews, author panels, radio and television appearances, attendance at major book conventions, interviews at book clubs, speaking engagements at related events—the successful authors are already doing that much. Are you going to do less?

Keep in mind that the major publishing and entertainment outlets are owned by corporations. Every dollar paid out has to be earned back with enough profit attached to it, or the entire operation fails. If too many of the publisher's books fail, then editors lose their jobs. Perhaps the publishing house folds. That's the sort of pressure that the person who is going to review your book for publication lives under every day.

The time for beautiful right-brain creativity is during the creation of your work. Then the right brain gets to rest while the reality-driven left side of the brain takes over the task of seeing to it that the word gets out.

If public appearances have already become part of your platform, then you have your general media skills in place. You have either grown comfortable with being in the public eye or you have learned how to fake it (both ways work).

HOT TIP!

If you are not thoroughly at home with the idea of speaking for the camera or on a panel of authors, then you *absolutely must* train yourself to speak on your topic.

Write It Out

How do you train yourself? Keep it simple. Begin by writing out your thoughts. Do it as if you were writing out your answers to the interview questions for a print interview. Practice describing your book to a stranger in *one paragraph* (seriously). Visualize what you would say if you wanted to describe your book out loud to a stranger in a coffee shop.

After you have done that until you are smooth in your presentation, consider the kinds of questions that people might ask about your book or any of its topics, then practice the answers. Write them down. Polish them until they really capture what you want to say.

Practice Out Loud

When you know what you want to say, practice the answers out loud, and be certain that you do it when nobody is around. You are particularly vulnerable at this time to interruptions that may include wisecracks or negative remarks. If you can practice in front of a mirror, all the better.

Then find a few tolerant people and practice the answers on them. Keep practicing until you can spell out your ideas with clarity and confidence. *The importance of this process cannot be overemphasized.* The less experience you have at this sort of thing, the more lead time you must give yourself before you first jump onto your platform. You will be competing with many other strong and smart personalities who all want a piece of the public's attention as badly as you do.

Happily, there is a double payoff to your efforts. Because long before you have a chance to conduct a live telephone interview for a talk radio station, appear on *Book TV*, or stroll onto Oprah's set and sit down for a heart-to-heart, you will have already benefited by smoothing out your ability to describe your book and its ideas. Smoothness has its own sound, like a well-tuned racing engine. It makes your story, your information, and your arguments all the more compelling.

ADJUSTING YOUR AUTHORIAL PERSONA

Quick informal poll: If you were going to read a historical western this weekend, would you be more likely to buy that book if the author pictured on the jacket is

(a) depicted in western clothing in an outdoor setting; or

(b) looks like an earnest researcher who lives in New York City and is photographed in front of a library?

That does not mean that if you have written a hard-boiled true crime book you have to be a hard-boiled street type to be credible, or to portray yourself as something you are not. It does mean that in representing yourself as the author of your particular book, you begin and end your platform with those aspects of your life and work that relate directly to the material. It is an essential part of your answer to the question that will hang on your reader's lips: *Who are you to write about this?* There are many ways to achieve your answer.

As we have said, anyone who does not have a built-in platform to bring to the table must create it. Fair warning: This will be an act of sustained willpower. Your platform will only be effective in recommending you to the extent that *it is the result of your fixed determination*.

The same thing may be said about the authoring of any worthy book. But take heart. Here are some specific ways to make the best use of any natural platform that you already have.

To begin you must find your hook. What little corner of the world of information and knowledge do you own? Author Geri Spieler took her friendship with Sara Jane Moore, the only female to shoot at a president of the United States, and turned it into a biography. Lisa Wysocky, a horse trainer and publicist in the country music industry, writes about country music stars' love of horses. Voice-over artist Joan Baker interviewed other voice-over artists to give readers a behind-the-scenes look at the voices we hear on radio and television, and in the movies.

Once you determine what your special and unique knowledge is, develop a one-sentence statement that sums it up. For example, your sentence might be, "I have been interested in the Civil War since childhood and am now a reenactor."

Then use the sentence to define your hook. What can you share with readers that others can't? You could research a day in the life of a family who was thrown into the middle of the war. Or maybe research the struggles of a town that was influenced by the war.

You must be sure that your hook is original and unique. A good way to do this is to do some research on BarnesAndNoble.com or Amazon.com. Are there any other books similar to yours? If so, how might you make yours different? What new information can you add?

When you have all of this firmly planted in your mind, you can begin to build your platform around your special area of expertise.

HOT TIP!

Keep your hook in mind as you begin to build your platform.

YOUR INTERNET PRESENCE: BUILDING A WEBSITE THAT ENHANCES YOUR PLATFORM

The first thing every savvy nonfiction writer needs to do is to create a presence on the Internet. That is often the first step in declaring yourself to the public. A website helps build your future platform while also serving as your current billboard. Consider the websites of authors you admire, especially those who are writing in your same category. See how they position themselves. Take note of the kinds of information they post about themselves and their books. These sites represent the industry standard;

it is a good idea to continue to refer back to them while you construct your site. A professional e-mail address to accompany your website is also necessary. Once your new professional website is constructed and ready to launch, be certain that everything is running perfectly and it is free of typos and visual flaws before you tell the world.

Link Your Site

Now that your website is up and running, you need to get the word out. Attract readers. The most effective way is to have other websites embed links to yours. Visit several websites that relate to your field of expertise. Contact them and offer to put a link to their site on your links page if they will do the same for you.

There is no reason to be shy about seeking links to your website. Just be certain there is an obvious reason for your connection to that particular site. The point is to increase the flow of visitors to your site. Even those who arrive indirectly while surfing other sites may find their interest captured by your clever and engaging website content.

Web Photos

We highly recommend that your website have a photo section where you can post images of you doing what you do best: working your platform. Never be without a digital camera at any professional event. Get plenty of shots of you speaking, attending book signings with well-known authors or recognizable experts in your field, and participating in other events that extend your credibility.

Once the photos are up on your website, contact a few of the other attendees and ask for their comments about the event. Also ask permission to post their comments on your site with the event photos.

In this way, you are giving the world a chance to meet *your* audience.

Headshot

Another key component of your profile is a professional-quality headshot. You can have a friend or family member shoot the photo of you, provided that they hold to professional standards as your competition will. No candid shots, and forget that good one of you at the beach. With digital photography, take as many appropriately posed shots as you need until you get the right one.

A few things to note about your photo: Do not wear white or black, or dress in vivid patterns. Be sure the background is in the light to medium range and not too busy. There should be no shadows across your face or body. Your wardrobe, the setting, and facial expression should match the tone of your book. Keep shooting with different variables (hair, lighting, background, pose) until you get the perfect shot. Let the public greet you the way you want to be seen.

Testimonials

It can be helpful to have advance praise for your book before it is published. Ask others who have a direct tie to your topic—preferably with some name recognition of their own—to read your manuscript and give you a quote. Then pull out short excerpts of these quotes to create a testimonial section on your website. A sentence or two from each person is enough. Your testimonial section will begin with these comments from people who are impressed with your writing, and will eventually expand to include reviews or comments from articles that you publish. It can also include e-mailed responses to talks or lectures that you have given, or those of colleagues in your field. Your testimonial page will grow as your platform expands, all of which can enhance a book deal. A good testimonial page (with entries that are all strictly true) can even help persuade a highly visible person to write a foreword to your book.

E-Mail Mailing List

Your site should have a prominent area where visitors can sign up for your newsletter or mailing list. Over time, this builds a nice mailing list that you can use to promote your book when it hits the market. Be certain that your website has a "Contact" section so that visitors can write to your e-mail address. You don't want to be hard to reach.

Newsletter

Another great way to build an e-mail list is to create an electronic newsletter to discuss your book project and alert readers to speeches, appearances, and signings, as well as to expand your platform. There are many new electronic newsletter services that provide attractively designed templates for your content. Ask Google or any Internet search engine for information on electronic newsletters. Use your mailing list for distribution. You can then monitor statistics such as: how many people opened your newsletter, what they specifically read, and whether they wish to continue receiving material from you. What was once prohibitively expensive is now quite affordable, with rates as low as fifteen dollars a month, depending on the number of names on your mailing list.

Blogs

Blogging may not be helpful until you have a good number of visitors coming through your website and reading your book, so don't sit around tapping away at your daily journal and waiting for things to get better. Instead, contact other blogs, ones you like and that are in the same area as your book, and offer to send them your column for free. Search online for electronic magazines and large blogs that actively seek and accept submissions from any writer if their story is compelling. Just set your search engine with keywords that apply to your subject. Also, consider the wisdom in avoiding the temptation to blog about your personal life. Anything posted online is permanently out there. It can easily come back to haunt you.

Video

If your story has caused any news footage, make a point to get video snippets mounted on your website.

If your video clips come from a mainstream media television show or an online news site with video, the station or site probably keeps a history of their episodes in archives, so you might be able to get permission to link their video directly to your site. That way you don't need to load the interview itself onto your site, saving on your site's memory load and raising your site visitors' scanning speed. The station may also be pleased to have more online hits through your site, so this situation is mutually beneficial. That's a good selling point when seeking permission.

If the video is an amateur YouTube sort of posting, try to contact the original source of the upload. You may have to load this sort of video onto your site because you don't want to lose the video if the owner's site shuts down.

You can create helpful video snips by shooting your own and mounting it on your site, so long as you do it in a way that evokes your professional image. Many nonfiction books are so true-to-life that they can support an interesting video segment just by having you sit before the camera and tell something about your story.

So make your own video. Invent a style for yourself. Address the camera in the "direct pitch" mode, or have someone off camera ask you brief questions so you have someone to respond to. For brevity, cut out the questions and play only relevant snippets of the answers. Viewers will understand that these are trimmed interview bits.

This is great practice for when you are actually doing a real on-camera video interview. Many televised programs will not book a new guest without seeing some existing footage, so this can also be used to send to stations on request.

WRITERS CONFERENCES AND WORKSHOPS

Be sure to join organizations that apply to your category of writing, if their membership rules permit. For instance, if you are a true crime writer, you might join Mystery Writers of America or International Thriller Writers and then attend meetings and conferences they hold. There is much to be gained by attending these conferences. The networking alone will help further your writing career and expand your professional network. In the natural course of conversation at these events, other writers will offer bits of information that will fall into place on your plan. These bits will pop up at times and in situations where you do not expect them. The learning never stops and the information is never stagnant. It is up to you to remain aware of the state of the publishing world. Part of the way that you do it is by attending conferences with fellow writers. (See the appendix for a list of organizations and conferences.)

OTHER WRITING THAT WILL FURTHER YOUR CAREER

While you are waiting for your book to sell, you will not just be sitting around. The process of researching and writing any nonfiction book confers a certain level of expertise. This may or may not place you among the world's leading experts, but your knowledge can go a long way in speaking out for you. Therefore, look for e-zines or printed magazines whose subject or readership matches yours. Then look at the length of the articles they publish, check for submission guidelines underneath the masthead or on a website's guidelines page, and write an appropriate article based on their specs.

 HOT TIP!

Unless you are a successful author, do not contact an editor until your article is ready for submission.

Be the Star, Yourself

Another approach is to get an article written about you. This is especially appropriate if you have become a writer because some dramatic event came about, and now you have a story to tell. Visit media websites and get an e-mail address. Remind them of a story or set of stories they did on your topic, or a similar one, and tell them you have a great follow-up. Describe your experience in two sentences. Yes. Two sentences. You will naturally want to take many more sentences than that to describe it, but two sentences is enough. Take two more to tell them why this is a new angle, then sign off.

If you plan to call a reporter or editor, write your short pitch letter first. If you hook his interest, he will most likely ask you to send him a written description so he can pass it around in a meeting.

Every bit of public exposure that you generate becomes another building block in the structure of your platform.

SPEAKING EVENTS

Use the same credentials for your book (an expert on your topic or having lived your story) to get yourself scheduled for speaking events. Any sort of speaking event will do, as long as it relates to your topic or to your field of expertise. Book clubs, library clubs, graduate school classes, professional organizations, benevolent organizations—all are places where you can cultivate a public persona.

If you are not an experienced public speaker, stick to smaller, less stressful group events until you have your remarks solidly in your mind and you have become more comfortable after giving several presentations. If you find public speaking difficult, sign up for a good public speaking class. Then practice, practice, practice.

Teaching

Don't despair if your particular skills or book subject do not lend themselves to speaking engagements. Instead, consider teaching a class related to your expertise. A teaching credit on your résumé goes a long way in boosting your credibility, assuring your prospective publisher that you bring as much capability to the table as ambition. Here again, document every event with photos, then get comments or testimonials from your attendees and post it all on your website.

Opportunities to speak, teach courses, or give seminars are always worthwhile—if they feel worthwhile to you. You're the expert, so you decide if any given group or location can be of use in solidifying your authorial persona. This is a subjective call. If it is practical for you to do so, you can appear at schools and community centers, or at religious, civic, and political organizations. The thing that matters is that the organization is related to your book's topic in a way that helps to bolster your image as an author.

In addition to making physical appearances, don't overlook online opportunities. For instance, if you want to do a course through The Learning Annex, contact them and find out if they are interested in having you teach an online class. This is a case where a quick phone call or an e-mail to their website's contact page might be enough to get you into their process for taking on speakers. If you decide to contact via an e-mail, follow the same principal as always in business correspondence and keep your letter concise and to the point.

A site such as The Learning Annex should have various pages and an FAQ section to tell you what you need to know about submissions, guidelines, and their query process. Don't make the blunder of introducing yourself as a potential "expert" by showing them that you did not do your fundamental homework about *them*.

Radio

Most stations do phone interviews these days. Never turn down a chance to do a radio broadcast. If you are an expert in your field, begin to solicit radio interviews in your area of expertise. Even though you do not yet have a book to sell, you can raise the visibility of your platform by tying your expert knowledge into current events of the day, annual holidays, or any other already newsworthy event. Start with local or Internet radio, then expand regionally and nationally.

How many variations can you get out of your basic theme? As many as possible without causing your listeners to roll their eyes or laugh in your face. Meaning that if you can find a way to connect expertise on Eighteenth Dynasty Egypt to a show on trout fishing in America, go for it. Who knows how many trout fishing enthusiasts are also amateur Egyptologists?

Contact every talk radio station in your region and offer to do a regular segment. This is different from an interview, as here you will regularly host a short program about your topic. If possible, make your initial contact over the phone instead of going the written query route. A phone call is an appropriate first contact because it allows you to demonstrate how you sound, and it actually becomes your first audition. If they want your pitch in writing—and they are likely to since you will have packed a lot of information into that single phone call—send a modified query letter (see chapter 7), altered to fit the specific radio station. Keep this contact letter short and sweet.

Here is an example: "Since many listeners of your Saturday morning show, *The Doggy Hour*, are real animal lovers, a regular listener call-in segment based on my book, *Therapeutic Massage for Your Pets*, will be of special interest ..." Modify the same sort of lead-in for whatever your product, subject, field, or topic may be.

Then, give a very brief description of yourself, no more than two sentences. Emphasize the ways your expertise gives you credibility on your potential book's topic and how you fit with their audience's interests. The details will vary with every author. The goal is to get you behind the microphone to embellish your platform while also offering something useful to the radio station and you both: listeners.

HOT TIP!

Proofread everything. Typos are truly sent by the devil and they will ambush you if you let them. Before sending any letter or e-mail, also be certain that the spelling and punctuation are spot-on.

Be especially perseverant about getting your voice onto the radio. Audience attention level is much higher in talk radio than it is in television because you have a captive audience of people at work or driving in their cars.

In nearly any form of talk radio, you can find specialty stations or shows that fit your particular platform. The early morning Saturday feed and grain report might not sound like a golden opportunity to you, but to the guy with the book about how America's farmers can survive in competition with the corporate farming conglomerates, that radio spot is a direct avenue to his prospective book's target audience.

Webcasts

A webcast is any radio or television show on the Internet. These shows go out to a specific list of subscribers, and often to the general public. Usually, a webcast can be accessed after the initial airing on an on-demand basis on the show's website as well as on the websites of many of the guests. Some of the shows will also be available on sites such as YouTube and Internet Archive (www.archive.org). Participating in a webcast is a great opportunity to raise your Internet visibility and grow your audience.

Wireless Internet has given real market power to webcast radio; there are now Internet radio and television shows, and websites covering every conceivable topic. Use a search engine to find those in your area of expertise, then e-mail or write to the producer or host. (The method that they prefer to be contacted by should be listed on the "Contact" page of their site.) Your letter or e-mail will be much like an initial query letter (see chapter 7), only here you will emphasize why you are a match for their show. Be sure to first check the *past guest list* and *topics of discussion* to ensure that you are a good fit. Then, if you have not already heard from them, follow up with a phone call a week after they receive your e-mail or letter. Ask if there is any additional information you can provide to prove that you are right for their show. If they do not provide a phone number, or if they give one that dumps you into voicemail, then send a courteous reminder note one week later using the same e-mail or postal mail form as you did the first time.

There are so many radio and Internet interviews that can be done online or over the phone that you can "appear" all over the country without leaving home. When your book is published, this is an ideal way for low-budget (or no-budget) promotional campaigns to get traction with the reading public.

HOT TIP!

In many cases, a radio tour will cost you nothing but time and effort, and can yield measurable results in terms of book sales.

Phone Seminars

Tele-seminars have also recently become a very popular way for nonfiction authors to gain readers. A tele-seminar is a seminar done via a conference call. You can share your information with others even though your book is not yet published.

They are fairly simple to set up. First, contact a service such as FreeConferenceCall.com that offer technology for a teleconference. With a few clicks you can sign up for a free conference call number that will hold a certain number of callers, usually close to one hundred. You will be given a conference call phone number and an access code. Then, through your website, interviews, social networking sites, and your newsletter, get information to any prospective listeners about the time, date, and topic of the call. You can even set up a generic e-mail address through your website so that people can e-mail you questions before and during the call.

Set up regular monthly tele-seminars and invite a guest to join you on the call. Before you know it, hits on your website and interest in your newsletter will both increase.

Social Networking

Social networks such as MySpace, Facebook, LinkedIn, and others allow authors to build an audience well ahead of any book they might write. A personal page on any of these sites is very easy to set up and can attract media, readers, and other professional opportunities. In many cases, others will stumble across your social network page and then go on to your website. Twittering might prove to be of some value, but then again, when will you get any writing done?

SIMPLY IRRESISTIBLE

The building of a platform requires time and effort in addition to the considerable investment of energy required to produce a book in finished form. Not to diminish the work on the book in any way, but the manuscript alone is not enough. The time that you spend defining and polishing your platform may well be the deciding factor of whether your book gets sold and whether it ever reaches a wide audience. When you match a fundamentally good story with an author—you—who is dedicated to performing quality work and who has constructed a credible platform of authority, you have a book that can become unstoppable in the marketplace.

The idea is to build such a compelling platform of author expertise, visibility, built-in audience, and quality of writing that a publisher will be simply unable to refuse you.

CHAPTER 4

GETTING THE RIGHTS
RIGHT

Depending on the kind of book you are writing, you may need to secure the story rights. Securing the story rights means getting *written* legal permission to document another person's story in book form. Often these rights are exclusive, meaning you are the only one who can turn the story into a book. Sometimes the rights are for a limited time, or for a certain geographical area, such as North America, or the United States and Canada. But in any case, obtaining legal written permission is necessary. Without it, publishers will fear legal repercussions and will not purchase your book.

Rights are a bigger issue for some forms of nonfiction books than others. For example, the author of a nonfiction book on the theory of a specific religion will not need to be as concerned about legal rights as will the author of a biography, true crime, or memoir. Depending on the actual subject matter, a current events author might not need to secure rights, but at the same time the rights for a different current events subject could make or break a publishing deal. Each book is unique in that regard, and by the end of this chapter you will have a good feel for those situations that call for obtaining written permission.

WHEN YOU NEED RIGHTS—OR NOT

So when, exactly, do you need to obtain rights? Prominent Beverly Hills media attorney Neville L. Johnson says that when you use an existing quote or song lyric, or when you simply talk about another person, permissions are determined on a case-by-case basis and depend on the type of use and other factors established by the federal courts. "In nonfiction, a quote of what someone said publicly can generally be quoted again, because it is a 'fact.' But that does not mean an entire speech can be quoted," he says.

Johnson adds that if a quote were given in a legislative or administrative setting, that is always permissible. "Under the copyright doctrine of 'fair use,' copyrighted material may be used depending on the interplay of four factors," Johnson says. Those factors are:

1. Whether the use is "commercial" and to what degree

2. Whether use is "transformative" because it has a different function from the original use

3. The amount and substantiality of the portion used (is only as much of the original work as necessary used?)

4. The effect of the use on the market for the plaintiff's work.

"Number four is the single most important element of fair use," Johnson says. "An author also does not generally need permission to write about another person unless rights of privacy or confidentiality are involved."

 HOT TIP!

Do not confuse your extraordinary writing ability with legal rights; you must have both.

SECURING THE RIGHTS

The surest way to help guarantee a book contract is to secure story rights from someone who is directly related to the story. That someone will usually turn out to be the story's protagonist, since people with the most information will be the ones in key positions. The source may also be a family member, or someone who is closely related to the protagonist. Your first step, then, is to determine for a fact that the person in question is a source of *exclusive access to important and interesting information*. That specific information will be the one thing that provides your book with market power whether you are a known author or not.

When you obtain story rights to a compelling story, especially when that story has had recent media coverage, you will have in your hands the *only* thing that has the possibility of blowing past all the rules about platform and public visibility in the effect of promoting your project. The energy that propels this kind of book forward will come from the publisher's natural hunger for the story, coupled with the exclusivity created by your signed story rights.

If you are enough of a salesperson to get that key person or persons exclusively signed to talk to you, then an agent or publisher is likely to decide that it's worth taking you on. Of course, you will be offering more than the fact that you have legal access to inside knowledge; you will also have made yourself more credible because of the skill and dedication that you display by obtaining it.

LETTER OF AGREEMENT

Templates of rights agreements are available on the Internet or in good bookstores. Download or copy one, edit it to fit your situation, then go get the signatures. Or, if you are more comfortable, ask your attorney to draft a letter for you.

If your subject is someone who may be put off by a legal form, draft a brief letter, as if it is written by the person, granting you his permission to tell his story—and have him sign it. If you are dealing with several people who are absolutely essential—meaning that the story cannot be told without them—you may have to offer them a percentage of your earnings. The amount can reach as high as 50 percent if they also share in paying commissions and promotional costs. However, for that much ownership in the book, your source would truly have to be at the heart of the story, and the story itself would have to be extraordinary enough to be worth your time.

HOT TIP!

Get it in writing!

If you are splitting a percentage of the book's proceeds with your source, it must be clearly stated in your Letter of Agreement that your source will also receive his agreed percentage on any ancillary deals, such as foreign rights, audiobooks, or e-books. Some sources may behave as if they are not concerned about that, at first. But they will absolutely become concerned if they learn that money is flowing and they aren't getting any. Additional income can be derived from foreign translations, ongoing royalties, and even film and television rights.

The most practical method for staying out of civil court with your source is to pay a fair share. All the fun will drain out of your publishing deal if the advance money and any future royalties have to go to your lawyer to defend you in court.

As the late Hollywood movie studio boss Samuel Goldwyn famously said: "A verbal agreement isn't worth the paper it's printed on." So we risk repetition for the sake of vital emphasis: Get it *in writing.*

PAYING FOR RIGHTS VS. BRIBING A SOURCE

Never pay for an interview. If you pay your source with any form of compensation—whether it is money, a vacation, or any other form of gain, it may later be construed as a bribe—and the truth of your entire story will be called into question. Usually writers who are tempted to pay believe that they are onto a "sure thing." But it is statistically disastrous to risk any amount of money on a "sure thing" in the publishing world, where sure things are essentially nonexistent.

Therefore, unless you are partnering with another individual—meaning that you are going to share a percentage of your book advance and book royalties with the person whose rights you formally obtain—*never pay your principal source or anyone else to talk to you.*

It will backfire on you in ways that you could never predict. Somebody, somewhere, is going to expose the fact that your information has been purchased. The pay-to-talk waters have been so heavily fouled by both the tabloid press and the true crime book market that most people, book industry executives and readers alike, will instantly dismiss the credibility of anything based on paid information.

The general public has seen too many examples of books that collapse shortly after their release because it is discovered that one or all of the sources were fabricated or contained fabricated information. (Can anyone say *James Frey?*)

The book *Angel at the Fence* is a good example. Written by Holocaust survivor Herman Rosenblat, the book was a memoir of his time interred in a concentration camp during World War II. In the book, and for the past sixty years or so, he has insisted that every day he was inside the camp his bride-to-be met him at the fence with an apple. Sounds like a great story, doesn't it? Oprah's people thought so, too. They invited Rosenblat to be a guest on the show not once, but twice. Additionally, a children's publisher released a children's version of the story and several overseas publishers bought rights. A movie was even planned.

Holocaust historians, however, said there was no way that a girl could have gotten to the same fence, the same time, every day, nor could Rosenblat, a prisoner, get to the other side of the fence for a regular meeting. Ultimately, the publisher, Berkley Books, withdrew the memoir after scholars, friends, and family members all said that

Rosenblat's tale was untrue. And this was after Berkley defended the book by saying it was a work of memory, and a story whose truth was known only to the author.

Consider the manner in which general awareness of the trend toward falsehood in memoirs has forced our society to a high level of cynicism regarding the entire category. We all wonder if a paid informant can give unbiased information or present his story in a way that is not self-serving.

In spite of your best intentions, when you try to obtain legitimate information from a source who is not a principal, but who is still valuable to the story, you may find yourself being held up for payment. In that case, you must explain that you cannot compensate any source because it will destroy your credibility as an author, while stressing that you want to give this individual the chance to *tell his or her part of the story*.

Most of the time that approach will work, even though some will feel they have to hold out for a while to be certain you aren't going to loosen up with some cash. With a little bit of time and your repeated assurances that they have the opportunity to be a part of history, most people will eventually come around. You should also offer to mention them in the acknowledgments.

PROCEEDING WITHOUT STORY RIGHTS

Keep in mind that not everyone wants a book written about him. In this case the rights might be difficult to get, if not impossible. Remember Goldwyn's quote about written contracts? Fortunately, it is at this point that you also encounter the following piece of good news: You can sometimes proceed without story rights.

Yes, there are certain situations where you can proceed with a true story without obtaining anyone's permission at all, and still remain within your own legal rights. All you have to do is tap dance your way across the legal minefield that lies between your right to free speech and any other person's legitimate expectation of privacy.

Let's say you can't get the rights to the story. Maybe the protagonist doesn't want to talk to you, or maybe wants money up front. Whatever the case, you've got no rights to the story. What can you do? Let's take a look at your options.

Write a Legitimate Work of Fiction

You can fictionalize the story, changing names, dates, and places enough so that the original story is unrecognizable. The problem with this scenario is that you have a good, true, factual story, which is worth much more as a nonfiction book than as a novel.

Find Peripheral Sources

As mentioned previously, you can obtain rights from people around the story, the peripheral characters that drive the manuscript along. In doing this, however, you must be very clear in your text whose point of view you are representing. It can be a tricky act of balancing many hats at one time, but it can work.

Public Domain

You can write the story based on public documents, such as newspaper articles and court transcripts, and public records such as birth, marriage, and death certificates. Land transfers, census records, and other official papers can also be of help. These documents are all considered to be in the public domain, and it is an arena where you can obtain information without fear of a defamation claim against you.

The best public domain source is usually an official court transcript. These transcripts may also include case depositions, along with any documents or interviews that are entered into the case record. Following a verdict, anything in the case record that has not been specifically sealed by the presiding court is available for fair use.

The most thorough method of research for these records is to physically visit the appropriate hall of records for the case file and obtain permission to read it right there. Since any other source that tells you what is in that court record has a potential for error, the only effective way to eliminate that doubt is to see the real thing for yourself and set aside at least one full day for reading and study of the evidence.

HOT TIP!

Complex cases may require many days of reading and review.

All other publicly filed documents are also legitimate sources of information, because (as with official court records) the parties to these public declarations of information have already accepted it as true.

Remember, though, that letters, memos, and personal documents of any kind retain a certain degree of copyright on behalf of their writers, *regardless* of who holds them now. So just because some brokenhearted lover gives you all of the letters sent by her ex, be aware that the ex still retains partial ownership of the words on the page.

HOT TIP!

No, they did *not* "give away" their U.S. Copyright protection simply by mailing the letter. You need to secure the rights from anyone to safely use their written words.

THE RIGHT APPROACH TO RIGHTS

The basis of your approach is simple. Anything you write that can be independently verified is safe. Also, most anything that casts a favorable light on the subject is also safe and not actionable in court, since there are no damages as a result of your words. Beyond that, you must be certain that anything you write about another person or group that is unflattering in any way is supported by at least one very credible source, and preferably two or more sources. Be assured that if you secure a book deal, the legal team at your publishing house will vet the manuscript for anything that could be considered actionable in civil court.

Remember, too, that even though the publisher's legal team will be going over your words with a fine-toothed comb, it does not mean that you can turn in vague or sloppy work. You must do all the due diligence that you can and turn in the most print-ready manuscript that you are capable of producing. This means that in addition to numerous formatting, spelling, and grammar checks, you must document your sources for each fact. If you can afford to have an intellectual property attorney review your materials before sending them out, that will be another layer of protection that you can give to your book. If you cannot, then at least filter every page of your work to guarantee that you have not libeled any person or organization, that you have written permission for any direct quotes, that you can cite where you obtained indirect quotes, and that any cutting of another's work that you employ is correctly credited and less than 100 words in length.

CHAPTER 5

THE NINE
ESSENTIAL ELEMENTS
OF A BOOK PROPOSAL

A book proposal is the primary sales tool for your book. If you secure an agent's interest, it will be used to attract an editor. The editor then takes the proposal to the publisher, and often to the key sales, marketing, and public relations people. Your proposal should give all of these people a good overview of you, your platform, and your book. Done correctly, it is a powerful instrument that can get everyone at the publishing company excited about you.

Because a book proposal is often a fifty- to sixty-page document requiring a serious investment of time and creative energy, you can convince an editor that you have what it takes to complete a book provided that yours is done exceptionally well. Many people can write a great opening and a couple of chapters, but then start floundering and somehow lose their way. Your first task is to assure a potential publisher that you are not one of them. No publisher can stay in business for long if they pay money in advance for books that are never completed to satisfaction.

Agents and publishers are also very busy. The number of e-mails, phone calls, and proposals each receive in a day is mind-boggling. Since it is not humanly possible for them to read through that many manuscripts, the shorter book proposal is a timesaver that your readers will appreciate.

Creatively, your book proposal will be your touchstone throughout the completion of the book itself. If, during the writing of the book, you find yourself off track, your proposal will nudge you back in the right direction. That will then allow you to deliver the book that the publisher bought, rather than something that will cause them to lose their enthusiasm.

FICTION VS. NONFICTION

You may wonder whether you should complete your book before approaching an agent or an editor. First of all, we must acknowledge that there are defined differences between fiction and nonfiction. The most important distinction being simply that fiction is made-up, while nonfiction is factual.

When writing fiction, it is important to finish the book to a polished condition, because the publisher is buying the complete package of plot, character, dialogue, and your particular narrative voice—sometimes that most of all. These things must reveal themselves before a decision can be made as to whether or not to publish a book. In addition, the greatness of a novel is sometimes only revealed in the last few pages, creating yet another reason why the book needs to be completed before pitching. Agents for more established fiction authors may be able to sell a two-book or three-book deal based on one completed manuscript, but unless you are a book star, that first one has to be finished.

The situation is different in the field of nonfiction. There, the publisher is buying the *idea* of the book, along with your platform, both of which can assure them that you are uniquely positioned to write and sell the book. And by buying into the project at the proposal stage, they also retain the option to have input on the direction that the book takes. This is usually a very good thing, and the process makes a lot of authors appear to be more polished than they really are. If you are a writer who can set ego aside and accept that these very smart and talented people want to make your book as successful as possible, then you have a winning attitude.

According to Michaela Hamilton, editor in chief at Citadel Press, speaking on the topic of an author's uniqueness, "At the Citadel Press, we want every book we publish to be the unique book that only its author could write. Whether it's a poker guide, a personal memoir, a narrative nonfiction work, a celebrity tell-all, a true crime book, a biography or autobiography—in any genre, the book must have something unique to offer. We are not interested in generic publishing or series publishing. Each book must stand on its author's unique qualifications to write it. For many titles, this concept comes down to platform— the author's ability to attract readers to his or her work through media interest. In presenting our list to major customers such as Barnes & Noble, Borders, and others, we have to be able to overcome their reluctance to support an unknown new product. Their question is always, 'Why do I need this new book if I am already carrying established titles that I know will sell?' We have to be able to answer, 'Because this book has something new and unique going for it.'"

Finding that uniqueness can be difficult, especially if you are not up-to-date on all the deals and trade industry news. A book proposal, rather than a finished book, gives agents and publishers the opportunity to tweak the basic concept to ensure your book is like no other and is ready for today's market.

THE BASICS OF FORMATTING

Before we address the specifics of your proposal, a few words regarding the format of your proposal are necessary. Today's publishing industry standard for writing proposals and manuscripts is to use Microsoft Word. Part of that software is its "Track Changes" feature, which tracks the edits and deletions of a file and is a powerful tool for authors and editors. If you are not up-to-speed on Microsoft Word, take a class, go through the software's tutorial, or read one of the numerous books available about it. Today, it is simply not acceptable to turn in a proposal using any other word processing software.

While each agent and editor may want to receive your proposal in a slightly different format, some things are standard to the form:

- Use 1" margins all four sides
- Times or Times New Roman 12-point type and double-spaced paragraphs
- A header with the page number, the title of the book, and your name on every page of your proposal
- [For print versions] Text on one side of the page only

This is also a good time to brush up on your grammar and punctuation skills. If you do not know the difference between *to*, *two*, and *too*, it's time to learn the correct usage of each word. Ditto for *their*, *there*, and *they're*; *buy*, *by*, and *bye*; *here* and *hear*; *your* and *you're*; etc. Equip yourself with a recent version of The Chicago Manual of Style (currently popular in hardcover in the fifteenth edition, and in various online editions for those who prefer to subscribe to a site service), from The University of Chicago Press. It is a major source for answers to countless questions of form, style, grammar, and punctuation. Remember that other writers who will be competing for your slot at a publishing house will tend to have impeccable grammar skills. Don't short yourself. You can gain permanent improvements with minimal effort.

HOT TIP!

Before sending your proposal to *anyone*: check, double-check, and triple-check to ensure that there are no typos, that your paragraph indentations are consistent, there are no extra spaces between words, and no extra lines between paragraphs. The statement of quality thus made by the manuscript is really about you.

THE NINE ESSENTIAL ELEMENTS

We propose nine essential elements to a book proposal. Each element is vital, though the details of each are of less concern. A solid and effective proposal will have all nine elements, even if they are arranged in a different order or are called by different terms. What matters is the quality of information that you give in your book proposal. The essential elements exist because agents and editors have discovered that there is a pattern to the information that they need in order to be able to decide whether or not to invest in your work. Experience has shown them that on top of needing a clear and concise presentation of the ideas contained in the finished book, they must also know about the author, the potential readership, and the author's ability to aid in promoting the book upon its release.

Even if you have already written your manuscript, we highly suggest you also create an accompanying book proposal to help market the complete work to agents and editors. In this case, the essential elements are the same as for any other proposal, with the exception of sample chapters and an outline. Since you already have the book, your efforts here are focused on showing your platform, your book's potential market, and the basic demographics of your projected readership.

1. THE TITLE PAGE

The impact of your title page is similar to the first impression you get the moment you meet a blind date for the first time. Sure, it's shallow, but we all respond to appearance. As you will see by the accompanying sample, the format of the title page is fairly standard.

Best-Selling Book Ideas:
Where to Find Great Original Concepts for Free—
and Use Them to Get Rich!

by
Seymour Keystrokes

(small author photo here)

Seymour Keystrokes
1001 Bookseller Circle
New York, NY 10010
800-555-1212
www.SeymourKeystrokes.com
Seymour@SeymourKeystrokes.com

Copyright 2009
by Seymour Keystrokes

The text on the title page is centered for impact. Place the title near the top of the page, with the subtitle on the line below. Some nonfiction books do not use a subtitle, but most do. You can take advantage of the accepted form by using your subtitle to tell your prospective readers more about what's inside.

Below that is your two-line byline.

If there is an image you think conveys your book well—i.e., an imaginary book cover or a professional author photo—place it below your byline. Make sure the photo is a low-resolution photo, roughly 100 dpi (dots per inch) and roughly 1½–2" x 2–3" (4–5cm x 5–8cm). This will allow the photo to be seen clearly without making the proposal file so large that it is impossible to open or send. If this were the only photo in the proposal, this would not be an issue, but you will be adding many more photos to this document.

Below that, place the appropriate contact information for your book. If you secure representation, this will be replaced by your agency's contact information.

Remember to include a copyright notice in the bottom right-hand corner of the page. You will be wise to ignore a toxic rumor that persistently floats around the literary business, saying that it is somehow insulting to the recipient to use a copyright notice. The facts are that a copyright notice is not technically required in order for you to retain your legal ownership of the material. However, your use of an official copyright notice is your clear assurance to the recipient that this is your full and final submission, presented as *you* intend it to be. In cases of ownership disputes, it is helpful to have that notice in place as an assurance to any third party that you took clear and reasonable steps to let people know that your material is not in the public domain. The truth is that no reasonable professional is ever going to feel the slightest "offense" by seeing your copyright notice. It is not directed specifically at them, anyway—this is material written to be read by many people.

When properly placed and formatted, it is another sign of your clear and focused intention.

2. TABLE OF CONTENTS

The table of contents (TOC) in your book proposal is a standard table of contents. You have probably done something similar before. If you have not, follow the example in chapter 6. In your TOC, accuracy is everything; therefore, the very *last* thing that you do before declaring the proposal ready to send out is to carefully go over your TOC page one more time just to be certain that all the pagination is correct. There is nothing worse than an agent or editor using the TOC to flip to a page, only to find she landed somewhere other than where she was supposed to be.

HOT TIP!

Be sure to format your page numbers with the tab feature set to "right justify" so that the page numbers line up at the right margin.

3. OVERVIEW OR SUMMARY

This overview section should only be one or two pages, but it will sum up the book so succinctly that your high school composition teacher would swoon to read it. This one really gets the re-read and re-polish treatment over and over again until it is letter perfect. The reason is that this very short section, *more than anything else*, is what will compel an agent or editor to want to embrace the whole book.

We caution you not to get bogged down in the details of your book here, as most first-time authors tend to do. Instead, cover the story in broad strokes and leave the details for the chapter summaries where they belong. We always have a number of overviews posted on the offerings page on our website (www.MartinLiteraryManagement.com).

These overviews are pulled directly from the book proposals that we were pitching at the time, and they will give you a good idea of the format and what to include.

4. ABOUT THE AUTHOR

All right, this time it really *is* all about you. Here is your opportunity to give us all the reasons why you are qualified to write this book. This is not the time to be humble. On the contrary, pull out all the stops and let yourself shine. Your author bio really cannot be too strong, but every word of it must be true.

Don't dress up your author bio by saying impressive things about yourself. You must cite concrete and specific (and provable) accomplishments that will reflect well upon your authorship. Be sure to include your:

- writing background
- post-secondary education
- civic and professional memberships
- awards and honors
- pertinent volunteer or community service work
- previously published work
- author's headshot

This section is usually one to two pages. Use the remaining space to provide links to articles you've written or that have been written about you, and interviews that can be viewed on the Internet to show off your media savvy. Include your website link here as well. It is critical that the end result portrays you as savvy and knowledgeable in your field.

Avoid delving into early life achievements. You don't need to go back to the womb; too much information is problematic because it takes the focus away from your ability to write this book. Keep in mind that the book proposal is a sales tool, first and foremost. Every single word in it must serve to direct the reader (the agent/editor/publisher) toward your goal of selling the book to a commercial publisher and then to a body of readers.

Fact Sheet

Another element of your author bio can be a one-page fact sheet. A fact sheet contains quick bits of information about you, including your likes and dislikes. Prospective agents and editors need to be provided with this information because it's only natural to want to work with someone who has things in common with you. Some of the things you might include are your hometown, favorite sports, hobbies, or most embarrassing moment. Just keep it short! None of us is as interesting to others as we are to ourselves.

For example, if you are writing an instructive how-to book on quilting, you might list as one of your hobbies the fact that you enjoy discovering and researching old patterns. Everything applies.

5. PHOTO INSERT

This section is for photos and graphs (and maps, if applicable). A few pertinent photos that can serve as a sample photo insert is usually acceptable, *unless* photography is a key part of your book. Remember that everything about your book proposal, including the images attached, must further define you as the perfect person to write this particular book.

 HOT TIP!

Check the dpi level of each jpeg used, so that it is big enough to reproduce well and yet still small enough to avoid pointless over-sizing and corresponding memory drain.

6. BOOK COMPARISONS

Next to your platform, your book comparisons (or comps) section is the biggest key to the success of your proposal. Your comps section must consist of three to six examples of recent books that are similar to yours, and which sold well. Take time and care in considering the right comps for your project. They must reflect well on the potential success of your book.

To find appropriate comps, you can start with online booksellers such as Amazon.com or Barnes & Noble (www.bn.com). Look for recent books that cover the same or similar subject matter as yours. Because trends and habits change, a book that did well thirty years ago will not necessarily do well today, and so it will not be a good comp. There is no use in comparing your book to a dinosaur. Additionally, new people are constantly moving into publishing, and they might not be aware of a book that old—or even one from ten years ago. Newer books give agents and editors a point of reference for current consumer buying habits in your field.

No matter what your book title and subject, you are sure to find a few comps that are close. Amazon.com offers several million titles; *a few* have to be similar to yours.

When you find eight to ten books that look promising and that are similar to your book, check those titles in terms of sales. The number one mistake that authors make here is that they list comparative titles without any thought to *the success of the books*. There is absolutely no point in holding up a book that tanked as a supporting example.

Many authors use the daily sales rankings at Amazon.com and Barnes & Noble to determine sales success, but these numbers only reflect very current sales and are not accurate indicators of the overall, long-term sales of a book. A better bet is to go to the best-seller lists in *The New York Times* or *USA Today*. Both publications archive their bestseller lists and you can check to see which of your prospective comps are on those lists. If you are lucky, you will find one or two of your comps have done exceedingly well. One might even have a blurb on the cover to the effect of "Sixty Weeks on the Best-Seller List!" or you might find a book that is in its fifth or sixth printing.

Then do your homework. Find the publishers of the recent comps that sold well, and go to their websites. See how many books they release each year and how large their backlist is. If you want to attract a large publisher, you need to use comps that have been published by a large publisher.

If these steps have completely eliminated your prospective list of comps, *go find some more*. If some comps are still on your list, go to an actual bricks-and-mortar bookstore or a library to find an actual copy of your prospective comp. Then assess it for quality. If the manufacture of the book is done as shoddy work, that publisher will not be among the respected in the industry. When you hold the inferior book in your hands, it becomes apparent that if you had used it as a comp, that would only draw an unfavorable comparison—something that you surely want to avoid.

As you can see, this process can take some time. After you finally get three to six suitable titles, pull information for the comp's title: author, publisher, publication date, page count, ISBN, and whether it is hardcover, trade paperback, or a mass-market paperback. Be careful: Many popular books have more than one edition, as well as large print and audio versions. You definitely want to choose the printed version that sold best. Often, but not always, it is the original hardcover printing of the book.

Pull a cover image so agents and editors can get a visual. Format the image as you did the other photos in your book proposal, then place it in your document near that book's title information.

Next, decide how best to compare and contrast your title with each of the comps. To do this, (a) develop a one-paragraph description of the comp, then (b) add another paragraph of analysis explaining how your book offers positive points that the other book lacks. The common theme for all commercial nonfiction is that your book is similar to others in ways that have proven successful, but it is also uniquely yours by virtue of *your* valuable perspective.

HOT TIP!

Uniqueness is important. What is unique about you? How do you set yourself apart from the pack?

CAUTION: More is not more, here. One prospective author sent us a proposal that included twelve comps, ten of which were from small, university, or self-published presses. If your goal is to be with a university press for the prestige, then by all means use those books as comps. But don't use these kinds of books and expect to get a sizable advance, as those presses pay very little in the way of up-front money.

With the proliferation of information on Internet, there is no excuse for an author to remain ignorant about the profession. Check out your references. For example, if the publisher of a prospective comp doesn't have a website, run! If the website is cheesy, run faster. Consider that the way this sloppy website looks to you now is how *you* would look to others, if they learned that this publisher was handling your work.

Never bluff. You must read your competition. Otherwise how will you determine the right way to position your book? You could easily end up looking like a fool by declaring a certain book to be a "comp" for yours, when your recipient is aware that it is not a good comparison. With today's tight budgets, accurate competitive analysis is more important than ever, but the onus of it is upon you, ahead of the publisher. When you multiply your book by hundreds of others, it is clear that editors at publishing companies have no time to do this for each book that they are thinking about buying. But if you try to bluff your way through with lazy work, you will never know how to predict what your recipient already knows about the topic. The accuracy of your comps is another arena where you can demonstrate that *you* are the writer for this book.

Regarding the language in your comparison: Certain words and phrases are the kiss of death in the comps section of a proposal. Never say, "This book is better than _____." Who knows whether your proposal might end up being read by the agent or editor of the book you just slammed. It can happen! A better way to approach is to say: "My book offers _____ in order to go deeper into the topic than other books have done so far."

Never try to get off with light work by claiming that "there are no other books out there" like yours. This is actually a very old and tired gimmick that has been attempted far too many times to carry any weight. Many of your competition will try it anyway, which is fortunate for you because it isn't going to work for them, either.

7. YOUR MARKETING AND PROMOTION PLAN

Provide potential agents and publishers with a specific and detailed list of everything you are capable of doing to help make the reading public aware of your book. When you compile your list, consider these questions.

- Do you have a regular media presence, such as a television or radio show, or a popular website or blog?

- Do you have any skills in giving interviews for print, radio, or television? More important, do you have existing contacts that will interview you when the book comes out? If so, who are they?

- Have you ever participated on camera in the national media? Your local media? Do you have access to the footage, or even to a promo snippet of it? Can the publisher use it? Is it on your website? (If not, it should be.)

- Are you available for an out-of-town book tour? If so, assuming that you are footing the bill, where can you travel to?

- Do you have contacts at any major bookstores? If so, who are they and will they buy your book?

- Do you have contacts with any book clubs or library associations? Who and where are they?

- Do you have the means to *contribute to the promotion budget*? No, it is not a bribe; funding your own promotion and marketing is an incentive for publishers to buy your book. It is often a form of partnership in the reality of today's business world.

You will sweeten your position if you can commit to hiring a publicist for a three-month minimum at the time of the book launch—or at least assure the publisher that you will pull out all the stops to do it your own. However, if you do it yourself, please note that you must be able to describe for the publisher *exactly how you will do your personal promotion*, giving specifics on the who, what, and where of it.

List all of the ways that you can help garner publicity. Avoid generalities. Every method on your list offers assurance that you have every intention of helping the publisher help the world to find your book. It lets the agent and editor know that you understand that the days are gone when you could leave it up to "Ye Olde Publicity Department," which in many cases has seen its budget and number of personnel slashed to the bone. Consider that an in-house publicist commonly oversees as many as twenty-five books in a single month. That fact alone should be enough to convince you of the need for you to augment their efforts with your own tangible promotional plans.

The topic of promotion implies the larger topic of marketing. *Marketing* your book, as opposed to merely promoting it, is about creating actual sales of the book in significant numbers. Consider the following questions as springboards to thinking about your own particular marketing assets.

- Do you have any experience at public speaking? Can you generate significant "back of the room" sales of your book following lectures or appearances?

- Do you have your own *established* book blog that could sell books?

- If you do not operate a blog, do you at least have an established website with documented high volume that could also sell books?

- Do you have some ability to directly market your book to appropriate topic-related organizations, teachers' associations, library associations, or book clubs of any size? (Never pass up an opportunity to speak for, write to, or blog with *any* book club.)

- Does your book relate to any specific business or industry, and might they be willing to place a "bulk" order and give them away as promotional gifts?

Every nonfiction book will have related businesses that can be contacted with the idea of promotional tie-ins. A travel writer, for example, could approach any business within the travel industry with the idea of using the books for promotional gifts to favored clients or customers. (Get your publisher to quote their lowest group rate so that you can offer the related businesses a significant discount on the cover price.)

Provide the publisher with an honest approximation of how many books you think you could move in a year. If you lack these potential book sale outlets, don't mention marketing at all. Instead, focus on how hard you intend to work to *promote* the book. Remember to be specific.

It does not count if you say, "I intend to work as hard as I can for this book." That much is assumed.

HOT TIP!

Be *realistic* in describing your own marketing and promotion abilities, so that the publisher cannot later claim that you defaulted on your promises.

8. CHAPTER OUTLINES

Chapter outlines lay out the book in step-by-step detail with two or three paragraphs to describe each chapter. Think of this as the blueprint of your book, and you are the architect. This section needs to be fully fleshed out to prove that your book will not collapse in the middle, and will steadily build to the final page.

It is unwise to fake descriptions of chapters that you have not actually thought through. For example, one chapter description in a book proposal that we received said, "This chapter lists all the things that can go wrong with your car on a dark and lonely road."

Vague generalities have never played well in the nonfiction world. Remember that these chapter summaries are the roadmap to completing your book. If you do not lay out a definite plan in the chapter summaries, you will break down in the middle of your book and flounder with nowhere to go. If you can't be clear and precise here, you need to step back and think your book through a little more.

HOT TIP!

In creating your book proposal, consider your ending. Your mission is to leave agents and editors in a similar emotional state to one that will be experienced by readers of the finished book.

9. SAMPLE CHAPTERS

Always begin with your first chapter. It's never a good idea to toss chapter 6 at them for your writing sample and hope no one notices. If chapter 6 has your best work in it, why isn't there some of that work right at the front to help pull readers into the book? Your purpose as an author is to demonstrate how your book will hook readers from the beginning.

Offer the first twenty to twenty-five pages of text, up to the end of a chapter and a logical cliffhanger or teaser. Even if you have more of the manuscript completed, don't send additional pages. Your proposal is a selling tool. All you need to do is give them enough to get fired up about you and your writing. Then politely end the conversation and allow them to go off and think about how much they want to publish your book. There is no magic number for sample pages, but the issue can be reasoned this way: Twenty to twenty-five pages should be enough to offer a picture of how the book will read and of your writing skills. More pages than that can make for burdensome reading at the proposal stage.

The "less is more" principal applies here; it leaves room for the agent or editor to come back and give a tentative yes to the book, provided that the manuscript is given more of this and less of that. Sometimes this sort of guidance can be just the thing that a manuscript needs. So when you submit a calculated amount of sample pages instead of throwing everything that you have at them, it leaves you room to accommodate such requests—if you choose. Anyone who is captivated by your proposal will come back and ask to see what else you have. You may then reveal the extra pages, if they fit, and your brilliance will stun them all. If they don't fit the requested changes, you can leave them in the drawer with none the wiser.

CHAPTER 6

THREE PROPOSALS THAT SOLD—
AND WHY THEY DID

The following examples represent three unique book proposals. They are presented here in abbreviated form, because the original versions run up to fifty pages in length. They can be viewed in their entirety at www.MartinLiteraryManagement.com or at www.AnthonyFlacco.com. While each of these proposals follows the accepted style, take special note of the various ways that the vision behind each book is spelled out. As you will see, these writers each employed a slightly varying format, but all included the necessary information for that editor or publisher who must be able to visualize the finished book. All three of these proposals sold quickly for a good price. The finished books emerged as compelling written works.

1. Book Proposal With Celebrity Association: The first proposal demonstrates an approach that shows real media savvy; it is less about proving the author can write the story than it is about promoting the subject's marketability and promotional potential. The proposal is for a fact-based book with a self-explanatory title: *Horse Country: A Celebration of Country Music and the Love of Horses*. It is an excellent example of how a non-celebrity author can raise her book's profile by harnessing the power of someone else's prominence.

In this first example, you can see how cleverly the author blended her personal love for horses with the natural interest that country music fans have in artists whom they know and respect. Her full proposal uses more visual aids and less text than the other two proposals, because of the uniquely visual nature of her two subjects. Please note that this proposal still conveys all the essential information.

2. Book Proposal for Historical Nonfiction: The second proposal, by co-author Anthony Flacco, demonstrates how to propose a book of historical nonfiction. *The Road Out of Hell: Sanford Clark and the True Story of the Wineville Murders* sold to Sterling Publishing at Union Square Press for release in November 2009. In this case, the subject was partially known by many readers, so the compelling nature of the proposal had to come from the fascinating aspects of the deeper story.

3. Book Proposal for a True Crime Story: Our third proposal is by Amanda Lamb—a previously published author in the parenting genre—and is titled *Deadly Dose: The Untold Story of a Homicide Investigator's Crusade for Truth and Justice*. This proposal would have sold even if it were her first book, because it is a solid demonstration of how to approach the marketplace with a compelling true crime case, one that has such stopping power for the reader that it will captivate the audience for an author, even when her name alone may not.

STORY RIGHTS

Each of these three proposals placed their authors in the thick of the story rights issue. The first proposal needed permissions for each of the celebrities interviewed, as well as sign-offs on the right to reproduce the photographs. The second proposal required signed story rights from Jerry Clark, the adult son of the late Sanford Clark, as well as quotation rights from numerous sources. The third proposal had the rights of the detective involved in the case, as well as court transcripts, interviews, and voluntary cooperation from everyone necessary to tell the complete story. Please note that in your proposal, each section should start at the top of a new page.

Horse Country:
A Celebration of Country Music and the Love of Horses

By Lisa Wysocky

Capitol Records Recording Artist
and World Champion Bareback Rider
Chris LeDoux (1948–2005)

.... *Insert Page Break*..

Table of Contents

[Note: The page numbers are *intentionally* deleted for the purposes of this example.]

[Note: This is a rare exception where an ongoing chapter outline was not used. The reason for the exclusion was that the book was sold before the interviews with the stars were completed, so the exact subject matter of each chapter was not known ahead of the interview. In this case, the publisher was able to visualize the book based upon Wysocky's overview and sample chapter—combined with her platform, marketing plan, and publishing history. In most cases, sample chapters must be accompanied by a chapter outline so the editor can see how you intend to structure the full book and, if it is a narrative book, how you will juggle the plot lines.]

.... *Insert Page Break*......................................

I. Overview and Format

Horse Country: A Celebration of Country Music and the Love of Horses combines two closely related subjects: country music and horses, and specifically, how horses have changed the lives of certain country music artists for the better. The stories are heartwarming, funny, touching, and uplifting.

Author Lisa Wysocky has been training horses and riders most of her life: first as a youth competing in saddle club and breed shows, then as a trainer and instructor to world-class Appaloosa horses and students. Now, she trains horses for therapeutic riding centers. Lisa has also been a publicist to the stars of country music and a syndicated lifestyles columnist, and currently splits her time between training, writing, and serving as motivational speaker and clinician to corporate clients and equine groups. She also still consults for artists and small record labels in the country music industry.

Horse Country is written in an approachable, easy-to-read format, and will contain twenty-seven chapters, approximately 55,000 words, and as many quality digital photos as the author feels are needed to illustrate key points.

Horse Country features twenty-seven stars of country music with heartwarming, funny, or touching stories, along with promotional photos and photos of the artists with their equine companions. The format will also include a brief bio of each artist's musical accomplishments, fan club contact information, a glossary of horse terms for non-equestrian readers, and an overview of the history of country music and horses, which dates back to the earliest cowboys who sang on the range.

The twenty-seven artists included in the book were specifically chosen for it. As a group, they offer a strong mix of traditional and contemporary country music, male and female, and bands. There are new artists, today's hot chart-toppers, and legends. A good mix of equestrian breed interests and riding styles are also included and range from Tennessee Walking Horses, trail riding, and cutting competitions, to wild horses, miniature mules, Friesians, quarter horses, and more.

According to the Country Music Association, country music accounted for 11.7 percent of all albums sold in 2005, with a total of 77.7 million units. Country was the only music format with an increase of sales in 2004, 2005, and, currently, 2006. Country radio remained the dominant format in 2005 with 2,031 radio stations in the United States, followed by 1,316 news/talk and 1,147 adult contemporary. More than 45.5 million adults listen to country radio stations nationwide each week, making it the highest cumulative audience of all formats. Additionally, country music radio stations are rated No. 1 or No. 2 in 43 of America's Top 100 markets.

A 2005 American Horse Council Foundation report found 9.2 million horses in the United States. Two million people own horses and an additional 2.3 million work or volunteer in the industry. Horses provide the U.S. economy with over 450,000 full-time jobs and have an annual impact on the U.S. gross domestic product of $101.5 billion.

Lisa is confident that the names listed below are interested and available for participation. Lisa also has contacts for each of the artists below and can get interviews scheduled relatively quickly. Great care was taken to ensure that each artist included is a true horse person, and not just someone who had ridden once in a video or for a magazine shoot.

Horse Country truly offers something for every fan of country music and every lover of horses. The list of specially chosen twenty-seven artists includes (in alphabetical order):

[Note: Consider the author's excellent use of industry statistics in her overview, which clearly shows there is a strong market for this book. The list of artists was placed at this point.]

.... *Insert Page Break*......................................

II. About Lisa Wysocky

Author, speaker, trainer, and entertainment publicist Lisa Wysocky was born in Minneapolis and raised in a nearby suburb. In her teens, a riding instructor taught her that by striving to "be the best you can be," you often become "the best anyone can be." That concept of success, and the instructor's insistence that how you won in the show ring—or in life—was more important than what you won, changed her life. Lisa studied to be a horse trainer at the University of Minnesota and then brought her ideas on success to the show ring. Early wins on the national and world championship horse show circuit took Lisa to all parts of the United States and Canada, where she was often asked to speak to groups of horse people, or to write articles for national horse publications. In her spoken presentations and in her articles, she stressed the key to success was "being the best you that you can be," and applied the thought to both horses and people. Lisa's passion for writing and speaking soon led her to a second run at college, where she studied communications and journalism.

A knee injury cut short Lisa's career as a competitive show horse trainer, but she took her unique skills and ventured into her second love, that of music. Six years as a correspondent for Nashville's paper, the *Nashville Banner*, and her reputation in the country music industry as a writer of quality biographical and promotional material, piloted Lisa to a career in public relations. She opened her own firm in 1989. Since then Lisa's innovative and aggressive style of public relations has earned kudos from clients and media alike. Lisa is also very active in assisting clients with their public image and with their interview skills.

In addition to running her public relations firm, Lisa has authored a narrative nonfiction book, *The Power of Horses: True Stories From Country Music Stars* (Lyons Press), which features true horse stories from eighteen of country music's top stars. Lisa has also edited countless books for other authors, written a weekly syndicated celebrity lifestyles column, and has been a regular featured guest on Jones Radio Networks syndicated overnight show, *Danny Wright All Night*.

Lisa is also the author of *Success Within: How to Create the Greatest Moments of Your Life* (Sourcebooks), and the co-author (with Brad Cohen) of *Front of the Class: How Tourette Syndrome Made Me the Teacher I Never Had* (St. Martin's Press), which was the winner in the education category for the 2005 *ForeWord* magazine Book of the Year Awards and the 2006 IPPY Awards.

Lisa Wysocky is a down-to-earth motivational speaker and equine clinician who gives her audiences step-by-step guidance on creating their own personal success stories. Learn more at www.lisawysocky.com.

[Note: Reading her bio, you have to believe that Lisa was born to write a book about country music stars and their horses. She definitely owns that little corner of the world. In the next section, Media Achievements, she described her credits in past books, articles, and documentaries as well as her television and radio credits.]

.... *Insert Page Break*.....................................

V. Comparisons to Other Books

[Note: This unique section is given in its full version for illustrative purposes.]

Most books in the marketplace about celebrities and their pets are photo driven, vs. story driven. However, there are a few that, like *Horse Country*, also focus on the heartwarming story of people with their beloved pets. Here is an overview of a few of those titles.

- *Chicken Soup for the Horse Lover's Soul* by Jack Canfield, Mark Victor Hansen, Marty Becker, Gary Seidler, Peter Vegso, and Theresa Peluso (Paperback, 380 pages, $14.95, HCI, July 2003, ISBN: 0757300987, 8.4 x 5.4 x 1.1 inches). This is a collection of heart warming stories that targets devotees of all things equine. The book is divided into seven sections, and contains ninety-three short stories about the horse's intelligence, versatility, and intuitiveness. However, there is no celebrity connection and few photos.

- *Chicken Soup for the Horse Lover's Soul II* by Jack Canfield, Mark Victor Hansen, Marty Becker, Teresa Becker, Peter Vegso, and Theresa Peluso (Paperback, 384 pages, $14.95, HCI, February 2006, ISBN: 0757304028, 8.3 x 5.5 x 0.9 inches). This follow-up *to Chicken Soup for the Horse Lover's Soul* combines the adoration people have for their horses with inspiring, funny, and tender stories. But again, there is no celebrity or country music connection, or photographs of celebrities with their horses.

- *Music Row Dogs and Nashville Cats: Country Stars and Their Pets* by Karen Will Rogers and Laura Lacy (Paperback, 192 pages, $18.00, Pocket Books, June 2004, ISBN: 0743491939, 9 x 7 x 0.5 inches). *Music Row Dogs and Nashville Cats* contains photographs of some of America's country music artists with their beloved pets, accompanied by short stories. While one or two of the stories include horses, most are of dogs and cats and the book is also more photo driven than story driven.

- *Pit Road Pets* by Karen Will Rogers and Laura Lacy (Hardcover, 163 pages, $19.96, Ryan Newman Foundation, February 2006, ISBN: 0977669904, 10 x 9.9 x 0.7 inches) features stories and photos of NASCAR drivers, their families, and their pets. No horse connection is present, and the book mostly discusses dogs, although the celebrity connection is there.

- *People We Know, Horses They Love* by Jill Rappaport, Wendy Wilkinson, and Linda Solomon (Hardcover, 170 pages, $39.95, Rodale Press, September 2004, ISBN: 1579548571, 10.1 x 14.3 x 1 inches). A full-color photo-essay celebrating the bond between noted equestrians and their horses, *People We Know, Horses They Love* features nearly thirty celebrity horse lovers who pay tribute to the special relationship between human and horse. While the celebrity connection is there, the targeted and focused country music connection is not, and the book is photo driven, vs. story driven.

Horse Country remains the standard in combining country music and horses, and balancing heartwarming stories with unique photos.

HOT TIP!

Use simple and effective points to contrast your proposed book with other recent, popular books. It works!

[Note: The comps were followed by two Marketing and Promotion pages full of descriptions of the market for her book and the specific efforts she intended to extend on behalf of the book. This was followed by an excellent sample chapter that convinced the publisher that she was the writer to do this book. The publisher was able to visualize the book based upon Wysocky's overview, the sample chapter, and her résumé.]

WHY THIS BOOK SOLD

The author's solid platform in both the areas of horses and country music established her as an expert in each field. Her writing was engaging and the subject matter was unique. Plus, in both the book comparison section and her overview she clearly established there was a market for this book, while at the same time demonstrating that this exact subject matter had not been covered.

Peter Lynch, editorial manager for trade books at Sourcebooks, Inc., said each of the sections that Wysocky used is critical for a successful proposal. Based on a similarly comprehensive proposal, he bought *The No Gossip Zone* by Sam Chapman with Bridget Sharkey, a guide for business leaders on creating a positive, healthy, and happy work environment. Like Wysocky's proposal, the first thing that jumped off the page for Lynch with *The No Gossip Zone* was the quality of the main book idea.

"It addressed a problem that is common in workplaces but rarely discussed, meaning I knew I could expect a big audience for the book and not have to compete against a lot of similar books on the topic," he says.

Also like *Horse Country*, the idea was presented in an eye-catching and interesting manner. That is important, according to Lynch, because "nonfiction readers don't have a lot of time to read, so they gravitate toward books that seem like enjoyable reads."

And finally, like Wysocky, Sam Chapman has a fantastic platform and runs a public relations firm. "This meant we'd have additional PR resources to help promote the book," Lynch says.

THE ROAD OUT OF HELL
Sanford Clark and the True Story of the Wineville Murders

Book Proposal—Historical True Crime

By
Anthony Flacco
with
Jerry Clark

.... *Insert Page Break* ....

[Note: This proposal contained a traditional table of contents, and a section of photo inserts that offered several of the fascinating crime scene photos. The sample chapters section contained two sample chapters for a total of twenty-one pages. The outline of the continuing story was fourteen pages, and offered compelling photos from the case.]

OVERVIEW

This stunning true crime case is the untold story of the 1928 "Wineville Murders." It follows young Sanford Clark, beginning at age thirteen, through two years of captivity inside the private human abattoir of Gordon Stewart Northcott outside the desert town of Wineville, California. The serial torture and murder of at least twenty young boys took place during Sanford's two-year term of capture while he was enslaved to the would-be concert pianist/rapist/murderer.

The book will continue through Sanford's lifelong struggle to recover, serving honorably in World War II despite flashbacks that were worse than combat, then completing a long career with the Canadian Postal Service, maintaining a fifty-five year marriage, and adopting two boys out of the local orphanage whom he raised into men who love and honor him. It is being written with the life rights and full cooperation of Jerry Clark, Sanford's eldest adult son.

THE STORY: Thirteen-year-old Sanford Clark was sent from his home in Canada to live with his uncle Gordon Northcott on a chicken ranch in Wineville, California, and soon discovered that his uncle was a rapist and murderer of as many as twenty young boys during Sanford's time there, and possibly many more beforehand. Most of the boys were young migrant workers who vanished easily, but three were cherished local boys whose disappearance sparked outrage.

Shortly after Sanford's arrival at the ranch, he was attacked by Northcott, raped and beaten, and eventually forced on threat of torture and death to help kill three of the boys. Afterward Northcott explained to the terrified Sanford that he was now personally involved in the crimes and therefore prevented from disclosing anything about the mayhem going on at the ranch. Sanford was so traumatized by the circumstances of his slavery that he believed it when Northcott told him that Sanford would be hung if Northcott were ever apprehended.

Sanford was forbidden all communication except for dictated letters that were mailed back home as if they were from him. For the next two years, Sanford was forced to help dispose of the bodies of Northcott's victims, digging graves, burying corpses, and grinding up burned bones, all while enduring Northcott's beatings and sexual attacks whenever there wasn't another boy to absorb his psychotic rage.

The truly compelling aspect of the story comes from the two female protagonists: Jessie, Sanford's older sister (by four years), and June, Sanford's wife in his adult years. It was Jessie who caused Sanford to be rescued after she became suspicious of the letters he was forced to send home. Taking it upon herself, she traveled to the ranch and risked her life to help free Sanford, but not before being attacked, choked, and nearly killed for her involvement, by Northcott himself.

When Northcott forces her to go back home without Sanford, she avoids telling the local California authorities, thinking they might kill Sanford in storming the ranch. Instead, she hurries back to Canada and contacts a private detective to act on her behalf and inform Canadian Immigration, who in turn notifies U.S. Immigration in California. But by the time they send men to the ranch, they find Sanford there alone, abandoned by Northcott, who has fled the country. Sanford is wandering the property in a state of shock.

Northcott, his mother, and his sister, Winnie—*Sanford's mother*—have fled the U.S. together to hide in their native Canada, where they are eventually apprehended. Sanford's mother is still voluntarily with her brother and mother in spite of knowing what had been done to her boy, such was the sickness of their family.

After the much-publicized trial, Gordon Northcott was found guilty and hanged. Young Sanford Clark was exonerated of responsibility due to the horrendous circumstances of his captivity and his defeated state of mind, which would later come to be known as Stockholm Syndrome.

This true crime evolved into a family love story, once Sanford was released from the ranch and spent two years in a therapeutic "boys' town" environment. Back home, he spent the rest of his long life as a loving and beloved local figure in spite of the public's knowledge and his lasting physical and mental trauma. His wife of many years, June, joined his sister, Jessie, in standing by his side through his debilitating depressions and fits of suicidal guilt. With their help, he later adopted two young sons who grew up loved and respected in his home, while he spent a successful career with the Canadian Postal Service after serving honorably in World War II.

To this day, Sanford's son Jerry reveals that *he never heard his father say an unkind word about anybody*. Sanford Clark, instead of allowing himself to be twisted into evil, used his long nightmare to become a gentle and tolerant man with many friends and a loving family, in spite of his lifelong struggle to claim victory over those horrifying years.

.... *Insert Page Break*...

AUTHOR'S NOTE

I see this as a captivating story not because of the sustained levels of demonic behavior that existed in the Wineville "slaughterhouse," but because of the magnificent way in which Sanford Clark managed to continue his life in the aftermath. He returned home to a town where everyone knew the story, and yet he held his head up among them. He served in World War II and saw close combat all over Europe with his artillery unit. His flashbacks were highly exacerbated by the sight of torn bodies and by having to huddle in foxholes that were so much like the pit where he was chained as a boy.

He served twenty-eight years at the post office in spite of a few co-workers who made it a point to torment him, and his fifty-five year marriage to June was the high point of his life. His lovable personality brought him public acclaim late in middle age, but the savage treatment by his own guilt followed him to his deathbed. I am passionate about writing this book because to me, the Sanford Clark story represents the very epitome of the human capacity to carry out one's life with genuine grace, even under the most egregious and sustained sources of fire. —A.F.

[Note: This section was accompanied by the author's résumé and some basic information about Sanford Clark's son Jerry, who was the principal source for the personal information in the book. These were followed by a standard book comparisons section.]

WHY THIS BOOK SOLD

The book sold in the same year that director Clint Eastwood released his film *Changling*, starring Angelina Jolie. The film sparked interest in the Wineville murders, but focused on one small aspect of the Wineville story. Flacco compounded that interest by securing the story rights of Jerry Clark, adult son of the late Sanford Clark, and then found support from the publisher by emphasizing the story as a psychological drama told from the point of view of captive Sanford, following him through the entire two years of brutal torment on the murder ranch and then throughout the arc of his life for the next sixty-five years. The driving question is how he salvaged a life of bravery, kindness, decency, and public acceptance out of those terrible years.

Deadly Dose

by

Amanda Lamb

*Her personal contact info was
placed here*

[Note: A standard Table of Contents was placed after this Title Page, followed by a two-and-a-half-page Overview. The proposal also contained a two-and-a-half page Prologue, followed by an eighteen-page Sample Chapter. The writing throughout was crisp, clear, and compelling.]

ABOUT THE AUTHOR

Amanda Lamb is a television reporter covering the crime beat for WRAL-TV, one of the country's top CBS affiliates, in Raleigh, North Carolina. She is a seasoned journalist with more than seventeen years of broadcast journalism experience and a highly respected reputation to match.

Amanda has also appeared multiple times on Fox News' show *On the Record With Greta Van Susteren*, and Court TV's *Catherine Crier Live* to discuss a recent high-profile murder case.

Raleigh used to be a sleepy little southern town that some compared to the famed fictional town Mayberry in *The Andy Griffith Show*. But times have changed. With a 19 percent increase in population since 2000, violent crime in the area has increased dramatically.

Every day Amanda meets with police officers, prosecutors, defense lawyers, and judges. Her world extends from sharing coffee and confidences with investigators, to sitting on the front row of death penalty cases. Amanda has become the premier voice in crime reporting in the Raleigh market. She is *the* reporter suspects don't want to see at their door, and the one that victims call upon most frequently to share their stories.

Amanda writes a regular blog for WRAL.com called *Dispatches From a Reporter's Notebook* that gives viewers a behind-the-scenes peek into the world of a television reporter, pounding the streets daily looking for the next big story.

Amanda is also an accomplished writer in other categories. Her first book, *Smotherhood,* a humorous, nonfiction, parenting memoir was published in the fall of 2007 as part of the first offering of Globe Pequot Press's new contemporary line from female authors called skirt!.

Amanda's writing is also featured in the recent compilation of day-diaries from thirty-four American women titled *This Day in the Life.*

For nearly three years Amanda has been a regular contributor to *DotMoms,* a community of women writers around the world who share parental anecdotes. Her work can be viewed at www.dot-moms.com.

Amanda received undergraduate degrees from Duke University in English and psychology, and a master's degree in journalism from Northwestern University.

> Amanda Lamb has the ability to find the soul of the story very quickly. Her level of intellect oozes from her writing, most uncommon in local television news. She provides the viewer with a concise and profound style of reporting. Most importantly, Amanda's heart is never more than a keystroke away from her writing.
>
> — *David Crabtree, main anchor, WRAL-TV News*

Amanda is an amazing storyteller. She can touch, move, and inspire with words. A woman of multiple talents, Amanda has an incredible ability to get to the heart of a story with ease. I have seen her tackle complex and controversial issues in the news, and simplify them in a way television viewers can fully comprehend. Amanda is a strong writer, journalist, mother, and friend.

— *Pam Saulsby, main anchor, WRAL-TV News*

[Note: Amanda followed this section with a two-page description of the detective and the psychiatrist who were her research collaborators.]

COMPETITIVE TITLES AND TARGET MARKET

Surprisingly, despite the number of movies on television portraying female killers, there are few books documenting the true crimes of these black widows. There are even fewer examples where the woman is well educated, attractive, and seemingly normal until she commits the ultimate sin.

[Note: Amanda followed this section with the standard presentation of Comparative Titles that you saw in the first proposal.]

Target Markets

One only has to look as far as your television set, which is probably ten to fifteen feet or so from your couch or the end of your bed, to see America's obsession with crime dramas.

CSI, now in its seventh season, has been the number one scripted series in the Nielsen ratings for four years. *Law & Order*, currently in its seventeenth season, is the longest-running crime series and the second longest-running drama series in the history of American television. The proliferation of these crime dramas is only second in volume to reality shows.

And it's not just prime-time television getting into the act. Documentaries on channels like A&E and Court TV have captured our obsession with the macabre. The audience can't get enough. They want the inside-baseball scoop with nothing left out. No gritty detail is too minute or tedious for a crime junkie to absorb. Like the driver craning his neck to see the car crash, the crime junkie needs to know *everything* about a case.

I suggest that the same people who are absorbed with crime dramas and true crime documentaries on television are the audience for this book. At the end of the day these people want something to keep them on the edge of their seats, to draw them out of their mundane lives into a world of intrigue, a world so bizarre that they are turning each page hungering for more.

But the best part of *Deadly Dose* is that while the story is bizarre, the reader can relate to it because the players are normal people caught up in an abnormal game of death and deceit. Chris Morgan, Ann Miller, and Eric Miller could be our neighbors, our co-workers, our friends, our family. They could be *us*.

MARKETING AND PROMOTION PLAN

To help promote the book, the author will:

- Be available for opportunities to speak about *Deadly Dose* to media outlets, bookstores, and organizations.

- Be a highly effective spokesperson for the project, as a television news reporter with more than seventeen years in the communications industry.

- Block out a four-month launch window dedicated to promoting the book, its publication and sales, and hire a publicist to help in this effort.

- Begin with local media and network affiliates of her current employer, Capitol Broadcasting. The company currently owns four television stations and two radio stations in the state. Its affiliates include CBS, Fox, and CNN. The author also has contacts at the network level, specifically with the morning network news programs. In addition, because WRAL has such a superb regional and national reputation, this will help open doors with radio and print media. WRAL already has a partnership with the dominant local paper in this market, *The News & Observer*.

- Use the Internet effectively in marketing and promoting the book. In addition to being one of the top CBS affiliates in the country, WRAL-TV owns and operates WRAL.com, which the Media Audit rated number one in the nation in market penetration in June 2006, surpassing even the *Washington Post*. Access to this website, which already contains the author's daily television stories and blog, *Dispatches From a Reporter's Notebook*, will be extremely helpful in promoting the project.

- Because the material in this book will be of special interest to people in the criminal justice system, the author will use her contacts to reach organizations like the North Carolina Bar Association, the North Carolina Police Benevolent Association, and Carolina Crime Writers' Association. She will in turn use her contacts to promote the book with the national counterparts of these groups.

- Being a well-known, highly visible television reporter in the area, in addition to in the national arena, will allow the author an entrée into promoting the book at more than one hundred book stores in the Raleigh-Durham market.

- The collaborators will also help promote the book free of charge by making personal experiences whenever needed as their schedules permit. This will give potential readers an opportunity to hear from the people who actually worked on this case.

- On the author's personal website, www.alambauthor.com, she will promote *Deadly Dose* by linking it to a separate site, which will be dedicated to the project. She will also have links to news stories she has covered relating to the Miller case. The site will also offer readers an opportunity to purchase the book.

WHY THIS BOOK SOLD

The author's platform is impeccable and, again, she tells a compelling story and writes it well. As you know by now, these are all key to selling your book.

Alan Rinzler, executive editor at Jossey-Bass/John Wiley & Sons, tells us of another proposal with a solid platform. "The author had just started a national memoir association with a solid plan in effect for expansion, including workshops, trainings, media publicity, and other events," he says.

Lenore Skenazy's *Free-Range Kids* interested Rinzler because, "First, the proposal was laugh-out-loud funny; she's such a good writer," he says. "Second, she takes a refreshingly common-sense approach that goes totally against current parenting trends, which encourage unnecessary over-protection, the so-called 'helicopter' parenting that drives parents nuts and infantilizes kids, preventing them from achieving maturity and independence. Let go, she says; give the kid the same free-dom we had as kids. Third, Lenore is media-genic and has a real knack for generating publicity."

The best book proposals, like the ones we've discussed, take a great deal of thought, planning, and preparation. If the idea of transforming your book *idea* into a *book proposal* seems overwhelming, simply break the job down into the essential elements that every good proposal must have (see chapter 5) and then work on each section step-by-step as we have illustrated so far. Go easy on yourself, but be persistent with your work sessions.

 HOT TIP!

You can eat an entire elephant if you do it one bite at a time ...

CHAPTER 7

THE TAO OF
THE QUERY LETTER—
AND BEYOND

We refer to "the Tao" of the query letter because the term *Tao* indicates a road or path—and there is a pathway that works, here. You will find a set of principles that recurs in virtually every effective query. There is also a range of bad habits that can overcome you at the outset unless you check to be certain that they are avoided. We will spend the next few chapters on the query letter because it is, next to your platform, the single most important element in getting your book published. Without an effective query, your prospective agent or editor is likely to ignore you. This is not done out of a desire to be mean—although it can feel that way—it is far more likely that your query simply failed to compel that person.

On the surface, a writer's query letter may appear to be no more than a page of correspondence that asks an agent or editor to consider your book proposal. It is far more than that. A powerful query is so important to a book's future that unless yours is done with maximum effectiveness, the world may be deprived of your work. The effect that you will do best to create was summed up in a famous line from the film *Jerry Maguire*: "You had me at 'hello.'"

So how will you get them at "hello"? That is going to be the fundamental question facing you when the time comes to bring your work into the marketplace. It is important to grab your desired literary representative or publishing house editor with your first attempt, or you are likely to lose the opportunity to reach that person. It is always a mistake to use the profession itself to help you revise your way through drafts, because it is much easier to get a first chance out of people than to get a second.

But a real point of advantage to you is that a large portion of your competition is made up of writers who are so uncomfortable with promoting themselves and their work that they will skim over the process. This failure is unfortunate for skilled writers who are touting perfectly worthy work—especially because they fail to realize they are shooting down their own hopes with their willingness to toss off a half-baked query. Never kid yourself; *your* query is no ordinary letter. It is foolhardy to write one as if it is.

HOT TIP!

Your query letter is a key step on your journey. It can make or break the rest of your efforts.

BEFORE BEGINNING THE LETTER

Before you begin your query letter, make sure your proposal is entirely finished and fully polished. If you are fortunate enough to hit on an agent who replies to you quickly (and, yes, many agents do respond in a timely manner), you will want to send your completed proposal back to the agent promptly by return e-mail or immediately via postal mail, whichever method the agent prefers.

If you delay in getting the proposal out once it has been requested, you will not only look unprofessional, you will tip off your recipient to that fact that your work is not organized. Worse, you will give the agent, who does not know how fabulous you are, the impression that your word can't be trusted. And with so many authors competing for representation, it is guaranteed that the agent will choose to work with the author who responds quickly and in a businesslike manner. This is all part of the query process.

The query process begins the moment you begin to actively seek the best literary representative for your book. For the most part you want to query literary agents rather than editors.

First, editors at major publishing houses rarely, if ever, respond to unsolicited queries. Unsolicited means that they did not specifically ask for it. So, coming out of the blue, your query will go right into the circular file or the "deleted" folder.

Second, the 15 percent commission that you pay to your agent will come back to you many times in the increased advance, foreign rights percentages, and other perks that your agent will negotiate for you.

Third, an agent can make suggestions to your proposal and manuscript that will increase its sales potential. Every effective literary agent knows exactly what editors at specific publishing houses are looking for and will pitch your work accordingly.

"Yes, it sounds high and mighty," says Ian Kleinert, principal at Objective Entertainment, a multimedia literary management and production company, "but more than likely the agent knows best, most of the time."

And finally, an editor will respond promptly to a query from an agent, especially if the agent and editor have worked together in the past. If the editor asks to see the proposal, she knows the agent has vetted the material, the document will be edited and formatted properly, and all the elements the editor needs will be in place. That way the editor is not wasting valuable time on a proposal that is not ready.

If you do decide to pitch directly to an editor, you now know what lies ahead. Really, the only time we suggest this is if you have had some personal contact with an editor at an event, such as at a writers' workshop or a book fair, and then only if the editor specifically asks for it.

For example, Marji Ross, president and publisher of Regnery Publishing, Inc., notes that they occasionally do well with books pitched to them directly by authors they know.

"Since we work in a very focused area, we know the authors very well, and they know us," she says. "Frequently we approach authors with an idea, and just as frequently they come to us with ideas, in both cases with books that are particularly suited to Regnery's core strengths and target market. We had a big bestseller in 2008, *The Case Against Barack Obama*, that was unagented, and our number one bestseller in 2004, *Unfit for Command*, was also unagented."

THE KEYS TO THE SEARCH

So, who will be willing to roll the boulder up the mountain with you? The answer to that question will arrive in response to a personalized letter that you will address to *each individual literary agent* (or editor). Because of the sheer volume of queries that agents and editors receive, this needs to be a letter with the ability to outshine the hundreds of others that may also arrive that week.

As a savvy writer, take the time to consider the interests, specifications, and requests of each person who will receive and evaluate your work, keeping a special eye on the individuals who will be receiving your correspondence. The more informed you are of the particulars of the literary market and the people who toil there, the more you will be in harmony with success.

The Researched Agent List

If you have not yet done a researched agent list, please stop and prepare it now, before you go any further. This is a list of agents who are actively looking for books in your category; you compile this list through research. The work you put into the list will not slow you down—it will substantially streamline your search.

Visit a well-stocked bookstore or library to find some good reference books for literary agents and managers. Two we like are *Writer's Market* and *Jeff Herman's Guide to Book Publishers, Editors & Literary Agents*. Both are updated regularly, so get the most current edition you can find (always check the book's release date). The best reference books are updated yearly and provide you with a thumbnail sketch of the kind of materials any given agent or manager will accept. These books also include specific information, such as whether or not the agent is willing to read work from unknown writers, or whether that agency only accepts queries upon recommendation from someone they know.

HOT TIP!

Wasted time is a form of blood loss. Don't waste yours by attempting to contact people who have made it plain that they are not available to you. There will be others.

You will also find many good websites that offer literary agency information. Ones we especially like are Publishers Marketplace (www.publishersmarketplace.com) and Agent Query (www.agentquery.com), with other good sites listed in the appendix. Every good agency will update their company site frequently, and with a little research you can determine which ones are "open" or "closed" to submissions at any point, preventing wasted time. Keep in mind that *this is a streamlining process*.

Here are the key factors in compiling a list of agents who are perfect for you.

- Are the agents open for submissions? Accepting new clients or by referral only?

- Do they represent the genre of the book you are writing?

- Do they have a proven track record that you can verify through previous sales?

- Do they have a website that showcases their sales history and client testimonials?

- Are their sensibilities in line with yours in terms of their previous book sales?

- Do they charge any upfront fees? (If so, run for the hills!)

- Is the specific addressee someone whose background you have researched and with whom you feel a connection?

HOT TIP!

Never skip this step! You can do the research on each agent or manager by spending just a few minutes per name. The resulting informed position will quietly demonstrate your research ability right from the start.

One word of caution: People move around a lot in the publishing world, so never rely on old contact information. Always use the most current reference books available.

Literary Agent, Literary Manager—What's the Difference?

You will notice when compiling your list that some literary representatives are agents while some are managers. There is a subtle difference between the two. Ideally, literary agents provide their writers with support and guidance throughout a book's preparation for submission to publishers, the eventual sale, the rounds of editing, and finally the publication. A literary manager does much the same job, but usually spends more time with each client in planning and building their career, including working with them on all of the ancillary opportunities like film and television spin-offs, and speaking engagements.

The customary fee for either an agent or a manager is 15 percent of all monies that the representative generates for you for domestic sales, and 20 to 25 percent for sales to foreign territories. Some agents also have a minimum fee, in case you decide to take a very low advance. Of course, any agent or manager may have a policy that varies from the norm, which is why it pays for you to do a few minutes of homework to check out an agent or manager's online presence.

Once you have your list of individual literary agents or managers, it is time to visualize exactly what your query letter is designed to do. Go on to the next step.

WHAT YOUR QUERY LETTER WILL ACHIEVE

Your query letter is more than a pitch for your fully polished and edited book proposal or manuscript; it is also a way to indicate your ability to grasp the overall concept of professional authorship. The subtext of your query will signal that you are the type of writer who, regardless of your artistic twists, can and will remain functional throughout the long process of writing and polishing book proposals or manuscripts, possibly enduring several rounds of publisher's edits. Your query must paint a portrait of you as someone who will truly *deliver what you promise*. It must demonstrate that you are a writer who:

- remains professional in the handling of contract negotiations

- holds to deadlines for completing book manuscripts

- remains cooperative during the editing process

- remains focused and cooperative during the legal vetting of your manuscript (which reminds some authors of being smeared with honey and staked out on a giant anthill, while others compare it to being eaten by piranha in slow motion)

- is competent in tending to the considerable promotional attention that any new book requires, including offering, whenever possible, to hire your own book publicist upon publication

- understands the importance of your platform, and displays that understanding within the first lines of the letter.

And yes, your written query will demonstrate all of these things while keeping to an approximate length of *one typed page*. Agents (and editors) are very busy people. Many handle hundreds of calls and e-mails every day and don't have time to read more than a page at the query stage. Plus, if you can't make your case in the equivalent of one typed page, then either you don't have the essence of your book planted firmly enough in your mind, or your writing skills are not yet where they should be.

HOT TIP!

Never query an agent or editor by phone. No one can assess the quality of your writing from the sound of your voice.

THE TONE OF YOUR LETTER

Even in this early stage of building your query letter it is important to understand that the overall tone has to match the narrative voice that you employ in the work itself. A surprisingly common mistake (and one you are now wise enough to avoid) is to adopt a jaded or hostile tone toward your recipient in the misguided notion that your frustration over previous rejections somehow warrants hostility now. Not only is this abusive tone rude and inappropriate, it's not helping your cause in any way. An abrasive approach from a writer will come across as a warning that whenever editors need some rewriting, they will receive back more attitude than content.

HOT TIP!

In your query, you may *describe* an abusive scenario as it relates to your work. You may even *quote brief examples* of abusive behavior or dialogue. You may *not* turn that abusive tone onto your recipient without getting your letter dumped and wasting your time.

If you are coming forward as an expert on any topic, you must sound like that expert at all times. Your query letter will take the same businesslike tone that you would use in your narrative. If your book is a breezy piece of pop culture, then your query letter will have a more informal or even whimsical tone, but you will never lose sight of the serious goal underlying your correspondence.

THE FOUR-POINT QUERY

As noted earlier, you only have one page to play with here. That means you've got a lot to convey and very little space to convey it. The best way to achieve this is to break your query letter into specific sections.

1. For each of the people on your agent list, craft an opening that tells the recipient why you are writing specifically to that person.

2. Follow that opening with a midsection that briefly describes your proposed book in a few paragraphs using the smoothed-out language and the clear and compelling terms that you have already polished in the process of your media preparation.

3. Describe your platform in a way that makes it clear why you should be published.

4. Close the query with a businesslike thank-you and sign off.

In chapter 9, you will see that this basic query structure can be expressed in an unlimited number of variations. Nevertheless, the best query letters are the ones that make clear use of all four of these vital query sections. The fact that you do so gives the message of professionalism that you want to convey *in addition to* garnering interest in your ideas themselves.

"Query letters must present a solid, well-developed idea, but the biggest turnoff is an unprofessional letter, one that wastes our time," says Kimberley Cameron, president of Reece Halsey Literary Agency. "I ask authors to please inform themselves as to how to write a nonfiction proposal, what it must contain, and how to present it. I look for unique ideas, but sometimes it's the voice in the letter that does it."

Before we get to the voice in the letter, let's take a deeper look at the individual elements of the four-part query.

For a well-focused query:

- Write in the same narrative voice that you use in the manuscript.

- Use a standard paragraph format.

- Keep to the one-page limit.

- Use black 12-point type, and we suggest Arial, Palatino, Times, or Times New Roman font. [Note: Industry cognoscenti already know that if you use a Courier 10 font, it will increase your book length by many pages without raising the word count at all. Don't use typeface for "filler."]

- Double-check the typing of the recipient's name and address as well as your own. *Never* resort to "Dear Agent," "Dear Editor," or "To Whom It May Concern."

- Use your opening to explain to the recipient specifically why you are contacting that individual. In so doing, you will avoid insulting your recipient and embarrassing yourself by submitting work to someone who does not handle that category. Let the recipient know you have done your homework by saying, for example: "I see how well you handled (name a similar book to yours that the agent or editor handled) written by (name the author and spell it right), and I believe that my work is just as viable, and perhaps more so, for the following reasons."

- Offer a concise description of your book and your platform.

- Avoid claiming "there are no books like this one." Why is this a bad idea? Consider that there are *millions* of books and uncountable millions of articles already on public record. Anyone who cannot produce a single example of similar or related work only reveals his own substandard research.

- Avoid the temptation to claim you are bringing this agent their "next big blockbuster." A positive attitude is good, but nobody likes feeling as if they are being hustled. Sadly, nobody can predict blockbusters, and writers never need to attach that sort of pointless arrogance to their work.

- Avoid promising that you will get an endorsement from the "O" word—Oprah. Oprah's show seems to be the Holy Grail for writers, but it is extremely difficult to get on and even harder to get an endorsement. It is completely inappropriate at this stage to mention it at the query stage, and a sure sign of amateurism if you do.

- *Selectively* include any early endorsements. Some agents and editors claim they ignore third-party comments about a proposed book. However, if you have an active writing group that has responded strongly to the work, or if you have a celebrity who will endorse it, there is no reason not to include a brief reference to them.

HOT TIP!

Keep this list in front of you while you begin to draft your letter.

Then sign off. Remember that even after all this work, many of the letters you send will fail to score. The fact is that they simply don't matter. It only takes one. This is the way you will seek out that one (or more)— and get them at "hello."

CHAPTER 8

CRAZY QUERIES: HOW NOT TO DO IT

Now that we've given you some overall ideas on queries, here are a few examples of what *not* to do. While the reasons for passing on these queries will be self-evident, and while we can specify what to avoid, we find it is quite helpful to also show you the ideas in action.

With that in mind, the following are actual queries received at Martin Literary Management and are typical of those hitting the inboxes of every manager and agent in the field. You might think that we "spiced" them up a bit. But they are reproduced here exactly as they arrived.

The sad truth is that we, along with most agents and editors, receive far more queries that are like the following than we do viable queries. So, take a deep breath … here we go.

Please note the spelling and printing are also exactly as received.

> Subject: *The Other Winfrey*
>
> I represent "_____" Winfrey. Miss Winfrey already has one book out, *The Other Winfrey*, that is self published through her own company. Now she is looking for a literary agent to help her get a publishing deal to either take over or work with her publisher. Miss Winfrey is planning on writing 5 more books this year.

This first one is an example of biting off more than anybody can chew. It takes at least four to eight months to write the average nonfiction book (working fast)—how can anyone possibly write *five* competent books in one year? (No doubt while killing spare time by writing operas in Sanskrit.) A better approach is to choose one narrowly focused book and succinctly give us its details. The harsh truth is that it is far more gratifying to make a series of glittering generalities about a list of brilliant projects than to focus on one at a time, because to do so would reveal whether or not they have been thought through.

The "five books" claim aside, the above query writer gives us no details. And other than having the same last name as Oprah, we don't see any platform here. (Remember, too, to spell out numbers of ten or less. Some stylebooks suggest writing out numbers of one hundred or less.)

Our next query shows that if you plan to write a book, it's always a good idea to understand the English language. It is often the case that the queries that contain poor grammar and punctuation are also the least professional in tone. Remember that your book is your business and your career. A publisher wants to know that they can count on you to represent them well.

Subject: P.S. 101

Dear Publisher or Literary Agent,

Attached is a small book called *Phone Sex for Everybody!* It is simply a Beginners Guide to Phone Sex (or cell phone sex)

If you are interested in publishing this or representing us, please contact me via email or by phone.

THIS BOOK IS PROTECTED BY COPYRIGHT,

IT'S CONCEPT BELONGS TO MYSELF AND TWO OTHER WRITERS:

Myself, Taresha, and Papa Do.

Well, alrighty then. The awkward line breaks in the middle of a sentence certainly make it fun to read, and while it is a good idea to include copyright information on your *actual work*, it is really not necessary to include it in the query. Possibly not a good idea to introduce yourself to someone by issuing a legal warning directly to them. You can see the difference between a defensive-sounding statement like the example above and a properly placed official copyright notice.

There is conflicting advice floating around suggesting that there is some valid reason *not* to use a properly placed copyright notice, as if a reader will be "offended" by seeing your copyright notice. This is nonsense. While it is true that a copyright is automatically granted to written work in the U.S., the placement of the seal is a clear indication of *the author's conscious intent to market the work.* This is a point of legal distinction that can come in handy under certain challenges. There is also the fact that nobody has a legitimate reason to object to the use of the standard five- or six-word copyright notice. Who is supposed to be "offended" by that? And why?

HOT TIP!

Remember your fonts: Arial, Palatino, Times, or Times New Roman. Some publishers will request a final manuscript in Courier New typeface. "Fancy" fonts are distracting and unprofessional.

Dear Literary Agent/Agency

Thank you for opening this email and apologies if you are offended by the mass mailout. I've been writing for over thirty years and this is the first time I am seeking representation. Mywriting includes a travelogue, a novel,poems, plays for children andadults, tv series, film scripts and plays theatre in development. Ifyou would like to know more about me, there is an outdated website youcan visit.

Thank you again for your time and may you be prosperous in all your endeavours.

Sadly, the writer of the above query did nothing right. In addition to the poor punctuation and the lack of a spell check, she used a flowery type that is okay for PTA newsletters but never appropriate in a business setting. Notice that she also included vague references to numerous writings, rather than giving specific and detailed information on one particular book project. Plus, she referenced an outdated (?) website.

Put yourself in the agent or publisher's shoes. In reading the query, what impression do you get of the writer? Is this someone you think is representative of your existing stable of professional authors and could make your company money?

The writer of the above query also committed what is probably the number one no-no in submitting to agents: the dreaded cc—carbon copy. The long list is omitted here to save space. Just know that each literary agency and each publishing house is a bit different from the other, and that it is useless to send a copy of a single letter to every agent and editor you can find. The cc list is a good way to get your correspondence deleted before it is read.

That will not happen to *you*.

> Dear Sir, Would you like to see some of my novel about a "love" affair in the red light zone of Amsterdam, in 2000 between a CIA torture victim and a German prostie. They have extra conversations. She gives clues, he offers to pay her rent; she teases.lures, and rejects him. Of their thirty conversations, most show four sides of irony per statement.

The query above had actually been forwarded twenty-six times before it landed in our in-box. The real irony, though, is the fact that our agency does not represent fiction. This is an example of a prospective author not doing his homework and failing to take the time to create a list of agents and editors who actually represent the type of project he is presenting. Of course, the poor grammar, formatting, and spelling would be a certain turnoff for any fiction agent who did happen to receive this. And finally, if your nonfiction book employs a narrative form rather than an instructive voice, avoid deadly generalities such as saying that a character "gives clues," or claiming that the plot has "twists and turns." Those are expected elements in any narrative book.

Other instant turnoffs, according to Adam Chromy, literary manager and founder of Artists and Artisans Inc., are queries that begin with trite declarative statements. "'Love conquers all.' 'Time heals all wounds.' 'There is nothing as strong as the mother's love for a child.' These are the conclusions I should come to after reading the book, not be hammered with as the opener," he says. "I also hate queries that waste my time by telling me in the first sentence how the author knows exactly how busy I am so they won't waste my time with superfluous introductions."

Openers aside, it also helps to understand the book industry and how the business of books works.

> Attention:
>
> I have compiled (twenty-four) of the most unique (Self - Help-Booklets) ever designed, while also writing over (Five-Hundred) funny stories. I'm offering all for sale at a (Basement - Bargain - Price) to anyone interested for ($650.000) total price.

So a 15 percent commission would be, what, $97.500? Waiter, we'll have the tranquilizers, please.

Agents and managers are all going to charge you for their knowledge. Why not let them be involved in setting the price for your work? They do, after all, work in the trade every day and realize that there are a host of serious considerations that go into a book sale; the initial selling price is only one of them. And again, a query has to have stellar grammar, punctuation, and formatting. Think of it as a short showcase of your writing skills.

Subject: VERY SPECIAL QUERY LETTER

It's almost not fair. Actually it isn't fair. It's so not fair. Here I am, left with a page, one page, just one page, to grab your attention and set aside my query letter from the rest of the hundreds and maybe thousands that you get on a weekly basis, so you contact me back to read my manuscript. But that's what they say about life right? It's not fair, or is it that it's like a box of chocolates? No, that was Forest Gump, good movie huh? If it was a true story then it'd be a great movie. I wanna be like Forest Gump, but I'm not slow, so I'll be the smart Forest Gump and go on and do great things (have I gotten your attention yet?) Well If not then let me keep going …

This writer used most of his one page and never got to anything remotely close to his book. You already know that a query like this is a waste of time. It is included here because it is important for you to see the context into which your efforts will play. In fact, according to Ian Kleinert, principal at Objective Entertainment, a query like this is one of the biggest turnoffs for agents.

"Horrible attempts at humor are the worst," he says. "If someone is trying to be funny and it comes out horrid, it does not bode well."

The poor attempt at humor, bad as it may be, does not pinch as hard as the voice of a bragging writer. Here's an example:

You don't know me, as an author, but you should. You know why you should? Well do ya? I'll tell ya why, because I am a best selling author. That's right a best selling author, if this was 8 to 12 months from now. Ooops, I know I'm not supposed to say that, boast about the books. So I just broke the rules of querying an agent with that one. But hey I gotta get your attention some how right?

I'm the writer of the rare kind who can write anything, any genre (oops I'm not supposed to say that too) but it is the case. I can evoke any kind of emotion with my writing; romantic sentimental material, tragic sad stuff, erotically stimulating stuff, witty humorous (perhaps like the opening of this letter)

This writer went on to mention seven or eight books of varying genres that were all unfinished. Some were not even started. All were bad ideas. When you consider that the tone of a query letter generally portrays the attitude of the writer, what would *your* gut response be to this one?

Subject: Taking A Chance

You know, I love to write. I don't know how to get in this business. I'm 23 years old and I'm now just taking a chance. If you like it, you like it. If you don't, you don't. But I can live for the time being to say "I sent my unedited story, that meant more to me than you reading it and I don't give a shit if you like it or not, but can you live with yourself and give me a chance to prove it will be worth your time …"

Of course the e-mail didn't actually give any information on the story—not that we were all that interested, strangely enough.

SUBJECT: LOOKING FOR AGENT/PUBLISHING HOUSE INFORMATION

ATTACHED TO THIS EMAIL IS A LETTER THAT POSES THE QUESTIONS THAT I WISH TO HAVE ANSWERED AND THE ITEREST WHICH LED ME TO CONTACT YOU. INCLUDED IS MY CONTACT INFORMATION, SHOULD YOU WISH TO RESPOND BY MEANS OTHER THAN EMAIL. THANK YOU FOR YOUR TIME AND ATTENTION TO THIS AT YOUR EARLIEST CONVENIENCE,

By now, most people know that the use of all capital letters in an e-mail is akin to shouting at your recipient. The tone of the letter is vaguely respectful and the writer of this query probably did not intend to "yell." However, it is also another breach of etiquette to include an attachment with your initial query. The recipient must beware of spam and infected e-mails; it is just not fair to expect a stranger to open an e-mail attachment. There is also a time element involved. No agent or editor wants to be "teased" into opening your attachments like a bird following crumbs.

You really can say everything that you need to say in the space of a single page.

Of course your subject line will be professional in tone and always pertinent to your book. It is the first line the recipient sees. Maybe the following query writer didn't get that memo.

> To: <sharlene@martinliterarymanagement.com>
> Subject: I'm SELFpublishing my book. ALL literary agents can
>   GO TO HELL!!!

> To: <sharlene@martinliterarymanagement.com>
> Subject: NO mother-f***ing agent is going to stand in the way
>   of my dreams!!!

> To: <sharlene@martinliterarymanagement.com>
> Subject: The internet has made it possible for authors to pub-
>   lish their work WITHOUT HAVING TO RELY ON
>   AGENTS! NA!!!!!!!!!!

> To: <sharlene@martinliterarymanagement.com>
> Subject: It feels SO GOOD that SELF-publishing allows
>   authors to tell agents to "go fuck themselves!"

The profanity aside, it's never a good idea to send repeated e-mails to an agent or editor. Trying to use e-mail to spew vitriol at a stranger does nothing more than reveal the writer's various neuroses while simultaneously wasting the writer's time. It only feels therapeutic—when you're done, you're still crazy. You know that and you just confirmed it for the person you were trying to assault by sticking out your tongue and wiggling your fanny.

> Subject: To Hon'ble Literary Agent--Sending my book /600 pages" attached...Seeking representation.
>
> Oct 8, 2008:
>
> Dear Honorable Literary Agent. At the outset its an astronomical honor to be writing to you.
>
> Am sending my book /600 pages appx." attached to this email in Word Doc. format. Am sending this email to all Literary Agents (which am including in the TO field of this email). I'd like to introduce myself a 31 yr old Poet. I'd be honored to have one of my most cherished poetry books /600 pages appx" represented by you .
>
> In this hour of gory terrorism, this poetry book of mine irrefutably proves that no matter how sacreligeously terrorism has stung the fabric of our society; Love conquers everything.... In perception of the same, I am attaching this poetry book of mine to this email in entirety in Word Doc format, (it is a 605 pages in Word doc. format).

Yikes! I think we understand that the manuscript is approximately six hundred pages. Repeating information is another common mistake that many query writers make. Of course, this query also was poorly written with many spelling errors, extra spaces between words, line breaks, and improper punctuation. Once again: Would *you* want to work with this person?

HOT TIP!

(1) Use the "Spell Check" feature in your software, and (2) also send a test e-mail to yourself before sending the final draft. If you follow these two simple steps, you might be surprised how many mistakes you catch!

The other issue is that Martin Literary Management does not represent poetry, and a quick visit to the website would have confirmed that to the writer. So, everyone's time and energy was wasted here. And we mean everyone—more than eighty agents were sent this e-mail. Obviously the writer did no research, and now, because he copied all possible agents who might have been interested in his book (had the query been viable), he has closed all those doors.

> Subject:
>
> Hello. I am trying to get my poetry published, ive been doing some research about publishing and came across literary agents,by the way i had no clue they existed. I just would like a direction to goin. im working on a manuscript, I know I need that. im a litle nervous cause i dont want to be taken advantage of, but I would love to have my work read, I also know that there is alot of rejection when it comes to thi industry, Im just hoping for some infor, cause i dont know where to goor how to go about it I know I want the chance to publish my work tho. Can you help?

You may think in reading this e-mail that we are loading the dice, so to speak, with queries written by poor spellers. Sadly, that is not the case. This e-mail, along with all the others, is representative of many that we receive each day. We're including it, however, not for the spelling issues, but because there was no text in the subject line. E-mails with nothing written in the subject line usually go straight into the trash and are not read.

It's also not a good idea to query an agent or editor if you do not have a book project to pitch. If, at some point in the future, you do have a book, the agent will probably remember you as the writer of an e-mail such as the following.

> Subject: My Sharlene (this is NOT a query)
>
> It's all in the name, your name!

Call it coincidence, female intuition, subliminal messages from the spiritual world, O Fortuna ...

my project, my Sharlene project, has many interesting twists and turns. I'm another writer who's had more than a passing interest in the Sheila LaBarre story. I knew Sheila when she managed her common-law husband's chiropractic clinic. She was a beauty, then, some 80 pounds lighter, a voluptuous shape oozing sex appeal.

She scheduled my appointments, and I ... I took her measure. Poor old Dr. LaBarre never had a chance, The official cause of death: heart attack. Perhaps so ... perhaps I let my imagination run wild.

Sheila ... Sharlene became my evil heroine, then, my fictional character. A psychological thriller, Sharlene is not an account of real events. Juicy sex scenes add sizzle. After all, that's what Sheila LaBarre was about - sex and dominance and death.

Why am I writing you? Should Sharlene ever hit book stores, I don't want you to think someone made a bad joke in very poor taste by using your name. My Sharlene has existed in manuscripts for a couple of years now. It's a freaky coincidence, and I simply had to tell you about it (lest I end up some day on your Query Madness pages, citing this as the latest trick of a desperate author gone mad, an author who makes the agent's name the title of a book, ha)!!

Our company website, like any other literary representative's website, clearly states that we are only interested in acquiring nonfiction books, yet this writer is employing this heavy-handed tactic to pitch us a thriller. She did lock on to the fact that we represented a book about Sheila LaBarre, and since her novel is apparently based on elements similar to that story, she changed the protagonist's name to Sharlene as a gimmick.

Another mistake (mentioned before but important, so we say it again) made by the above writer was to describe the book as "having many twists and turns." When you see it written down that way, you can tell that this over-used phrase doesn't really say anything and see why you are wise to avoid it.

If an agent should pass on your query, and most likely some will, then you should understand that, assuming you crafted an excellent query letter and have a strong platform, you and your book were just not a good fit for that particular agent or publisher at that time. The e-mail below is a good example of the many query writers who have to find a reason the agent or editor passed on their query. This writer blamed it on ageism and completely ignored the fact that, based on the query letter, he does not possess even rudimentary command of the essential writing skills. This person also used a bold font, another pointless way of "shouting" that does not work.

> Dear Ms. Martin,
>
> I didn't have a chance to look at your website or I would have seen that you are GREEN NOW...which is GREAT. Your name was given to me by a friend in the industry..who recommended you as an agent since you like tomes that are easily adapted to T.V. and FILM.
>
> After seeing your Website tonight , and the books you have represented , I can see why we are not a match. I need an agent who has a younger audience. Your's seems to be with the over 50 age group, which is understandable for books on Tennese Ernie Ford and Mary Jo Buttafucco and some of the others I've seen on your site dealing with "Wellness and Spirituality".
>
> My tome is for a much younger reader ... and I need an agent who has connections with film directors who target this particular age goup.
>
> Good luck to you ... and Happy Thanksgiving.

The following writer also chose to take issue with our pass. Our reply is in regular type and the writer's text is in italics.

"Based on your query we don't feel we'd be the right advocates for your material."

"Pretty amazing how you can figure that out based on my query."

"As a result, we must respectfully pass on representing your worthy project."

"It has now been rejected 169 times, so apparently it isn't so worthy."

At some point, prospective authors should realize that if agents and editors are all passing, there has to be a reason. Rather than pitch over and over and over, it is a good idea to realize that what you are doing is not working. Then take time to stop and reassess the writing, your platform, and the project itself. Fix whatever seems to be the problem, then try pitching again (but not to the same people).

The following is another response to a pass. This writer, however, took it a little better, although the letter came in formatted just as you see it below:

Subject: Re: RE: Query submission:
SMALL BUS MKTG MADE EASY

Thank you for your prompt response. If you ever tire of the glamorous world of publishing and decide to open a fried chicken franchise in Queens, call me right away. As a small business specialist I'm the man who can help you.

Hey, times are hard enough. The sender's address will stay on file—you never know when you might want to wear a hat with a chicken on it.

Here's another query and response. In this case, we hope the writer took our advice.

I submitted a couple queries yesterday and today I get a rejection reply on a totally off the wall and unprofessional proposal I sent a month ago, meaning I've learned a lot in the last month.

What I have not learned anything about is, why nobody want's my book? I don't understand, is incest such a hush,hush sweep it under the rug subject that nobody wants to touch it. Could you be so kind to enlighten me on this matter, I spent hours last night actually reading your website thinking that you will be the agent that won't be afraid to touch this controversial subject that know one want's to talk about or wants to believe happens.

I respect your busy, but if you get a moment even if your not wanting to offer any type of representation could you tell me if I wasting my time and if I should just stop writing right now?

Dear Writer:

You do not have command of the English language and do not understand punctuation and grammar, and I must tell you that this is why your query is being rejected.

It is true that a good story is essential to selling a book—but great writing is even more important. I suggest you work on your writing skills or take on a writing partner who has them.

Best,

Sharlene

We do hope that everyone who receives a long series of rejection letters will realize that while the story is sometimes there, the quality of the writing may not be living up to it. You can often remedy that by taking on a collaborator or ghost writer.

As you will see in the next letter, sometimes it is better to leave a few things out of your story.

Best described as Autobiographical Existential Action Thriller Technical Instruction Manual. No shit. It's my life story with drugs, nitrous balloons, cops, dance music, road trips, snowboarding, flashbacks, long legged women, a Dog named Townsehnd, a Killer African Grey Parrot named Sasha, fake hippies, avalanches, a castle, a reservoir, near death experiences, dream sequences, journeys into the space time continuum, funny lights the explanation of life and death, and our higher purpose, or at least mine, puzzles, verbal diarrhea, Bob Dylan as a used car salesman, David Letterman as David Letterman, Dr. Dre as the voice on my phone, propagrandiose material that could be a conspiracy to overthrow the government, so you need good lawyers if you go anywhere near it.

It is all true, except for the part where I smoke out of a hookah on the side of the road with a giant caterpillar, but you should know that.

Im looking for the people who have been looking for me, but I dont know them, so if you see them, tell them where I am, and that Ive been looking for them, for almost two thousand years. tell them to hurry, because Ill be checking out soon, with no forwarding address. It makes sense when you read the book.

contact me by phone, as it may become difficult for me to access email soon. Even my phone will be turned off, so hustle. Im not sure what freedoms they allow you in such places.

A HOST OF CRAZIES

You might already be aware that our agency handled the sale on behalf of the Goldman family of the O.J. Simpson book *If I Did It*. We weren't involved in the original sale of the book to ReganBooks at HarperCollins. At that time, the royalties were still going to "The Killer," as the Goldman family refers to him. However we did become involved when a court decision moved the majority of the proceeds to the Goldman and Brown families, and to the Ron Goldman Foundation for Justice.

HOT TIP!

If the issues of grammar, syntax, and narrative voice are not within your skill set, then by all means *find an editor or ghostwriter who can help you.* This is a perfectly sound business strategy. The only foolish choice would be to attempt to bluff your way out and waste your own time as well as everyone else's.

Our involvement is mentioned here because the huge wave of national press the book brought us also brought a number of unusual people out of the woodwork. Here are a few:

- Oprah's "boyfriend" from the 1980s who made damning accusations about her

- A would-be celebrity who publicly claimed to have killed Jon-Benét Ramsey

- The lead investigator for the O.J. *defense* team

- The son of a famous actor who was acquitted of having murdered his wife

- The sister of a young movie starlet who was killed by Charles Manson's zombies

- The niece of the another woman from another crime scene, who was also murdered by the followers of Charles Manson

- An aging boy band star who wanted to blow the whistle on a renowned boy band manager

- The brother of a recently deceased gorgeous sex symbol, who wanted to "tell all"

- Someone claiming to be Oprah Winfrey's cousin with a "tell all" about her family

- A prominent member of the wedding party at the O.J. Simpson Las Vegas wedding debacle, who made it a point to mention that O.J. had specifically suggested that they call Martin Literary Management for their literary management needs.

We were whelmed.

Your professionalism, however, can immediately leave all such prospective writers far behind you on the pathway to the world's bookstores.

CHAPTER 9

WHY YOUR QUERY
WILL WORK

Now that you've seen how *not* to write a query, here's how it should be done. The following six query letters are actual queries that got their writers noticed and signed for representation. These winning queries teach by way of example. You will find each sample letter followed by our comments.

As you will see, not every letter follows all of the suggestions for a great query, but in each case you will see why the query offered something compelling enough for us to respond positively. Not one of them is obnoxious or self-defeating. Well, okay, one is, but it was a gag used for a book on personality disorders and a unique example.

Please also note that none of the letters attempts to employ self-pity to motivate the reader. As painful as it may be for you that your finances are in drastic shape, or that you have suffered great injury or have endured great injustice, it is not appropriate to refer to such personal travails unless they are a direct part of your proposed book. Considering that *there is no way to know the personal situation of the person who reads your letter*, you could put yourself in the position of whining to someone who is suffering to a much greater degree. Also notice that all of these letters stick to the pitch itself.

The following queries represent a mix of first-time authors, celebrity authors, teachers, and others. By the end of this section you will be aware of the common themes of effective queries. Most important, you will gain a clear idea of how to create an equally effective pitch for your own book.

Dear Ms. Martin:

When I was 18 years old, I moved from my home town in Oregon (population: 7,500) to live with the most powerful man in Hollywood and be a nanny to his 3 children.

In my memoir: "You'll Never Nanny in this Town Again! - The Adventures and Misadventures of a Hollywood Nanny, I describe my unusual experiences with the rich and famous and provide a peek into their private lives. I also share humorous stories about my girlfriends [who were] working for celebrity families. The book describes my short education at the Northwest Nannies Institute in Portland, Oregon. It also describes my journey to being a 24-hour a day modern servant, while juggling medical emergencies, as well as toddler AND adult tantrums.

This book is a cross between *People* magazine and *Seinfeld*. One example of the bizarre priorities of the wealthy that I encountered was a family who had a small painting in their family room that cost 5 times as much as my parent's home, but I was told not to take anything from the hotel honor bar when we were on vacation, because it was too expensive.

I self-published the book last year and was selected for a distribution contract through IPG small publishers program. I have consistently been ranked in the top 5% of Amazon sales. I have already sold over 4,000 copies in 12 months and garnered great reviews. I have a popular website—*www.HollywoodNanny.com*.

Some of the media attention I have received includes: E! channel "Will Work for Stars" red carpet interview for the Screen Actors Guild awards. I am featured on an upcoming A&E special "Fathers and Sons in Hollywood," have been interviewed on many radio programs, and speak nationally.

So now I'm ready to go mainstream with a major publisher. Apart from writing this book, I am a mother of two, an RN and have worked as a high-risk labor and delivery nurse, lactation specialist and childbirth educator.

I can send you a copy of the book by e-mail or regular mail, and hope to hear from you to discuss this further.

Suzanne Hansen

LETTER #1 ANALYSIS

The instant appeal of a nanny who worked for a major Hollywood player is obvious. And paragraphs two and three make a clear description of the work, so that when the "spoiler" comes in paragraph four, telling of the book's self-publishing past (which is often a deal killer), the author builds upon momentum she has already established by quickly pointing out that her self-published book enjoyed real success in online sales and garnered a following by word-of-mouth and in the blogosphere. This first-time author displays real savvy about writing and marketing.

The Follow-Up

- The supposedly "impossible" happened. Suzanne Hansen's previously self-published book sold to Crown Publishing Group/ Random House for a six-figure advance, was published to fine reviews, and quickly went into multiple printings. It was a *New York Times* and *Los Angeles Times* bestseller. Suzanne appeared on *The Today Show* and is now a frequent guest for foreign and U.S. entertainment shows on nanny and parenting issues.

- The television rights to her book were optioned to a television network and a major studio.

- Dare to dream.

LETTER #2: SAVVY AUTHOR, BABIES, AND ENVIRONMENTAL CORRECTNESS

Subject: Query: The Smart Mama's Green Guide

Dear Ms. Martin:

Over 4 million babies are born each year in the United States. With a new baby to introduce to the world, parents often worry for the very first time whether exposures to toxic chemicals may harm their child. The newspapers headlines about toxic chemicals in common household products scare new parents, and frequently prompt interest in green or organic products. In fact, new parents frequently turn to organic food for the first time as a way to protect their children, and the purchase of organic food results in the purchase of other organic items. The organic food market is growing at a rate of more than 30% per year, and the natural baby products market is growing similarly.

The Smart Mama's Green Guide: Simple Steps to Reduce Your Baby's Toxic Chemical Exposure will give a new parent simple, practical advice on how to reduce or eliminate a baby's exposure to toxic chemicals found in and around the home. It gives advice from a mom who knows that utility and convenience are the hallmarks of parenting. Rather than simply recommending to "buy green" as other competitor books have done, *The*

Smart Mama's Green Guide focuses on easy, sensible solutions. It is organized by rooms in the home, with checklists to evaluate the risks of exposure and simple steps to reduce exposure. It does not preach adopting a natural lifestyle or overwhelm with dense scientific information. Instead, it helps you hug a tree without getting dirty.

In addition to being a mom of two small children, I have an engineering degree and formerly worked as an environmental engineer. Currently, I am an environmental attorney, focusing on consumer product labeling issues. I lecture routinely on simple steps to reducing exposures to chemicals to new moms, and draw on this experience, as well as my own efforts to reduce my children's toxic chemical exposures, to provide a simple, practical guide for parents to reduce toxic chemical exposures.

I look forward to hearing from you.

Jennifer T. Taggart

LETTER #2 ANALYSIS

This potentially dry topic was made fresh by this author's savvy connection of a checklist book and the current politically correct wave of "green" awareness. There have always been books about how to keep babies safe from household items and various dangerous situations, but this book has been converted into a cutting edge prescriptive book for all the fresh green moms and dads out there. The writer has an excellent platform and a terrific, fully developed website (www. TheSmartMama.com).

This one was another of the easy ones. Gotta love it!

The Follow-Up

- Sold to the Center Street division of Grand Central Publishing.

- The author uses her book as source material for her many lectures and workshops as a "Smart Green Mama" and environmental attorney.

LETTER #3: ATTENTION-GRABBING BOOK TITLE AND DESCRIPTION

Subject: Query

Dear Ms. Martin,

It must be nice to have such power. You must get quite a rush as you read all of these query letters from us little people, and have the clout to accept or reject our pleas.

How did that statement grab you? Imagine dealing day in and day out with such provoking comments from your spouse, your co-worker, your boss or someone else with whom you frequently have to deal. Even when we think we are handling things, this kind of garbage from others makes us feel miserable, frustrated, moody, and angry. I have written my book,

STOP YOUR MISERY

The *Definitive* Guide to Recognizing

People Who Make You Miserable,

How They Do It,

And How to Eliminate Them From Your Life

to help people recognize and deal more effectively with those insufferable individuals who daily bleed happiness from our lives. These difficult and manipulative people have unique attitude problems called personality disorders. My book explains to readers in clear, simple language and many down to earth examples how we get trapped in these relationships, how to recognize them for what they are and then what to do about them.

I am a board-certified psychiatrist presently practicing in Florida. I have extensive clinical experience dealing with the book's subject. I write a weekly psychiatry column for a large circulation newspaper with the column well received. My verbal and writing style is clear and down to earth and free of psychobabble. My past media experience includes a weekly call-in radio show, frequent TV interviews and my own local cable network TV show on health issues.

I hope you find my book unique, fresh, and rewarding as well as publishable. I look forward to your reaction.

Stanley Kapuchinski, M.D.

LETTER #3 ANALYSIS

A *risky* attention-getter opens this one. The author dares to expend the first two sentences in the kind of talk that generally begs for the delete button. But he accurately calculates just how close to the button the recipient's fingertip is, before he drops the mask of obnoxiousness to reveal his true purpose. Want the scary truth? It was only the prominent placement of the title and subtitle in the middle of the page that captured our attention long enough to keep us from simply going on to the next entry. So this letter is included to acknowledge that any rule can sometimes be broken. But can you see how such an opening could backfire with a recipient who is working through dozens of queries?

Here is a clear-cut example of platform in action, including a tie-in website, www.stopthemisery.com. And, a working psychiatrist has an excellent vantage point from which to comment upon subtleties in relationship issues.

The Follow-Up

- Sold to HCI Books.

- Dr. Kapuchinski was invited to present a speech on topics from his book at the 2007 BookExpo America convention held in New York City.

- He is still a practicing psychiatrist and is also a frequent contributor for print and radio media on the topic of personality disorders.

LETTER #4: EMOTIONAL MEMOIR WITH CELEBRITY TWIST

Dear Ms. Martin,

I'm sure I've browsed to your site several hundred times if once, and I continue to come back; drawn primarily, I think, by the evident priority that you place on your authors.

Ernie and His Lovely Wife, Betty is a narrative recounting the lives of Betty Jean Ford and her husband, Ernest, the man known to the world as Tennessee Ernie Ford. In a career that lasted half a century, Ernie Ford achieved a degree of fame that went beyond his success as an entertainer. It was a fame that weaved him into the fabric of popular culture, and earned him a permanence in history: three stars in the Hollywood Walk of Fame, walls of Gold and Platinum records, and a television legacy spanning generations.

But *Ernie and His Lovely Wife, Betty* is not a biography of Ernie Ford, but rather, a record of the lives of *two* people. It is a portrayal of the complex and beautiful woman who shared his life; a gifted artist the world would never know, whose own star might one day have eclipsed even his, but instead, slowly faded over the years, paling under the weight of the lengthening shadow unwillingly cast by the man she loved—a shadow she believed she could escape, but only by taking her own life.

From their first meeting on a desert airbase at the dawn of World War II, to their last moments together nearly half a century later, the story of Ernie and his lovely wife, Betty, is an American love story, an American tragedy; a portrait of an ordinary family changed forever by an extraordinary life. A family whose story is also my own. Ernest Jennings and Betty Jean Ford were my mother and dad.

I am haunted by the memory of these two souls. I am gripped by the arc of their radiant lives, and wounded by the memories of their deaths. This book is my hope of healing those wounds; a hope bound with a promise that one day I would tell their story.

The book stands completed at just over 92,000 words. I would be honored if you would consider reviewing a partial submission.

Jeffrey Buckner Ford

LETTER #4 ANALYSIS

As you see, there is a blood relation in this nostalgic celebrity memoir, but it is a mistake to think that just because you are related to somebody famous, you have an actual book in you. Relationships are one thing, but you are either able to write about them with alacrity and depth of insight, or you are not.

This author is careful to explain his protagonist in paragraph two, so that you know what the scope of his story will be. But it is in the third paragraph where Jeffrey Ford demonstrates why he was not merely born into this family; he was born to write this book. The paragraph is consumed mostly by the second sentence, and after reading it, can you doubt that this writer possesses the sensibilities required to tell this powerful tale of quiet frustration?

There is also a subtle sense of mystery in the query that left us wanting more, and that is a fine line to straddle.

HOT TIP!

Them words is tricky! It's often a good idea to let someone else read your query before you send it to an agent or editor, just to be certain that it delivers the tone and feel that you want it to have.

This author also took the impressive step of writing a complete draft before seeking literary representation, although this can sometimes work against you. With memoirs, which are more narrative in nature, writing a full draft can be helpful. However, many publishers of nonfiction books like to have some input into the flow of the information and the text. Before the book is sold it usually is best to put your time and energy into your platform, your proposal, and then your query—*in that order.*

The Follow-Up

- *River of No Return* sold to Cumberland House in Tennessee Ernie Ford's hometown of Nashville. Jeffrey is actively working on the film treatment of his family's story.

- Following the book's release in May 2008, Jeffrey embarked on a four-month national multimedia tour that included readings, signings, and interviews in Baltimore, Memphis, Los Angeles, Houston, Denver, Nashville, and Indianapolis. In June 2008, he was a guest author at BookExpo America in Los Angeles; in October 2008, he signed copies at the Southern Festival of Books in Nashville. Jeffrey appeared on more than eight hundred Sirius, XM, and Westwood One radio affiliates coast-to-coast, and he was a guest on John Seigenthaler's flagship PBS series, *A Word on Words*.

- The book has been consistently strong, garnering positive reviews in multiple national print and online periodicals, including *Library Journal* and a starred review in *Publishers Weekly*.

- Ford's highly interactive websites, www.jeffreybucknerford.com and www.ernieford.com, have increased visitor traffic.

LETTER #5: FUN TITLE, RESEARCH, AND CONCISE INFORMATION

Subject: Query from Janet Horn, M.D.

Dear Ms. Martin:

My co-author and I would like to send you our proposal for *The Smart Woman's Guide to Midlife and Beyond: A No-Nonsense Approach to Staying Healthy After 50.* I am specifically writing to you because of your profile on the AgentQuery website, which indicates an interest in the fields of health/fitness, medicine and women's issues.

From caring for aging body parts, to relevant psychosocial issues and specific subjects of concern to our generation (cosmetic surgery, weight control and body image, sexuality, cancer, among others), our book will cover the spectrum of women's health issues, including a chapter on Integrative Medicine (alternative medicine) and another on herbs and vitamins. At the end of each chapter will be the important "take home" points in the form of "Hot Flashes."

Our backgrounds and life experiences make us exceptionally qualified for this project. An experienced board certified internist, Dr. Miller is also an Integrative Medicine Specialist, having trained with Dr. Andrew Weil at the University of Arizona. She is an award-winning medical correspondent for KOBI, the NBC affiliate in southern Oregon and is seen nationally on the Patient Channel and MSNBC.com. She has been a national speaker for "Speaking of Women's Health" and has published two books for young people concerning health.

I am board certified in Internal Medicine and Infectious Diseases, with training in Obstetrics and Gynecology. I've had a solo private practice in Baltimore while continuing to teach as a faculty member at the Johns Hopkins School of Medicine for many years. My major areas of interest are women's health, sexually transmitted diseases, and AIDS, about which I have published many articles in medical journals and written chapters in medical texts.

Dr. Miller and I would be honored if you would agree to review the proposal.

Sincerely,

Janet Horn, M.D.

LETTER #5 ANALYSIS

In a fun way, the title clearly describes the book she proposes. But what really impressed us is that this author took time to do her homework. She had researched our agency and our interests, and used her query, in part, to speak to those areas. You just have to read the second sentence to understand why she contacted us for this book.

The second paragraph offers a clear sketch of the proposed book and the range of issues it covers. The last sentence of the second paragraph reflects a comprehensive visual of how the book will be structured by noting the "Hot Flashes" bits that will cap each chapter with prescriptive information.

And by paragraph three it's hardly fair anymore. This pair is so highly qualified in their respective fields that their platform for writing the book is thoroughly compelling. We were especially impressed that the author of the query was a board-certified physician in two areas with additional training in two others. This puts her far above the "average" physician. The fact that she maintains a solo practice while also teaching at one of our country's top medical teaching hospitals, and the fact that she is previously published in both medical journals and books, led us to believe that she was respected among her peers. To us, her professional platform was both impeccable and marketable.

The Follow-Up

- *The Smart Woman's Guide to Midlife and Beyond: A No-Nonsense Approach to Staying Healthy After 50* sold to New Harbinger. We initially approached this publisher because their entire list is essentially health-related books. Our research indicated this book would be a good fit for New Harbinger and we were thrilled when they thought so, too.

- The book also has a great website, Is There a Doctor in the House (www.myhousedoc.com), which includes a weekly blog to update the medical information in the book as information from new research studies is released. The blog supplements the book and gives updated information. The authors' audio and video interviews to date may also be accessed. There is space for readers to e-mail questions to the authors, as well as an area on the blog page for reader comments.

- *The Wall Street Journal* did a full page on this book and that really propelled sales. In fact, the publisher had to do an immediate second printing, as they couldn't keep the books in stores.

Library Journal and other trade publications also gave the book great reviews.

LETTER #6: UNIQUE FIRST SENTENCE AND GOOD INDUSTRY INFORMATION

Dear Ms. Martin:

I make loud barking sounds I can't control. I've been hit, teased, and kicked out of class. The first 24 principals who interviewed me weren't willing to hire a teacher with Tourette Syndrome. When I finally got in front of my own second-grade class, I went on to become First-Year Teacher of the Year in Georgia. In my book, "Front of the Class: How Tourette Syndrome Made Me the Teacher I Never Had," I will tell how I grew up with no friends and no support from teachers at a time when even doctors knew little about the neurological disorder called Tourette Syndrome.

When I landed my first teaching job, people worried that my students would be too distracted by my noises and twitches to learn. Once I explained Tourette's to my class, my kids were unfazed. By year's end, I had not only taught them addition and subtraction, I had showed them how the right attitude can make being different an opportunity rather than a disability.

This 15-chapter, 60,000-word book—envisioned as a trade nonfiction narrative—will appeal to the some 200,000 people diagnosed with Tourette Syndrome as well as 3.3 million teachers in the United States alone. I will market my book to parents of children with special needs, especially those that often accompany Tourette's such as attention deficit disorder, obsessive-compulsive disorder, and learning disabilities. My audience does not stop there. This book will appeal to anyone who loves an uplifting, laugh-and-cry-out-loud story about success in the face of adversity.

Without seeking coverage, I have been featured in more than a dozen newspaper and magazine articles and made several television appearances. I am making a name for myself as a motivational speaker and continue to reach new audiences as a mascot for the Atlanta Braves. I will make use of all contacts, including a vast network of friends and extended family in marketing my book.

Sincerely,

Brad Cohen

LETTER #6 ANALYSIS

When it comes to opening lines with the old grabber effect, it's hard to beat "I make loud barking sounds I can't control."

Brad Cohen has had a lifetime to consider his condition and explain it to others. As a result, look at how much information he packs into this letter, and at the same time, look at the economy of expression. Although he uses the full page, all of the facts he mentions are crucial to his story in ways that we can clearly understand. For example, he succinctly covers the story arc, describes a defined audience, and gives compelling reasons why he is the perfect person to write this book. Specifically, he has Tourette syndrome, but teaches grade school, and is so successful that he has won major teaching awards. He has a sense of how to publicize himself, and also has some experience at it. *You* would ask to see this one, wouldn't you?

The Follow-Up

- Because Brad had difficulty writing due to his Tourette tics, we put a co-writer with him. The book first sold as a hardcover to

VanderWyk & Burnham, and then the trade paperback sold to
St. Martin's Press.

- Since the book was published, Brad appeared on *The Oprah Winfrey Show*, who devoted an entire segment to him. He also had a full segment on *Inside Edition*.

- He received a four-page spread in *People* magazine and *Front of the Class* was reviewed in over forty newspapers and magazines.

- Brad now speaks as a keynote speaker on disabilities and educational issues.

- The TV movie rights sold to Hallmark Hall of Fame and was adapted by an Emmy Award-winning screenwriter. The film premiered on CBS in December 2008, starring Treat Williams and Patricia Heaton. It was nominated for a Movieguide Faith and Freedom Award.

COMMON THREADS

So you see the common quality among the queries. First, each query writer has an exceptionally strong platform. But while several of these proposals do have celebrity connections, don't worry if you lack them. Whatever your field of expertise, you can build your own platform enough to interest a publisher with or without a celebrity tie-in. The advantage of a celebrity connection is simple, in that you can tap into their fan base. However, if you build your own platform and your own fan base—as each of these authors did—then there is no need for you to hook onto someone else's coattails.

Another thing you will find is that many of these authors have advanced degrees in their subject matter. Degrees are very helpful to have, but not absolutely necessary. What is an absolute must, though, is that you have specific and unique knowledge in a narrow field of expertise.

You must also be able to express that knowledge in an informative, entertaining, and educational manner. And that brings us to our next point.

HOT TIP!

Deploy your bullet-point list to be certain you have touched all the necessary bases.

Each of these queries gives us everything we need to know in very few words. As you have seen, there was little room for the writers to discuss their book or themselves. Each query quickly and succinctly got its point across and made us want to know more.

And finally, no matter how different the queries, the author's passion for his or her subject is evident in each of them. A strong, passionate query sells the book's salient points while avoiding useless or distracting information. With that in mind, *before beginning your letter,* the most important thing you can do is to isolate those few aspects of your writing and your story that will tell your recipients what they need to know about you and your book.

Once your query letter is perfected, we'll show you the best way to submit it … and why it is done that way.

CHAPTER 10

SUBMITTING YOUR QUERY

Your query is completed, and it's perfect. (If not, go back over the last few chapters and work on it until it is. It is essential for you to have the query polished before you proceed here.) "Perfect" here means that you have trimmed the wording to a minimum, made certain to address your recipient(s) with individual reasons for writing to each one, and expressed your book idea in a clear and compelling manner. You followed that with a brief description of your specific platform as it relates to your expertise. You are ready to submit it to a prospective agent or editor. The way that you go about doing so is just as important as the content of the query itself.

ELECTRONIC VS. HARD COPY

Until recently it was universally considered appropriate to send your query by postal mail. But that was when the world was trapped in the land of hard copy. Now that virtually everyone has access to the Internet, we are saving millions of tons of paper every year. Not to mention the substantial cost savings of e-mail compared to any form of postal mail service. More importantly, e-mail somewhat speeds up the slow and burdensome process of reading and responding. Most agents today want to receive their queries by this method.

In fact, many agents today will only accept electronic queries, including Scott Hoffman at Folio Literary Management. In addition to the benefits mentioned above, Hoffman finds it much easier to read, track, and respond to an electronic query than it is with postal mail. If he is interested, he requests a hard copy. Some prefer electronic submissions but will reluctantly accept hard copy in instances where it seems genuinely necessary (usually having to do with extensive use of photo or graphic files).

WHAT DO I SEND?

How do you know which communication method to use? Your first source, of course, should be the agent or editor's website. Most agents and publishers have a button on their site that says "Submissions," or something similar. If you click on that button, their preferred method of receiving queries and manuscripts will be listed. You can also consult annual directories like *Writer's Market* that have entries listing the preferred guidelines of agents and editors. While we provide general guidelines here, be sure to follow the specific agent or editor's exact instructions when you submit your work. This is just one more reason why you do not write one query and send it to 138 addressees—which insults everybody who receives it by telling them that you don't have the time to address them as individuals.

Recently a woman looking for literary representation sent Martin Literary Management an unsolicited manuscript—not a query or a proposal, but an entire manuscript. She included with it a postage-paid envelope for the manuscript's return, but the manuscript weighed over one pound, meaning that its return required a specific hand delivery to the post office. She was quite upset when she learned that it would not be returned.

Imagine if an agent or editor made a special trip to the post office for every unsolicited manuscript received. A single daily trip would involve the use of a minivan and a forklift. When would they do their work? That is only one more reason to follow the submission instructions to the letter. Any agent or editor who asks for something to be sent in hard copy form bears the responsibility to get it back to you. But whether you use electronic or postal communication, never send anything unsolicited except for your query itself.

Sending Hard Copies

If an agent wants to receive your query by hard copy, and a few agents still do, include a self-addressed, stamped envelope (SASE) so the agent can send a reply back to you. If you question the need for the SASE, keep in mind the number of queries that agents and editors receive. It would bankrupt them to mail a reply back to everyone who sent in a query or heavy manuscript.

If you choose a hard copy submission, use a fresh ink cartridge to print your query. If your ink is splotchy or faded, or if your paper is crumpled or stained, it reflects poorly on your professionalism. For a postal query, use standard white copy paper and a white No. 10 business envelope, or a professionally printed business letterhead on a higher grade of light-colored paper.

And as with electronic submissions, never type in bold, in all caps, or in a flowery type.

 HOT TIP!

Attention to detail in everything you do is the surest way to prove your professionalism and set yourself ahead of the pack.

Polish your work! Make sure that the text of the query letter, envelope, and SASE have no typos. Double-check that all addresses are accurate, and that you have the correct amount of postage for both envelopes.

Supporting Documents

While attaching anything to an e-mail query is generally ineffective, you may, if you have received recent national press on the topic of your book, include a link to the video or article. Be certain to place those links directly into your regular query.

If you send the same information via hard copy, know that most agents probably will not take the time or trouble to type in a website address that you reference in a postal query. Time is always short. An agent might, however, take a look at a one-page newspaper clipping or magazine article if it is included in the same envelope as the postal query. Be sure it is a nice, clean, legible *copy*, and not an original document. Remember that if you send anything that has not been specifically requested, you cannot fairly expect to get it back.

PLAYING THE WAITING GAME

Whether you send your query electronically or by mail, the hard part for many authors comes after you have sent it away. There is a tendency to begin second-guessing yourself, thinking that you should have changed the second sentence, perhaps, or wondering if the strength of your platform was somehow unclear.

It is tempting to quickly send a follow-up to be certain that your recipient understands exactly what you meant. You absolutely must resist this. Don't do it. It could doom a budding relationship between you and your prospective representative.

At Martin Literary Management, we try to respond to e-mail queries within two weeks. E-mail queries are funneled into a specific computer file folder and normally we go through them twice a week. Other agents might do this once a day or once a week. The primary business for all literary representatives is to sell the work of clients whom they already represent. If agents have their hands full with a list of title submissions to editors, they simply cannot have much time left over to take on new authors. That is not to say that they won't, but all experienced agents know that they must be very selective about asking to see a project because the process of screening them is such an uncertain and speculative investment of time.

So, follow the instructions on the respective website of the company and individual who will be receiving your correspondence. If the site predicts a query response within three months, then avoid e-mailing, calling, or sending flowers during that three-month period. And if you submit hard copy by mail, remember that the advertised three-month period dates from the time that your query is actually received—*not* from the date that you mailed it. Adding a week on either side for traveling through the mail, and you are really looking at three and a half months.

HOT TIP!

Use this secret to protect yourself from undue anxiety: *Apply* three and a half months of patience to this time period the same way that you would *apply* a bandage to a cut. Once it's on, leave it alone while the clock ticks. Your automatic response to any urge to hurry is that patience has already been applied for this time period, so there is no need to wonder whether or not you will be doing anything else during that time—you have already determined that you will not. *Give in to that. Then give in to it again and be prepared to give in to it once again immediately after that if need be. Repeat as needed and keep on repeating until the full time period has elapsed.*

Some agents never respond to queries that fail to interest them. Their view is that there is not enough time in the day to do so. Adam Chromy, literary manager and founder of Artists and Artisans Inc., is one who does not respond to queries that fail to interest him. His response is,

"We are not here to run a public service, gently letting down aspiring authors regardless of how inept their queries."

If you don't hear from an agent within the time frame specified on the company website, assume that there is no interest and walk away. You have so much else to do. If a literary representative *is* interested in seeing your proposal, you may be sure that they will contact you.

At Martin Literary Management, we generally respond to everything, even queries for projects that we cannot get behind. We do not respond if the query is spam or if the e-mail is part of a copy list to multiple agents, or the query contains abusive language. It is often encouraging when brief thank-you notes arrive after we have had to pass on a query, because it means that there are prospective authors out there who are courteous and considerate, and who keep their sights set on the future.

This is not about kissing up to anybody; it shows wisdom in handling oneself in a difficult situation. The people who work in that marketplace every day are in the best situation to appreciate what it takes for you to show refined behavior in the face of disappointment.

Be sure you also resist the temptation within, say, forty-eight hours after you send the query, to then e-mail the agent a second time with something like, "I sent you an e-mail two days ago and was just checking to be sure you got it." That is a transparent attempt to engage an agent that will produce the opposite effect.

In terms of contacting an agent after you have sent your query, there is one more thing to consider. At various times of the year, certain agents and publishers will be closed to submissions even though the agency itself is still humming away. An agent might be overwhelmed with the existing workload, or at a trade show, or out of town for a holiday. So, it's always a good idea to check before sending your query to be absolutely sure that an agent or publisher is currently open. (But don't call!) If there is nothing on their website that indicates they are *not* currently taking submissions, then it is fair to assume that the door is open.

EXCLUSIVE READS

It is never appropriate to send your work to a literary representative or an editor unless it is requested. When it is, the reading period may cover anything from a single weekend to a week or two, sometimes even longer. Since you have already researched this person or company and you know that you want them to represent you, it is a common courtesy to grant that brief period if it is requested. This means that you are agreeing that during the agreed span of time you will not submit that project to anyone else. If there is someone else who is already considering the work, congratulations, but be sure to put that information out on the table. Your recipient may choose to ignore it, but they deserve to be honestly informed.

If you agree to an exclusive reading period, you must stick to it. It is more than just tacky to break that promise; it can come back to bite you in all sorts of unexpected ways. The book world is a relatively small industry. Everyone knows most everyone else; they all talk to each other—a lot—and a great deal of what they talk about is other people. So beware of any associate who attempts to convince you that it is okay, in that wink-and-a-nod kind of way, for you to quietly continue submitting your work in spite of a commitment not to do so. Never make the promise of granting an exclusive read unless you fully intend to keep it.

HOT TIP!

When others hear that you are faithful to your words, cynics may sneer at your naiveté, but the people you actually want to know will begin to seek you out as your positive reputation precedes you.

FORMATTING FOR SUCCESS

The current standard e-mail format for transmitting your manuscript is Microsoft Word, whether your system is a PC or a Mac. A book manuscript or proposal that is written on obscure software may not display well (or at all) on another system. Plus, Microsoft Word is currently the publishing industry standard. Its "Track Changes" feature, which we will discuss shortly, is used extensively in the editing process. You will need to be fluent in its use if you are to communicate with anyone in the publishing industry.

The first page of your proposal or manuscript must contain your contact information, including address, phone number, and e-mail. Then, start each chapter or proposal segment at the top of a new page. Be sure that the title of your book or proposal and a page number is on every page. The header feature works well for this. Most often this information will all be at the top of the page, but your prospective agent or editor may have specific requirements.

If you are sending your requested material by postal mail, do not bend, fold, cut, or staple any of the pages. The same goes for two- or three-hole punches. Your pages need to be loose because often copies will be made of your work. That way several people can read it simultaneously.

If sending electronically, send the entire manuscript as one file. *One single attachment.* No broken sections, no individual chapters sent in separate files like the world's most annoying daisy chain, unless your recipient requests it that way. Otherwise, you are expecting them to do your clerical work for you in sorting your materials. You are not trolling for an assistant; you are appealing to an established advocate for a speculative investment of *their* time and energy on *your* behalf.

 HOT TIP!

Many of your competitors will weed themselves out this way ...

Track Changes

One of the essential features of Microsoft Word is the "Track Changes" feature. An editor today is more likely to work electronically than on a printed manuscript, requiring you to make necessary changes using the "Track Changes" editing feature. So learn it. It's an absolutely necessary skill for a writer today. If you focus on it, you can learn everything you need to know about using Track Changes in an hour or less.

Track Changes, as the name implies, keeps track of the changes done to a manuscript by any person at any time. It keeps track of all the original work, new comments, and proposed additions and deletions, and displays them neatly color-coded and arranged. The feature optimizes the ease and speed of communication, since multiple people can edit the same document: the agent, the editor, the copyeditor, and you, the author. Later, your editor can make any necessary notes directly into the manuscript using Track Changes *without altering the original version*. That's the fundamental benefit of the Track Changes function. It is a consistent and verifiable way to track the exact progress of any revision whatsoever to the original document or to any subsequent draft. Track Changes defines all edits using colored typeface and other markings, such as underlining and redlining, along with who made the change. The beauty of the system is that it allows the writer to receive the suggested edits and then accept or reject each one. As you can see, Track Changes represents a quantum leap from paper manuscripts and postal mail. It is by far the most efficient way to electronically edit.

Track Changes is not difficult to learn or use. If you take time to familiarize yourself with the feature, you will acquire a powerful tool for handling suggested changes in a fully documented fashion. Track Changes is also especially good at minimizing mistakes in handling the heaps of minutiae that accompany a book-length work of nonfiction.

HOT TIP!

The Track Changes feature will protect your chain of authorship.

As you have seen, the switch to e-mail saves time and costs for all concerned. When a writer has to make that long trek through a series of submissions before landing a book deal, the quicker responses to e-mail queries—and the use of Track Changes, if there is back-and-forth communication concerning the work—allows everyone to cover more ground with less time spent waiting for a response.

MAKING CONNECTIONS AT BOOK FAIRS, FESTIVALS, AND WRITERS' CONFERENCES

Paper and electronic submissions aside, there's nothing like a face-to-face encounter to help get the attention of an agent or editor. We mentioned earlier that it is a good idea to go to different book events. And you should, as long as you remain professional and businesslike by conducting yourself in a manner that will further your career.

First, it is important for you to understand the purpose and intent of the event. At a writers' conference, it is expected that meetings and interaction between writers, editors, and agents will happen both formally and informally. But even though the people who hold your holy grail in plain sight are readily available, you must not be obtrusive. This means you do not interrupt agents or editors when they are eating, in the restroom, or in the middle of a conversation. It is about fundamental respect, and poor conduct will be remembered.

Many times appointments with key people in the book industry are generally scheduled well in advance, so be sure to check out the event's website and contact the organizers if it looks as if meetings of this type will be scheduled. Sometimes you can get a list of attendees from the conference organizers or from an advance copy of the program directory.

If so, take time to write a short, carefully crafted e-mail asking for an appointment during the event.

If you can't obtain a meeting, or if the event is not scheduling meetings for its speakers, the best way to attract the attention of a person you want to meet is to sit in the first row during his presentation. At some point during the presentation or the discussion afterward, ask one appropriate question. Just one. Be sure your question is carefully thought out and that you ask it in a poised and confident manner. Then, after the session is over, introduce yourself, give the person your card, and ask if there is a time during the event where you can meet briefly. This shows your interest, intelligence, and patience. Chances are the person will not have time to meet with you, and in that case, ask if you can meet by phone or send an e-mail after the conference. This is a great way to open the door without barging through uninvited.

Trade shows such as BookExpo America (BEA), however, are intended as a venue for publishers to sell their wares to libraries and to bookstores. And while some prescheduled meetings with a publisher's existing authors do take place, this is generally not an event where publishers have time to meet with prospective authors. BEA is an excellent event to attend if you want to learn about the book industry, though, and we feel every prospective author should try to go at least once. Their educational seminars are outstanding and the trade show gives you a feel for the enormity of every aspect of the book industry.

So be sure to align your expectations to the purpose of the event. If you want to learn about the craft of writing and network with other authors, go to an event where that will actually happen.

 HOT TIP!

Never discount anyone you meet. Today's interns and assistants are tomorrow's full-time agents and editors. And today's unrepresented authors can be on next year's best-seller list. Fair warning.

The True Purpose of a Pitch Fest

Another wonderful kind of event for authors is a pitch fest. Many writers' conferences use them, wherein they set aside special times for agents and editors to take dozens of pitches from conference attendees over the course of a single afternoon, with each pitch lasting no more than two to three minutes. This is a wonderful way to practice pitching your book, and who knows, maybe you'll hit a home run!

CHAPTER 11

FROM AGENT TO DEAL (OR NOT):
TACTICS
FOR PRESENTING YOURSELF

When your query has grabbed an agent's attention and your submitted proposal or manuscript has lived up to the hype—then you are at the point where a contract for literary representation will be offered to you.

You should have already made certain that this particular representative is right for you (see chapter 7 on researching agents), so that if representation is extended to you, you are prepared to accept. Remember that no honest agent or manager charges an up-front fee for representation, other than sometimes charging for nominal office costs of making photocopies and mailing the author's work or materials pertaining to it. Legitimate agents are paid via commission, meaning that they are paid if and when their faith in you pays off and they successfully sell your book.

In being offered representation, you are not only being offered that person's time and expense in representing you, but also their personal financial loss if they guess wrong. So, if an agent is interested in representing you and your work, read his contract and reply to the offer within a week. One week. If the agent is met with a lazy response from you or with any gamesmanship in negotiations, he or she is likely to remember how many other sincere and hardworking writers would love to have their representation at the quoted terms ... and rescind the offer made to you.

The commission rate of 15 percent is the industry standard in today's market. Some agents will also have a minimum representation fee, in case you choose to take a lower advance and a higher deal on the back end. Agents need to be paid for their work, and your agent will have done the work by selling your book to a publisher. It is not a good idea to try to negotiate an agent's fee. Established, best-selling authors may have a degree of leverage here, or lesser-known writers if they have secured rights from a sports hero, political giant, or international film or television star, but those rare opportunities are exceptions to the rule.

However, if you have reason to believe that the contract has room for amendment, have your legal advisor ready to respond soon after it is received. This advisor needs to be well versed in intellectual property law. Make all of your requests for changes in a single pass. If you drag out the process, it may cause the agent to question your overall judgment. After all, *you* are the one who sought them out!

The length of your literary contract will probably be for a term of one year and, depending on the amount of work your agent thinks needs to be done on your platform and your proposal before submitting it to publishers, is likely to include an option to represent your next book if the first one sells.

TACTICS FOR PRESENTING YOURSELF

In this single, all-important step of obtaining representation in the literary marketplace, you have launched yourself far ahead of many thousands of other prospective authors who have not. So what comes next? Hint: A well-planned submission list of potential publishers and their in-house editors is in your immediate future. From this moment on, every move that you make should be calculated to demonstrate that *you* are the perfect person to write your book.

How you present and conduct yourself during the next leg of your journey can make or break your book publishing deal.

Be the Perfect Author

Every agent and editor has thoughts on what qualities make for a good author-client. Obviously the talent for writing is paramount, but right behind it is the need for the depth of dedication necessary for seeing a long project through.

Jamie Brenner, an agent with Artists and Artisans, Inc., hopes her authors will communicate their expectations and concerns along the way. "Be honest with me," she says. "Work hard and then harder. And trust me to do the same."

Heidi Krupp-Lisiten, CEO and founder of Krupp Kommunications (K2), hopes that her authors will work in tandem with her. "The best way an author can help us is to be our partner. We are in this together. The more we are clear on their goals and objectives, the easier is it for us to deliver and exceed their expectation."

We once asked another agent for his description of the perfect author. He said, "a dead one with a trunk full of incredible manuscripts." He was kidding … sort of. So are we. (No we're not.) If you cannot muster a *consistent* level of creative passion and professionalism, your book's chances of finding a readership take a nosedive.

A passion for reading is also important. It is difficult to be a great and dedicated writer unless you are also a great and dedicated reader. Do you find it hard to eat your breakfast without reading the morning paper, your e-mail, or the back of the cereal box? If you are the kind of person who is not happy unless you are writing on a regular basis, and if you can pursue it while remaining dedicated and professional in your manner, you may be able to become your agent's "perfect author" yourself.

Understand That Publishing Is a Business

It cannot be overemphasized that publishing is a business and that you, as the author, are an entrepreneur in this business world. The ware that you are selling is your book. Everything you do should be done the most effective way possible toward the goal of selling that book. Think of it this way: You want to climb the corporate ladder and become CEO. To reach that status from the mailroom, you must conduct yourself in all of the ways that move you closer to the CEO position.

Do Your Homework

Become familiar with every stop on the road to publication. The more you learn about the book business in advance, the better it is for your future. The time that it takes for you to attend a book conference or to study the industry in detail is time well spent. You are also using your time wisely if you are able to join a writers' group, attend book signings, or take an online course—provided that these things help you to actually get your writing done.

Your increased familiarity with all aspects of the profession will help you understand the way that the current publishing climate will always affect book advances, back-end deals, and a host of other clauses in your contract. In today's market, the big six-figure advances that we saw in the early 2000s are the anomaly, not the norm. That will change as the overall economy changes, but right now it is not realistic to expect an advance of that magnitude unless your story is truly spectacular and international in its appeal.

Martin Literary Management represented one author who possessed national name recognition through a TV reality show, and this person continuously e-mailed us to ask why the book was not selling in numerous foreign markets. Even though this author had achieved minor celebrity status, American "reality TV" is more of a phenomenon here in the U.S. than anywhere else. Our client got a little burst of media-generated fame and had erroneously concluded that this kind of celebrity status was something more than "fifteen minutes" within a narrow media market.

The other plus in educating yourself is that you will come to know your competition very well, a key component in the success of any business. One way to do this is to read current titles that are in your field and to watch their success (or failure), learning from both results.

Build Your Platform

We've said this before (and devoted chapter 3 to it): Start to build your platform right away. The biggest single mistake new authors make is waiting too long to start this part of the process. You must establish yourself as a credible author with name recognition in your subject matter before you submit your agent query, because once you have an agent, the process is already moving along much too quickly for you to fix up a platform. Remember that your agent will be pitching you to editors who must then feel very confident that your platform will move enough books to not only cover the cost of the advance, editing, and production of the book, but to actually make the publisher money.

Michaela Hamilton, the editor in chief of Citadel Press at Kensington Publishing, relates a story of two authors who did it right.

"When I acquired *What Really Sank the Titanic: New Forensic Discoveries* by Jennifer Hooper McCarty and Timothy Foecke, I knew its authors would be the key to our publishing plan," says Hamilton. "As metallurgists who had personally examined the artifacts of the sunken vessel, they had all the right credentials. Their work had won attention in major newspapers in the United States and throughout the world. They were practiced speakers who regularly gave standing-room-only presentations about their work. Their book broke new ground in bringing together key findings that at last showed the reason for the great ship's tragic demise.

"Further, I believed that interest in the *Titanic* remained strong after many successful books on the subject as well as the blockbuster film. Happily, my hopes were realized when the book was published; it received a front-page write-up in *The New York Times* and extensive coverage in media around the world, including morning television, evening network news, and an author's appearance on *The Colbert Report*."

Now that is the kind of platform-driven success that every author should seek to emulate.

Take Your Time

When it comes to your query, proposal, platform, and book, it is *never a good idea* to shoot from the hip. To be effective, each part must be carefully and methodically planned out and executed. No, this is *not* slowing you down. It is actually speeding you up by giving you what you need to do it right the first time.

Don't be in a hurry to send out your query or proposal. The savvy author will have other people read and critique the work before sending anything off (and will go over each word to be certain that the grammar, spelling, context, and formatting are perfect).

Be Considerate

At Martin Literary Management we like to think of ourselves as a "considerate literary management" company, and we hope our clients will reciprocate by being considerate authors. This means first and foremost doing what you say you are going to do. Failing to follow through on your promises is bound to make anyone leery of working with you.

As a considerate author you also understand that your agent is working in your best interests, and so you heed the advice that you are given (or seriously consider it). Remember that your agent's business is your book.

HOT TIP!

Even if you find a literary manager who is attentive to your career, never allow yourself to be blind your situation—no matter how unskilled at business you may consider yourself to be.

Although a good manager will spare you the drudge work of operating the various facets of your platform, public relations campaign, website, book signings, or other aspects of your career, the final responsibility will always rest with you. Your name is on the cover of this book that you are carrying in your head. You are the one who will be singled out by reviewers for praise or condemnation.

"Authors sometimes don't recognize that their entire team (including agents, editors and publishers) are all pulling in the same direction," says John Willig, president of Literary Services, Inc. "Ultimately, we are all in the same boat in helping make your work a great book. So recognize the professional expertise and experience of your partners and listen to their advice at every turn."

The observation makes a lot of sense. After all, you are paying your agent 15 percent of your gross, so you should seriously consider the advice that you are paying to receive, even if it is not what you want to hear. Sometimes, telling you what you don't want to hear may be the most important thing that an agent or manager does. If your representative thinks that your book needs more work, up to and including another full pass through the manuscript, then instead of resisting the advice, consider being thrilled that you have a wonderful representative who can help guide you, if you are so lucky. Then buckle down to work.

The Nice Things in Life

While many authors (sadly) never thank their agents (not even in the Acknowledgements section, a venal sin), there are a few authors who go overboard the other way and wear agents out with cards and gifts. A Christmas or holiday card is nice, but a Valentine's Day card is, honestly, a little weird. Sending flowers or a gift card to your agent to celebrate the sale of a book is appropriate. But unless your book is about the history of the Fourth of July, a basket of flag-shaped cookies to mark the holiday is not.

Like anyone else, agents want to feel appreciated, but remember that this is a business relationship. If you wouldn't send it to the CEO of a company that you work for, don't send it to your agent, your editor, or your publisher.

Phone Etiquette

When it comes to phone etiquette, less is definitely more. It is far better to communicate via e-mail whenever possible. Remember that every phone call is a demand upon an agent's time and a distraction from ongoing work, even if you "just have a quick question."

It feels good to speak directly to your representative and it is a form of hand holding that many authors seem to desire. But the problem with phone calls is that they occur in real time, requiring the person on the other end to stop work and communicate things to you that could be handled more conveniently via e-mail. The lag time created by e-mail also gives the recipient breathing room, especially if your agent has a set time of day for handling correspondence. This small courtesy on your part allows your agent to address your concerns without having to interrupt something else to do it. Remember, you only have one literary representative, but any agent or manager can have dozens of active clients at the same time. Telephone time gets multiplied to the point that it becomes highly burdensome, even if every client only has a quick question.

The Permanence of the Internet

Any time that we do business over the Internet, we must remember that we are working inside of a transparent box. The illusion of privacy is exactly that. The search engine company Google offers a service called Google Alerts where a user can receive e-mails when a certain search term or phrase pops up on the Internet. Many professional people, including agents, receive Google Alerts whenever their name is used.

That means that if you trash your agent, or former agent, or agent-to-be on the Internet, she will probably be sent an e-mail from Google, complete with a direct link to your disappointing words.

Of course it works both ways. If you've written something praising your agent on the Internet, they'll get an e-mail regarding that post, too.

E-Mail Etiquette

Whether it is a phone call or an e-mail, every communication you have with your agent or editor should pass the "essential communication" rule. This means that every time you pick up the phone or open a new e-mail and type in your agent's address, you need to ask yourself if this communication is absolutely necessary. If not, over time you will flood your representative with phone and e-mail communications and eventually it will become a turn-off. There just isn't enough time in the day to answer unnecessary calls or e-mail.

HOT TIP!

Use e-mail to minimize phone time and be sure to adopt a civil and positive attitude. You are its main beneficiary.

E-mail can be a very casual way of connecting with someone but it doesn't give you the right to be casual in your communications. Remember that your book is your business. All of your e-mails should reflect the high standards of all your correspondence.

REQUESTS MADE OF YOU

There is a good chance that your new literary representative will make a few requests of you while preparing to take your proposal or manuscript to potential publishers. You may be asked to provide materials such as award documents, photos, or press articles in addition to your book proposal, to help sell you. Treat all such requests as opportunities for you to be directly involved in the sale and promotion of your work, and respond quickly with whatever is needed. This is you helping you.

However, as a considerate author, never e-mail huge documents to your agent. Ever. If the material is requested and is enough to choke the recipient's inbox, a hard copy may be the best way to go, via secured postal delivery. If electronic format is important, consider delivering the storage medium itself: flash drives, DVDs, CDs. We needed some supporting photos from one author who put them on a flash drive and sent them to us, which works well. Another put their information on a CD, and while we are generally timid about putting unknown CDs into our computer, the fact that it was requested and came from one of our authors relieved our anxiety. Slightly.

Take-Backs

Never attempt to "recall" your work in favor of a new draft. It is a common temptation and the urge is powerful, but once you have submitted your work, it is done. If you attempt to call back one version and replace it with another, you will demonstrate that you did not fully prepare your work before it was submitted. Worse, it shows that you have no confidence in your own judgment. Yet another reason why, when you are ready to submit, it means that you have made absolutely sure that your work is properly done, down to the smallest detail.

 HOT TIP!

No take-backs!

HANDLING WRITERLY INSECURITIES

Throughout this chapter we have discussed how to present yourself and your work to your literary representative. Your relationship with your agent is professional, and while it should definitely be cordial, it is not personal and there is no need for you to behave as if it is. There is no ongoing contest to see who can send the most flower arrangements to their representative. Also, please do not yield to the temptation to relate any of your insecurities to your representative in an attempt to engage their empathy and speed the response process. Life is hard. But before you cry the blues to one who has placed faith in you, consider that you are not your representative's only client; your agent is juggling multiple clients and multitasking through multiple submissions. You are trying to publish a book, not win first place in the Misery Olympics; you will quickly alienate your representative by showing impatience or anxiety.

We had one client who called to see if we could wire an advance because he was on a ski vacation in Aspen and he was "broke." Another client, this one an accomplished executive, told us that he was in such poverty that he was eating cat food. Both were impatient for their advance checks. The apparent implication was that we weren't working as hard as we could, but that an "emergency" would cause us to go back to the publisher and ask them for a loan on the writer's behalf. It was an invitation to madness. We don't want to know if you are crazy, falling off the wagon, or getting divorced (although an e-mail letting us know you are getting married is nice). Save it for your spouse, your drinking buddies, your pastor, or your shrink. This is one of those areas where maintaining a noble silence is the most attractive accoutrement to your persona.

It is not uncommon at this point for a writer to snap under the pressure of waiting for responses, waiting for a check, waiting for a major review. As for *you*, whether or not your representative keeps you well posted on submissions, whether or not any helpful feedback arrives, your mantra must remain: "It only takes one." It only takes one editor, one publisher, to turn you from an aspiring writer to a published author.

Know that the suspense here is far worse than it was when you were waiting for an agent to respond to your initial query. You await a publisher's response fully aware that you could be a hair's-breadth away from your goal. The wait is agonizing no matter how swiftly the process moves. Time slows down for the waiting writer, and the imagination goes to work, fears expand, paranoia growls. If you allow yourself to give in to your insecurities, then before long, tense phone calls are placed and nervous e-mails are sent. Take a deep breath, chill, work on your blog and your platform, outline your next book. After all, if you are relaxed and happy when the call that you have been waiting for finally comes, you will enjoy it all the more. Yes?

CHAPTER 12

DEMYSTIFYING THE PROCESS: HOW YOUR SALE IS MADE

If you remain on this pathway, then the day is drawing closer when your agent will call to inform you that one or more offers have been received for your book. But just how does your agent get your book to that point?

Let's demystify the process by going through exactly what a competent and enthused literary representative does concerning the sale of your work.

A MASTER OF MULTITASKING

A good agent needs to be a master of multitasking. There are any number of things that must be done to achieve a sale, and your agent needs to do them at the right time for every one of the dozens of active clients who are currently in the submission process. There are also ongoing issues with books that have already been sold: sales of foreign rights, audio and e-book rights, and film rights must be tended, not to mention the continual phone calls and e-mails regarding the dozens (or hundreds) of books that the agent has previously sold.

Query to Publishers

After you have scrubbed and polished your proposal, the most important thing that your representative can do for you at the beginning of your relationship is to absorb your work. Every properly prepared literary representative must be able to break down your book into a concise and compelling pitch for a third party, and do so with such clarity that the vision you brought to the book becomes contagious. Your representative may take elements directly from your query letter to compose a pitch letter to a publishing house, or may extract parts of your proposal for the same purpose.

A Researched Submission List

Just as you did the research necessary to draw up your agency submission list (as featured in chapter 7), your agent will research publishers to compile a list of appropriate editors and publishing houses for your work. The choices are based upon each editor's pattern of past book acquisitions as the primary indicator of their potential interest. Many agents will also prioritize submissions based upon their working relationships with specific editors.

The point is that every conscientious agent or manager keeps a list of publishers, imprints, and individual editors, and constantly updates it so that whatever kind of book needs to be sold, all the necessary information is easily available. Few agents will rely on memory alone; the database is enormous. In addition, publishers go out of business, editors change jobs, and the list of correct places to submit your book six months ago may be very different from the list of the best places to send it today.

Many of the larger publishers have several imprints, or groupings of books of similar subject matter. There are complicated rules about submitting to editors from different imprints at the same publishing house, but you must never submit to multiple editors simultaneously at the same imprint. Another of your agent's tasks is to choose which editor is best suited for your work. Some of that comes from knowing the editor personally. Some comes from knowing the editor's history of acquisitions.

In preparing to approach a publisher with your work, your representative must consider each publisher and publishing imprint's *backlist* of books. This term refers to books that have already been released and are still being sold. Part of your representative's responsibility is to have a working knowledge of those backlists, in order to be able to determine in advance whether or not a publisher has a conflict of interest, or conversely, if the publisher needs a book like yours to round out their list of acquisitions.

Other considerations include the agent's knowledge of how individual publishers treat authors, the publisher's budget, and whether it is a small independent publisher or a large major house. It's important to determine whether the publisher pays on list sale price or net sale price (see page 197 in chapter 13) , as the difference can mean double for an author's royalties.

Some agents just don't submit to certain editors. This might be because in the past the editor has not responded in a timely manner, or perhaps promised something but failed to deliver. It is a real concern to you if an editor does not respond in a timely fashion. Let's assume your agent submits to Editor A at a house with three imprints. If the editor asks for the submission and then sits on it, that disqualifies your agent from sending your work to any other editor at that publisher's other imprints. The same professionalism that is so important for you to employ is equally important all the way up the book industry ladder. Your representative must know something about each editor's style in order to protect you from slow-response logjams.

Finding the perfect editor to submit to can be a time-consuming process, because on top of everything else, it is important to consider the editor's personal interests. An agent who is submitting a book on men's health will most likely search for a male editor. For a book on parenting, the ideal editor will probably also be a parent, and a book on gerontology would not be a likely fit for a twenty-five-year-old associate editor. Consider how long it took you to come up with your book idea, define it, refine it, write the perfect book proposal, and then write a query that jumps off the page. With that in mind, allow your representative the time to go through a similar process so that your material has been digested well enough to be explained clearly to a stranger on your behalf.

So as you bite your nails and try to distract yourself from the process, begin by showing patience with your representative. It takes time to fully absorb your words, ideas, and intent, and then to craft a carefully researched editor list with a query that sparks enthusiastic responses.

 HOT TIP!

Authors cannot possibly have enough inside knowledge of trends, publishers, editors, and backlists to make the best pitches to the most appropriate publishers. This is just one of the many reasons it makes sense to be professionally represented.

Cause for Dismissal

No good literary representative ever sends a writer's work out *unsolicited*. That sort of a casual toss-off of something so important to you is a sure indicator that you need to seek out another representative. The right representative for your book will take care to assemble a list of appropriate editors, and will always ask those editors if they are interested in reading your work before ever sending it to them. There is no other acceptable order to this part of the process. Any time a lazy agent or manager tries to get away with just throwing your work against the wall to see if it sticks, your work and your professional image are both devalued by it.

WHEN EDITORS REQUEST YOUR WORK

When an editor requests your proposal, you have reached another milestone on the road to becoming a published author. Since most editors don't want to interrupt their day to listen to random phone pitches, your submission is likely to go out via e-mail. Postal mail and messenger service also may be used, and if so, you will reimburse those delivery charges.

Remember that the voices in your head that encourage you to bug your agent for updates are actually little demons trying to lead you astray. Consider that if your representative presses the publishing house editor on your behalf, it is likely to simply irritate that person and achieve nothing of value for you. An agent can always get an answer by pressing for one, but it probably won't be the one you want to hear. Once an editor has your work, it is important for the agent to leave the editor alone to process the information.

However, if you are continuing to work on your book during the submission process, and if you have *additional* edited and polished sample chapters that are newly available, make your agent aware of that. Sometimes, if an editor is on the fence about your ability to complete the manuscript, additional writing samples may be the very thing that generates an offer.

Your representative has placed faith in you and your work with every one of the editors contacted on your behalf. Return the gesture of faith even when your insecurities may be giving you hell. That means enduring the wait with patience and good grace. It absolutely will be noticed and appreciated by your representative, whether or not it is ever mentioned.

One thing that is reasonable for you to request of your representative is a list of publishers to whom your work has been submitted. Here it is especially advisable to avoid the phone call, as e-mail assures that you have reliable records of that request later.

Although we have mentioned that an agent can only pitch to one editor at a publishing imprint, if more than one editor from an imprint is listed, this is most likely because an editor may have passed on the proposal, but referred your representative to another editor within the company. Hopefully it's not because your agent is doing simultaneous submissions to the same house.

Literary agent Scott Hoffman of Folio Literary Management warns, "Publishing is a slooooow industry. Figure out what you think should be a reasonable time for everything to take place, and then triple it and add a day. It will keep your blood pressure down."

Everyone in the book world is aware of how difficult it is for a writer to await a response on a book. But you also have the opportunity during this time to give an effective demonstration of your professionalism by showing grace under pressure. You can accomplish that by avoiding those insecurity-based e-mails and calls to "inquire about news." Agents and managers will rarely keep news from you—and never hold back if the news is good.

You will often hear initial reactions within a few weeks. Sometimes feedback is received in just a few days, although that usually only happens if a book is considered to have strong potential as an international bestseller. But remember, it can also take months for an editor to get to your proposal in the stack and then sit down to read it.

IF PUBLISHERS REJECT YOUR WORK

If, as does happen, a publisher rejects your work, take solace in the principle that one person's pleasure is another's poison. Even if you have avoided the pitfalls of a conflicting book by another writer or a publisher's secret project, even if your project was not too similar to a book the publisher lost a ton of money on last year, there is always the issue of personal preference. If you are rejected and you carefully considered all that we have outlined for your submission, then the rejection means nothing more than that particular reader's bell was not rung by your clapper.

HOT TIP!

There are people who don't like Hemingway or Faulkner, or even Shakespeare. If a writer fails to understand that, any rejection can strike hard.

All published authors, no matter how successful and esteemed they may be, write with the certain knowledge that there will be people who do not like their work. There will always be critics—and there is beauty in that. It lies in the understanding that everyone who writes is in the same boat. The democracy of that fact snuffs its power to sting.

There also may be a project in development that is too similar to yours for a publisher to be able to get behind you. Or a publisher may have already filled their internal quota of acquisitions in your book's area, leaving no room for interest in your work even if it is of the highest quality. That particular problem may be a little easier for your representative to foresee if there is a reliable contact within the publishing house, but there is never a guarantee that your work can be completely kept away from such an obstacle. It is difficult, if not impossible, for any literary representative to completely protect you from things going wrong, but the depth of knowledge and the level of energy that he or she is willing to expend on your behalf can keep the odds tilted in your favor.

Keep in mind, too, that sometimes publishers have projects under *embargo*. This term describes projects that are being prepared for publication in secret. Nonfiction books occasionally have legal reasons for being played close to the vest, while other projects may be timed for a surprise release that coincides with a particular date or event. In such cases your book may present a conflict that would not be known by your representative.

Editorial Opinions

If the first editor—or the first few editors—do not have a positive reaction to your submission, it may be nothing more than errant opinion. But it may also be something else. The primary reason, as we have repeatedly emphasized, that today's editors reject an otherwise fabulously written and highly salable nonfiction book comes down to the writer's platform. Few people who have not encountered the publishing system can grasp how closely the publisher's marketing and sales department will look at the writer's platform.

Consider also the position of any editor who has two or more prospective books that they would like to acquire (as often happens) but they are only budgeted to buy one. You understand why they are most likely to go for the book that is written by someone who can guarantee plenty of public exposure, someone who projects an air of media savvy. (You *have* been working on your sound bites and your single paragraph descriptions of your book, haven't you? If not, stop *here* and catch up.)

Publishers are charged with the task of bringing in more money on books that they buy than the amounts that they have to pay out to get them. Many times publishers serve corporate overlords who will fire them if they fail. Their corporate overlords also answer to higher-ups: the owners and stockholders. All that accumulated pressure comes to a point at the top of every writer's head.

Editors and publishers frequently do not want to get into details about why they are rejecting a book, since their decision is not an invitation to a debate. However, if the thing that stops them from going ahead with the book is doubt about the writer's platform, they often feel free to speak right up about it. Perhaps it is a little easier to deliver bad news if the objection is over an external quality, such as the writer's platform, rather than a disparagement of the work itself.

What Passes Really Mean

If there is no criticism of the writer's platform, but the passes and rejections keep coming back with a similar ring, this indicates a trend. The chance that all your dissenters are wrong grows smaller every time a negative reaction is given. But it can take weeks or months to gather enough feedback so that you know whether this is true or not. Usually, there is no way to predict what will happen with the project until a good number of publishers have come back to you, perhaps as many as ten.

There are some instances when several of the editors who request material just happen to read it right away, and then coincidentally send back their responses within a few days. It is wonderful when that happens, especially if at least one good offer is forthcoming, but statistically the speedy message will tend to be that there is something flawed about the project.

In that case, the writer who has carefully considered the nature of the marketplace does not meet with failure, merely with the decision of whether to fall back and give it a serious rewrite, or to conclude that the critics are wrong. You and your representative may be deluding yourselves into thinking that your work is better than it really is, but here is your dilemma: There will always be those rare instances when the rest of the band happens to be marching out of step with *you*.

If that scenario presents itself, have a heart-to-heart talk with your representative, who has shown faith in your work so far. Together, you should decide whether submissions should proceed. You may find that both of you are on the same page. If your mutual conviction remains strong, then a second round of submissions may be in order. However, if you are not in agreement on this, your representative may bail on you at this point. It's a common occurrence. A few, if they are passionate about the book, will stick with you until there are no other potential publishers left. That kind of dedication is rare. Rejoice if you find it, and immediately get back to work.

There is a big "however" here. Even if your work is roundly rejected and your literary representative releases you from your contract, *it does not alter your true challenge of getting your book published*. That may seem like a cold response to a gut-wrenching experience, but consider this: You already know how to deal with securing an agent or manager. You did it before and you can do it again. With or without new representation, the real question remains one that only you can answer: Will you or will you not rewrite prior to resubmitting your work?

Reject any thought of giving up at this juncture. Even if you are prepared to happily make any changes requested, capitulation to incoming viewpoints is not necessarily the way to go. Consider that Mark Victor Hansen and Jack Canfield gleefully tell of *Chicken Soup for the Soul* being rejected by 140 publishers before finding HCI, where they loyally remained for many years. What do you think it was like to make that long, uphill slog? Would you have been willing to hold out through 140 rejections? Is your belief in your book that strong? For many of your competitors, the answer is no—and they will fall by the wayside here. Their ranks will not include you.

The conclusion is simple: There is wisdom in maintaining a flexible and open-minded stance about the feedback that your work receives—but you must not be too quick to abandon your own ship.

 HOT TIP!

Remember our mantra: *it only takes one*. It only takes one editor at one publishing house to get the ball rolling. Sure, it's a competitive field, but sometimes the force is with you.

PUBLISHER MEETINGS

An editor may ask to meet with a prospective author, or if an editor is hanging on the fence about accepting a project, your agent might suggest a meeting. Such a meeting is very important and can make or break the sale of your book, but at the time that it happens it will be easy to fear that the future of the universe hinges on this meeting. The illusion quickly passes, and you will have sailed through the experience by calmly discussing your writing and your book with clarity and passion. You will drop a few remarks that indicate that you have read up on how the industry functions outside of the writer's experience.

It's a good idea to have your agent along with you if you meet with an editor, even if you have to pay travel expenses. While the bulk of the publishing world still resides in New York City, the Internet has made it possible for agents, editors, and publishers to thrive anywhere that there is Internet access and overnight mail delivery. Your agent might work in the heart of Manhattan, while your prospective publisher might be in Chicago, Dallas, or San Francisco. Personal meetings can be ideal, if they are possible, but there are now a number of effective alternatives to long-distance travel. And with the proliferation of conferencing websites, you may even take your meeting on webcams in cyberspace.

If you and your agent agree that a meeting is a good thing, be sure to dress professionally, arrive on time, and let your agent take the lead— whether you are there in person or you will be a figure on a screen, you are the author. *Be* the author.

THE BEAUTY OF EXCLUSIVE OFFERS

Sometimes an agent gets a book proposal that is so perfect for an editor or a publisher that she really can't believe it. When that happens your agent might offer the publisher an exclusive for a short period of time, say one week. Your proposal then goes to the very top of that editor's reading list and also to the top of the publisher's weekly acquisition meeting. If you are lucky, the publisher will come back with a pre-emptive offer, which is a carefully thought out offer that the publisher hopes is attractive enough that you and your agent will take your book off the market and sell it to them—without pitching it to any other publishers.

Is that a good thing? Usually, in that a contract is completed immediately and most pre-emptive offers are positioned to remove the book from the market at a premium price. The potential loss arises from the lack of any chance for competitive bidding. Of course you and your literary representative will consider more than just the monetary aspects of a publisher's offer. If an editor and publisher are that excited about you and your book, rest assured that you will be a top priority at the house throughout the entire publishing process. There is real value in that.

THE AUCTION BLOCK

Another way that your agent can sell your book is to put it up for auction. This can happen in two ways: when your agent receives multiple offers for your book, igniting a bidding war, or when an agent senses that a book will be a hot commodity and thus spends days setting up a declared auction. This involves notifying publishers of the details of the project and its impending auction, and then setting up the auction parameters, perhaps presenting a minimum bid, then declaring deadlines for publishers' responses. The auction itself can last several days or even weeks if your agent has to conduct multiple rounds of bidding in order to secure the best offer.

There are quite a few things to consider in deciding which auction offer to accept. The following form outlines the information we usually require in our auctions. Other agents may request more information or less, but if an editor fills out this form completely and returns it to us before the auction deadline, we'll have an excellent idea of the scope of the proposed deal.

AUCTION OFFER FORM

Title of Book: _____

Author: _____

Agent Contact Information: _____

Editor: _____

Publisher: _____

Opening Minimum Bid: $ _____

Please circle the rights that you are bidding for:
NORTH AMERICA   WORLD ENGLISH   OR   WORLD RIGHTS

Initial Print Run Estimate: _____

Hardcover/Trade/Mass Market: _____

Anticipated List Price: $ _____

Anticipated Publication Date: _____

Subsidiary Rights Splits: _____

Royalty Scale: _____

Additional Considerations: _____

Payout Schedule: _____

Publicity and Marketing Support: _____

Escalators/Bestseller Bonuses, etc.: _____

Other Comments: _____

_____

Auctions happen rarely and only when there is significant interest from several houses. You should be jumping up and down with joy if this happens to you. Unfortunately, not every author understands the significance of auctions. We had one celebrity client who refused an offer from a major publisher because she said that she had "shoes that cost more than that."

Remember: The best deal for you is also the best deal for your agent, and agents work hard to make the most of your opportunities.

HOT TIP!

Be realistic in your expectations and look at the whole deal, not just the financial part.

AN OFFER ON YOUR WORK

By now, you have a good sense of how well your literary representative handles business. You should be able to trust her judgment in bringing you back the best possible offer. There are genuine advantages to allowing your agent to take care of the contract's fine points, such as royalty rates, subsidiary rights, foreign translations, performance rights, and more.

Unless your agent or manager just got off the bus, she is already familiar with the industry's going rates and percentages, as well as the low and high end of each scale. Perhaps your agent has done previous business with your potential publisher and knows how far to push the negotiations *without* jeopardizing the offer. This is why literary representatives earn 15 percent, and this analysis and advice is part of the way they earn it. It is also how the agent continues to earn it from her share of your royalties. The best deal for an agent is to get the best deal for you. This is very unlike the situation you have with an advisor, such as an attorney, who is in for an hourly fee.

Once your literary representative has secured an offer and negotiated the best contract possible for you, you should get a deal memo, a brief listing of the deal's major points. If it is agreeable to you, the next step is to review the publisher's contract before signing it (see chapter 13). If you use an outside advisor or attorney, find one that has intellectual property and literary contract experience. General contract experience is not enough for an advisor to give a safe and reliable analysis of your situation.

Deal Killer Alert

Never allow your attorney to get between your agent and the publisher! The purpose of outside counsel is to help you be certain that you understand every clause of the contract, and to alleviate concerns you may have over whether your agent is bringing you the best deal possible. You did not hire counsel to cause the destruction of your opportunity.

The toughest part of the contract, however, is one that nobody can negotiate away for you. It is the part that states that if you blow your deadlines, turn in inferior work, or fail to meet your contracted minimum word count, the publisher retains the right to drop you. Furthermore, if they are offended by the quality of your efforts, they can and will utilize their right to cancel your contract and require you to return all the advance money.

Of course, that is never going to happen to you. You have considered your position—and theirs. And you would rather gargle razor blades than miss a deadline.

HOT TIP!

Publication of your book is never guaranteed until you meet the delivery and acceptance clause of your contract. Your manuscript must be formally accepted before you are home free. In other words, don't turn in anything but your best work.

SO, THEN ... WHO ARE YOU TO WRITE THIS BOOK?

From the moment you signed your publication contract, you agreed to provide a specific written product on a specific date, one that you created out of nothing but the force of your imagination and your own persistent labor. Every writer claims to be able to do that in the beginning, but some will fall by the wayside before seeing it through. The reliability that you display will set you apart from them, and you will achieve that reliability by focusing on each task at the time it presents itself—and by giving it your concentrated effort until it is done. Then you move to the next task and do the same thing with that one.

These individual steps keep you from becoming overwhelmed by the size of the journey.

CHAPTER 13

HIGH FIVES:
THE BOOK CONTRACT

Oh yes, contracts can be boring. But it is very important that as a prospective author you familiarize yourself with every contract that you sign. One reason you must do this is so you can actually collect what you have earned instead of watching other people rationalize taking it from you. As in any business, it is never a good idea to sign any representation contract or book-publishing contract that you do not understand. To fully comprehend that contract, you must know the respective roles that you, your agent, and your publisher will each play in the life of your book.

While agents can guide authors through a contract, most agents are not lawyers. You should trust your agent to represent you in a legal situation to the best of his or her ability, but an agent's strength is in selling books and negotiating deals, not in the legalities of contract wording.

If the contract is not so straightforward that you can grasp its meaning right away, then by all means, hire an attorney to review it. But keep in mind that while agents are not lawyers, neither are lawyers agents. Many lawyers do not understand how the book industry works, or what is standard in the business. If you do bring a lawyer in, make sure it is only for contract review, and not to step in the middle of the deal and muck it up.

Because the ultimate decision is yours and you must understand a contract before you sign it, we will go over the basic points of a contract here. We are not lawyers, but we do deal with literary contracts on a daily basis, so we can give you a general overview along with some specific observations.

Many areas of a literary contract are standard and require no negotiation. But you should closely read every word anyway, because one misplaced word or one single typo by an office assistant can change the entire meaning of the clause or the contract. Even the most standardized of contracts can have a few sticky areas, though. The following information will prepare you for the day when your agent begins negotiating a contract for your book.

THE AGREEMENT

The "Agreement" is traditionally the first section of your contract. Its wording is standard and it simply lays out the date of the contract and the parties involved, usually the author and the publisher.

After the Agreement there will be a number of paragraphs under a section the begins with "Whereas." For example, this section might read something to the effect of:

> WHEREAS the Author is compiling, has written, compiled, or edited a literary work at present titled "My Nonfiction Book" consisting of approximately 85,000 words and 10 illustrations (hereinafter called "the Work").

The paragraphs, or clauses, that follow detail a number of things, including the due date of the manuscript and how it is to be delivered (disc, hard copy, e-mail, etc.). This section can also specify when the publisher will publish your work. Unless a publication date has already been set, which is unlikely at this stage, this date is often vague. The contract might say "within eighteen months of delivery of an acceptable manuscript." There are usually some "out" options here as well, giving the publisher the right not to publish in situations of *force majeur*, when acts of nature or man-made disasters make the publication of your book difficult or impossible.

The Importance of Permissions

The publisher will stipulate in the contract that it is understood that you have written permission to use any copyrighted material in your book, such as photographs, maps, charts, and other artwork. The keeps the burden of rights and permissions squarely upon the author's shoulders (meaning you).

We are referring to *express written permission*, and never to a verbal agreement or a handshake. What is needed is a simple one-page signed and witnessed letter of agreement that specifically, or "expressly," gives you permission to use the artwork or other copyrighted material.

If you do not have this permission, the contract usually states that the publisher will secure this permission for you, but will charge you whatever it costs to do this. They may deduct it from future royalties, or they may require you to pay this to them in cash. It's always best if you can take care of this yourself, as it is usually more cost-effective for you. Plus, delivering a manuscript that doesn't need a lot of work from the publisher will please your editor greatly.

Delivering Artwork and Your Manuscript

The contract will state the preferred method for delivering the artwork and stipulate that even though you are sending the material to the publisher, they are not responsible for it in case of fire, flood, or other unexpected situations. With that in mind, it is a good idea to make copies of everything you send to the publisher, just in case. Never send original versions of supporting materials unless they are specifically required.

The publisher will see to it that this section of your contract covers the possibility of your failure to deliver the manuscript by the due date.

There will sometimes be a grace period of sixty or ninety days after the due date. After that designated point, the publisher does not have to publish the book and you will be required to repay any advances. If this happens, you also have to repay any amount that went to your literary agent, because by this time agents have done the job for which they are paid. Final responsibility remains with you.

There will be another "out" clause here, too, that says if the work you turn in to the publisher is not acceptable to them, either in content or in form, they don't have to publish it. This essentially means that if you turn in work that is very different from your proposal, or if it is very sloppy and requires a lot of developmental editing work on their part, your book will not be published. In this case you are often allowed to submit your work to a second publisher; but if a second publisher buys your manuscript, the money will normally go to the first publisher until their investment in the manuscript (and in you) is fully repaid.

Proofing Your Work

The publisher will also want to be sure that you agree to read and correct any proofs that they send you in a timely manner (usually ten to fourteen days). If you request changes after that point, they will charge you a fee.

HOT TIP!

Proofing requires a rested and focused mind, so stay in touch with your editor regarding the timing of the proofs before they arrive. That way you can clear your calendar so that you are ready to go when the proofs arrive. (Multi-tasking is a killer, here.)

The Originality Clause

Another clause in the contract will ensure that the work you turn in to the publisher is original, and that you are the sole owner of the work. Plagiarism of any kind is never acceptable.

Truth in Content

Most publishers ask that the work not contain anything obscene or defamatory and that you certify that everything you have written is true. There will probably be some legalese at this point in the contract about indemnifying the publisher (keeping them from harm) in the off chance you or the publisher is sued over something you have written. If the publisher incurs legal fees to defend you or your book, don't be surprised if you later receive a bill from either the publisher or their attorney.

In the event you have written anything that the publisher questions, your contract will most likely require you to edit or revise those areas to the publisher's specifications. By the way, if you have sold world rights to your publisher, everything you agree to here extends to any other publishers who may publish your book in foreign countries, or in audio, e-book, or other formats, even if their contracts do not specifically state it. This contract that you are signing now will become the "original contract." It will take precedence over all others, meaning that every other contract that branches from it is considered fruit of the tree.

Never Compete Against Yourself

As the publisher is buying the work for a certain geographical area, such as the "United States," or "North America," or "The World," they want to make sure that you do not sell another work similar to this one to another publisher, as any work that is too close to the one they pay for may negatively affect the sales of this work. If you should find yourself in that position, there really is no point in taking the risk. The easier and better way to spend your time and efforts is in promoting this book.

The Right to Index

Sometimes publishers will decide that adding an index to your book is helpful for readers. If they do, you will be the one incurring the cost of having the indexing done. Even if you offer to do it yourself, the publisher will probably prefer to use one of their experienced and trusted indexers, because they know that readers hate to look up something in an index and then find the page number is incorrectly listed. The work of creating an accurate index is exacting in the extreme and perilous in its level of detail. Professional indexers know exactly what words and terms to put into the index, how to list them, and what subject matter to leave out. Experience gives them the ability to do the job with reasonable speed.

Learn to Pick Your Battles

Literary agent Kimberley Cameron, president of Reece Halsey Literary Agency, said that when authors and publishers disagree over the terms of a contract (such as the question of who is doing the index), she asks the author to trust her judgment. Like most agents, she negotiates a contract as a deal maker whose primary responsibility is to facilitate a good sale. Nobody profits from lost opportunities.

"Usually the author knows that I'm doing everything I can to make the best deal in his/her best interests," says Cameron. "I discuss the contract terms with them as much as possible, but I've had more deals fall apart because the author didn't want to work with the changes that the publisher requested."

Cameron's advice is good to keep in mind when it comes to the actual production of your book. You probably have a good idea of how you think your book should look, but your publishing contract gives your publisher complete control of this area. They might give you some input on the cover, but often will not. This is an area in which you need to let go and trust your agent and your publisher (another reason why the original research you did in selecting your representative remains so important to you throughout the process—it is the reason that you know your trust is well founded). The final cover of your book is determined by a number of people, including your editor and publisher; the publisher's key public relations, sales, and marketing people; and the publisher's distributor, among others. These people analyze the image or images, typefaces, styles, and colors on the covers of books that sell exceedingly well. They take into consideration your subject, your direct competition, and the predicted tastes of your target market.

As a case in point, Martin Literary Management represented the co-authors of *Front of the Class*. At first they were not wild about the design of the cover of their book and they voiced their concern. Their publisher asked them to trust in the process and they agreed. The hardcover book not only sold very well, it went to trade paperback and was then purchased as a Hallmark Hall of Fame television movie.

So when the publisher dictates the number of pages, the selling price, and whether your book will be a hardcover or paperback (and when they show you a cover that is completely different from what you think the cover should look like), do your best to smile and remember all the hapless writers out there who would love to be in your shoes.

"Once the book is sold, it becomes a collaborative process with many people involved," says Jamie Brenner, agent at Artists and Artisans, Inc. "Sometimes the way a publisher does something doesn't totally match the author's vision. An author and agent can win some fights in this arena, but others we cannot, and will not, win. New authors need to learn to pick their battles, and to trust their agent to help them in this process."

Remaindering

If your publisher decides to "remainder" your book, they usually will give you first refusal rights for purchasing the "remaining" stock. This price is usually a low percentage of the original list price. Remaindering happens in several scenarios. Usually it is at the end of the book's sales cycle and the publisher either has a lot of books remaining in stock, or a lot of returns coming in from bookstores. The other scenario is if the book tanks from the get-go and the publisher decides any further effort on the book is a lost cause.

In dealing with remainders, the publisher can drastically change the price of your book and set it so low that you essentially do not receive any royalties for those sales. But the publisher is the one who put up the money in the first place to edit, design, print, and ship your books to the stores, so they can sell the book for any price they choose.

Royalties: How You Get Paid

During the term of your contract, everyone hopes that your book will sell exceedingly well. The mutual goal that all parties involved in the contract have for your book is that it earns out the advance money and sells enough copies for you to earn lots of royalties. Keep in mind, though, that some books never sell more than a few hundred copies and that many others never break the five thousand sales mark.

HOT TIP!

The strength of your platform ultimately determines the strength of your sales.

Royalties are paid in two ways: *List* is the retail price of the book; *net* is the price that the publisher receives for the book. Publishers usually receive somewhere in the neighborhood of 40 percent of the list price from their buyers. Depending on the buyer, special sales initiatives, and the quantity ordered, this price can range anywhere from around 38 percent up to 50 percent.

In dealing with royalties, publishers also hold a *return reserve,* a percentage of your earned royalties (often around 25 percent) that the publisher holds back in case any of the books they sold to bookstores are returned. Books, videos, DVDs, and music are the only products that are sold on a "fully returnable" basis, and can legally be returned months after the sale. So, if, for example, ten copies of your book are sold to the XYZ Bookstore and eight of those books sat on the shelf for several months, the bookstore can then return them to the publisher, even though the store has already paid for them. It's not an efficient system, and a lot of other people in the book industry think so as well, but that is the way that the system works—at least for now.

The publisher will pay you on the number of actual books sold, less the return reserve. You will eventually get royalties from the return reserve, as long as the number of books returned does not exceed the level of reserve.

But what, exactly, will the publisher pay you? Whether you are on a list or net percentage, standard figures begin in the neighborhood of 8 to 15 percent. There also can be sales bonuses built in to your royalty rate. For example, your contract might state that for the first 5,000 sales of your hardcover book, you might receive 10 percent of the list price, for sales between 5,000 and 10,000 you will receive 12.5 percent, and if your book sells more than 10,000 copies you will receive 15 percent. Some contracts also have a best-seller bonus that could be a flat fee for making *The New York Times*, *USA Today*, or other best-seller list.

Most publishers offer deep discounts to clients who order books in bulk, so there may be a clause in your contract that says for those copies sold in bulk, your royalty rate will be a few percentage points lower than for regular sales.

Royalties for trade paperback sales are traditionally a little lower than for hardcover. Your royalty rate for these books, for example, might begin at 6 percent and escalate from there. The bulk rate discount applies here, too, so your rate for those sales might be in the neighborhood of 5 percent.

You may be thinking that this doesn't sound like much. It isn't. But consider this scenario: A publisher is paid 40 percent of list for your book. For a $20 book, that is $8. Ten percent, or $2, goes to you. That leaves $6. It might cost the publisher $2.50 to print the book, so that leaves them $3.50 to cover editing, typesetting, book design, cover design, public relations, marketing, salaries of their sales staff, office rent, utilities, office supplies, computer equipment and software, insurance, warehouse space and staff, shipping, administrative support salaries, Internet access, phone, and the list goes on and on and on. Granted, your publisher will publish many books in addition to yours, and they (hopefully) will sell many copies of each. But the reality is that there just is not that much wiggle room in the price of a book.

At least not on domestic sales. Domestic sales are typically sales here in the United States, Canada, or, depending on your contract, North America. Outside that area, you may receive as much as 50 percent of the net, or even more.

Subsidiary Rights and Royalties

Simply put, subsidiary rights are rights you might grant to the publisher for additional sales such as book club rights, dramatization rights, electronic rights, audio rights, first serial rights, etc. Depending on the publisher's offer, your agent may include these rights with your initial contract, or he may suggest you hold those rights back and sell them separately. His advice will depend on the amount of the advance, the public relations support, the release date, and a host of other things that the publisher offers. While royalty rates for subsidiary rights can vary widely, the chart below will give you some idea of the possibilities.

Rights	Author	Publisher
Translation rights:	50%	50%
Anthology, book condensation, digest, quotation, microphotographic reproduction, xerographic, strip cartoon or picturization book rights, book club rights and reprint rights (including the use of English text overseas) licensed to other publishers:	50%	50%

Dramatization and film rights:	100%	0%
First serial rights:	90%	10%
Broadcasting and television rights, and rights of reproduction by record, tape, or other mechanical means:	75%	25%
Second serial rights:	50%	50%
Paperback reprint rights:	50%	50%
Commercial or merchandising rights in the Work and/or its title:	90%	10%
Electronic rights, including but not limited to CD-ROM, Internet distribution, or any other means of reproduction of the Work or part thereof in electronic form:	50%	50%

The Timing of Advance Monies

You should know that if your agent is able to negotiate an advance for you, you do not get it all at once. Generally, there are two payment methods. In the first, you receive half the money within thirty days or so of signing the contract. The money will be paid to your agent; your agent will deduct his commission and then send a check to you. You will get the second half of your advance upon delivery of an acceptable manuscript. In the publishing world, an "acceptable manuscript" can be somewhat subjective. Some publishers "accept" a manuscript after the first round of editing, some not until it is in the typesetting phase.

The second method of payment consists of one-third of the advance around the time of the contract being signed, one-third on receipt of an acceptable manuscript, and one-third within thirty days after publication. In any case, the publisher will always pay your money to your agent. Some agents will deduct their full 15 percent commission from the first payment rather than spread their commission over the entire payment schedule. After all, the bulk of their work is done.

Remember that advance money is not a gift. It is an advance against future sales, so your royalties will not kick in until your book has sold enough copies to "earn out" the advance. Also, the publisher will not pay any royalties on free copies of your book that are given to you (usually only a handful), or copies that are given free to media, reviewers, and others who will promote your book in some way. Your royalties are based on actual sales, so if the book is not actually sold, you will not be paid.

Updating Your Work

Depending on the subject matter of your nonfiction book, the publisher may require you to update your work periodically. Depending on your contract, you may or may not be paid for this update. If, for some reason, you are unable to revise the book when the publisher asks, the publisher may hire another person to do the work for you—and deduct their fee from your royalties.

Financial Accounting

As stated, royalties are only paid after your book earns out its advance. When royalties are earned, they are usually paid two times a year. Your contract will state when the payment periods are and when your agent can expect to receive a check. Along with the royalty check your agent will receive a statement detailing the number of sales and returns. Many times these statements are difficult to fathom, but it is important that you, as the author, look it over carefully so you can understand exactly how your book is selling. If your publisher also holds subsidiary rights, these will also be detailed in your statement.

HOT TIP!

Sometimes, depending on the specifics of the publisher's offer, it's better to agree to a lower advance and a higher percentage of royalties.

Your contract will also have a clause that if your royalties are less than a certain sum (often as little as twenty-five dollars) the publisher can hold this sum over to the next payment period. If for some reason the returns on your book exceed the returns reserve, and if you have already been paid on those copies, then that amount will be deducted from your next royalty payment.

Let's look at an example. Let's say your book has already earned out its advance and your publisher sold 1,000 books to XYZ Bookstore. If you had a 25 percent return reserve, at the next payment period the publisher would pay you on 750 books, and hold back payment on the remaining 250 books. But in this case XYZ Bookstore only sold 650 books and returned 350 books to your publisher. There is a difference of 100 books for which you have already been paid, so royalties for those books will be deducted from your next check.

Author Copies

No, sadly, you don't get an unlimited amount of free books from your publisher. The industry standard is ten, however sometimes exceptions can be made. You will probably want a dozen copies of your book. After all, you will be selling your books at speaking engagements and at book signings you do outside of traditional bookstores. To address this issue your contract will list a price for which you can buy your books directly from the publisher. This price varies, but will be somewhere in the neighborhood of a 50 percent discount off the list price of the book. You will also have to pay to have the books shipped to you or directly to your event.

Copyright

Another clause in your book contract addresses the copyright. Usually the publisher will bear the cost of securing the copyright in your name here in the United States, and also in other countries if your publisher holds foreign rights. It never hurts, however, to check to be sure the copyright was done correctly. Even with the best of intentions, someone at your publishing company could make a typo or just forget to do it. To check online to see if your copyright has been registered properly, visit www.copyright.gov/records.

When Your Book Goes Out of Print

If your book should go out of print (meaning it is not available for sale in any form or edition, including reprints and there is not an existing contract with the publisher for a new edition), your contract should state that your Agreement with your publisher terminates after a certain period of time. This time period is often six months, but can vary. If this happens, all rights you granted to your publisher revert back to you.

Sometimes this can be a good thing, especially if you feel the publisher produced a poor quality book or didn't market it properly. Many authors take books whose rights have reverted back to them, update the text, typesetting, and cover, and put it out as a self-published book. With the variety of print-on-demand and e-book options, this path can lend new life to your book, especially if you do well with back-of-the-room sales at speaking events.

The publisher can also terminate your Agreement after a specific period of time stated in the contract if they determine your book is not selling well enough for them to continue publishing it. The publisher will give you whatever advance notice is listed in the contract (often three to six months) that lets you know they are discontinuing your book.

In either case, you as the author should have the right to purchase the publisher's remaining copies, and original artwork for the book cover, typeset files, etc. If you do not choose to purchase these items, your contract will most likely state that the publisher will destroy them after a given period of time.

The purchase option also holds true if your publisher should file for bankruptcy, except that instead of an agreed-upon price between you and your publisher, your purchase price will be the "fair market value" of the items as determined by the bankruptcy court. If you choose not to buy the remaining copies of your book, your contract may state that your bankrupt publisher can legally sell your books for whatever price they can get, and that they do not have to pay you royalties on these sales.

The Option Clause

Some literary contracts state that the publisher has the first option of publishing your next book-length work on terms to be mutually agreed upon at a later date. While it is flattering to know that the publisher is optimistic enough to think there might be a second book, this sometimes can backfire on an author, especially if the publisher turns out to be passive about marketing and promoting your existing book. The terms of any future option must be skillfully negotiated to protect the author's interests.

Notice

Most modern contracts include wording about how to notify the other party of important information, and literary contracts are no exception. Your contract might state that any notice should be "sent by registered or certified mail, return receipt requested, addressed to the other party at the address given on his portion of the contract." The contract will also probably say that either party can designate a different address by the method listed above.

Breach of Contract

The breach clause is another standard contract clause and basically means that if either party to the contract is in violation (or breach) of any section of the contract, the breach does not affect any of the other clauses in the contract. So, if your publisher is a week late with a royalty check, it does not mean the entire contract is null and void.

Waivers and Modifications

There are times when a contract does need to be modified. To address this possibility, your contract should have a provision for that event. Something to the effect of "no waiver or modification shall be valid or binding unless it is in writing and signed by both parties" works just fine.

A Binding Agreement

This clause should state that in the unfortunate event of your death, your contract will be binding upon and benefit your heirs. It should also say that your executors, administrators, and assigns will be recognized by the publisher, and confirm that you can assign your royalties to anyone you choose as long as you give the publisher official notification. For example, some authors may assign their royalties on a particular book to a favorite charity, or a family trust. Depending on the wording of the contract, the publisher may or may not be required to agree to your assignation.

Some literary contracts have reciprocal wording, meaning that the author also has to recognize the successors and assigns of the publisher. If your publisher is sold, or "assigns" themselves to another publishing company, your contract might state that you have to agree. Not all contracts state this; however, publishing companies are bought and sold every day, so it is good for you to know what your particular contract calls for.

Somewhere in here the contract should have some wording that addresses the fact that your contract will not be binding upon either the publisher or you unless it is properly witnessed and signed.

Governance

Whatever state the home office of your publisher is located in is probably the state that governs your contract. This state will be listed in your contract.

Your One and Only

Your publisher will want to be clear that this contract, this particular Agreement that you are signing, is the only agreement between the two of you regarding this specific work. This section of your contract will also say that it contains the whole understanding of both parties, meaning that if something is assumed and is not specifically listed in the contract, the assumption has no legal standing. To be certain everyone understands this, your contract will specifically state that this contract contains the whole understanding of the parties, and that it supercedes all previous oral or written contracts.

Formats

Your contract will also detail the specific rights you, your agent, and your publisher have agreed upon. For example, it might read something to the effect of: "The Work, as used throughout the above agreement, shall include printed books, e-books, computer disks, CD-ROMs, computer databases, network servers, and all other means of distribution, electronic or otherwise, whether now known or hereinafter discovered." Or, your contract could simply read, "The Work shall include printed books only."

Excerpt Usage

From time to time your publisher may want to use excerpts of your work in other publications. Your contract will detail the number of pages that can be used and what the payment to you would be. The money here is typically not significant.

The real advantage in excerpts is the exposure it will bring to you and your book as each excerpt introduces your work to an audience that may not have heard of you or your book.

Signatures

Finally, at the end of the contract, there will be places for you, your publisher, and any witnesses to sign. Unless you are in New York and are signing the contracts at the publisher's office, this can be a process of several weeks via hard-copy correspondence.

First the contracts are sent to your agent, who will look over them thoroughly. Remember that a single typo can change the entire meaning of a clause, so your agent will be quite diligent here. After your agent has vetted the contracts, they will be sent to you. Be sure that you also look over the contracts thoroughly and also that you understand what you are signing. Usually there are three or four copies.

The publisher will then request that you send your signed copies to them, where they will also sign. They will keep one or two copies and send the others to your agent. The agency will keep one copy for their files, then send the last copy to you.

When you receive the fully executed copy of your contract, you are entitled to celebrate with a nice meal or an evening out. You deserve this!

Besides, the real work has just begun.

CHAPTER 14

THE SELF-PUBLISHING
OPTION

All right, time out to speak out about the elephant in the room: the question of self-publishing. For many years the terms "self-publishing" and "vanity press" were the book industry's equivalent of slumming. That is because once an author exhausted all possibilities of attracting a traditional publisher, he or she often turned to self-publishing, either using the services of a company paid to produce the book, or setting up a small publishing venture.

Typically, these books were poorly written, poorly edited, and had cover designs that weren't competitive compared to books on the shelves of bookstores. Bookstores have never carried these self-published tomes because they have not gone through the editorial phase under expert supervision. Also, since they are not published by a traditional publisher, they are not carried by any of the regular wholesalers or distributors that supply the bookstores. It has always been too much trouble to buy one title from a small one-or-two-book publisher, when a store buyer could order hundreds of titles through a major distributor. And it was only by ordering through a distributor or wholesaler that the store buyer was guaranteed that the book would be up to industry standards in writing, editing, design, and manufacturing.

Today it is a somewhat different story. Bookstores are still reluctant to carry self-published books due to the same writing, editing, and ordering difficulties. But improvements in printing and print-on-demand technology, the ease of use with current software for editing and page layouts, and the increase in the number of viable self-publishing businesses that walk new authors through the process, all combine to make self-publishing viable for some authors. The question is: Are you one of them?

We have been spending a lot of time talking about the things that you must do to attract an agent and editor so you can secure a larger traditional publisher. And yes, we can hear you thinking, "If self-publishing is now a legitimate road for authors to travel, why don't I just do that?"

That's a great question and for some of you it might well be the best route. But by the end of the chapter many others of you will decide that traditional publishing has more to offer. Before you start designing your book cover, let's first take a closer look to see whether or not self-publishing is for you.

ENCOURAGING STATS

In 2008, the industry tracker company, Bowker, reported that nearly 480,000 different book titles were published in the United States. That's a lot of books! The good news is that figure shows an increase of more than 100,000 books, as compared to 2007. Even more importantly, Bowker credited a significant part of the increase in book sales to a rise in the number of self-published and print-on-demand books.

On first glance, this looks exciting, especially as it arrives on the heels of declining sales in traditional publishing and a struggling national economy. The other encouraging news is that literacy rates are also up for the first time in several decades. "Reading on the Rise: A

New Chapter in American Literacy," a National Endowment for the Arts report based on data from "The Survey of Public Participation in the Arts," which was conducted by the United States Census Bureau in 2008, found that for the first time since 1982, the number of adults eighteen and older who said they had read at least one novel, short story, poem, or play in the previous twelve months had risen, especially among readers in the eighteen to twenty-four age bracket.

HOT TIP!

Good news! More book titles are being published, and more people are reading them.

SELF-PUBLISHING VS. TRADITIONAL PUBLISHING

There are some real perks to self-publishing, but with those perks come some additional responsibilities and financial investment. Is it worth it? Only you know, as the situation for every book and every author is different. Some authors use traditional publishing for most of their books, but self-publish a title that is close to their heart, or has such a small niche market that they know it will not sell more than a few thousand copies.

The Control Factor

You do have a lot more control over your book if you self-publish than you do if you go with a traditional publisher. You will have final say over the editing, layout, and cover design, whereas if you sell your book to a regular publisher, they will usually dictate the final result in these areas. While it is nice to have that control and vision, most publishers do know what they are doing, so their suggestions and advice can be invaluable to you in creating a finished book that is attractive to readers in both look and content.

The Title Game

A book's title is a typical bone of contention. Many times an author has come to us with the "perfect title" only to have it shot down by their publisher. The publisher might not like the title because there are too many other similar titles. Unfortunately, you cannot copyright a title, so often two (or three or more) different books have the same title. This can be a problem when readers and store buyers are looking for *your* book. Or, your publisher's sales and marketing team might shoot your title down because they don't think it's catchy, or it's too long, or doesn't accurately describe your book. This is a battle you can't win if you are with a traditional publisher, so move past it as quickly as you can.

Here are a few great titles that might give you some ideas for your own:

- *You'll Never Nanny in This Town Again* (a memoir of a young woman who nannies for Hollywood's most powerful film agent)

- *Horse Country* (top stars of country music discuss their love of horses)

- *River of No Return* (the story of Tennessee Ernie Ford and his lovely wife Betty, and her eventual suicide, with the title taken from Ford's hit song)

- *Tabloid Prodigy* (the story of a young woman's descent into tabloid journalism)

- *Taking Aim at the President* (the story of Sara Jane Moore, who shot at President Gerald Ford and was the only woman in American history to shoot at a president)

- *Wicked Intentions* (a true crime story of a female serial killer)

- *The Road Out of Hell: The True Story of Sanford Clark and the Wineville Murders*

Financial Investment and Reward

If you decide to self-publish, the reality is that you will have to put some money up. Instead of the publisher paying you an advance, you are paying an editor, book designer, and printer (or a service that provides all of that). That means the initial outlay of cash can run well into the thousands of dollars.

The other option is to go with a company that fronts all of that for you, but then charges you a lot when you want to buy copies of your books. If you are reselling your book at your speaking events, this is probably not the best option for you, because there will be very little profit margin in your resale price.

While the initial outlay can be steep, the rewards of self-publishing can sometimes be greater than with a traditional publisher. If you handle the printing, you have an immediate stock of books at cost that you can sell for full price on your website or at your speaking gigs.

You can also set up online accounts with Amazon.com and www.bn.com (Barnes & Noble's online site). Here you will receive 40 to 55 percent of your book's retail price, which is the industry standard. Some of the variation is due to how quickly you choose to be paid. The longer the payout from the time of sale, the higher the percentage you are paid.

HOT TIP!

Both Amazon.com and www.bn.com welcome books from small and self-publishers.

While 40 to 55 percent is a far cry from full price, it is certainly greater than the 10 percent you might get from a traditional publisher, after your book has earned out its advance.

While all of that sounds pretty good, if you think your book has a mainstream audience, if you think your book will sell more than a few thousand copies, be aware that the average number of copies of a self-published book that are sold is less than two hundred. Some of that has to do with the fact that most self-publishers do not have a marketing budget, do not advertise to the book trades, or let store and library buyers know their book is available. But even if they did, remember that these buyers are still leery of self-published books due to the lack of oversight in producing the final product.

So, if you have a *lot* of speaking engagements with large audiences and know you can sell a ton of books there, or if you want to document your life story for your family, friends, and future generations, then self-publishing might be the route for you.

Financial and real estate guru Donald Trump, who published several best-selling books with some of the world's largest publishers, eventually decided to self-publish because he speaks regularly in huge arenas to sold-out crowds. As a result, he moves thousands of books. He also has the resources to produce a quality product, so it makes financial sense for him to self-publish.

THE TWO FORMS OF SELF-PUBLISHING

There are two basic forms of self-publishing. The first involves setting up a traditional publishing company, getting ISBN numbers and bar codes, and getting all the editing, cover design, book layout, printing, and shipping done yourself. The second involves getting a self-publishing service to do all but the writing for you. There are pros and cons for each method.

If you are a business professional and expect to do more than one book over the next few years, you might want to find your own sources for editing, design, bar codes, and printing. If you do, you will have more control over the finished product because you are paying for each element individually, not buying a package of services. We won't lie to you and tell you this will be an easy process. It won't. In fact it will be full of tension and uncertainty, but you will have an inordinate amount of pride when you hold your new book in your arms for the first time. Producing a book yourself is, in fact, much like birthing a baby—complete with problems and frustrations wrapped into a little bundle of joy.

Using a Self-Publishing Service

As traditional publishers slash their rosters and rely on hopes of a bestseller, self-publishing service companies are dramatically adding to their list of titles. The reason? Because the author pays for the production of the book, companies such as these can make money on a book that sells just a handful of copies.

These companies should take away the hair-pulling frustration that can come with the DIY method. We say "should" because there are a number of services out there, and some are more reputable than others.

HOT TIP!

If you decide to use a self-publishing service, do your homework online to see what other people have to say about the company.

If this is the best method for you, know that you will pay a little more per book than if you do it yourself. You also may be limited in your size of book, page count, cover design, and other elements of your book production. But those limitations shouldn't hinder you too much as long as you know ahead of time that they exist. A few well-placed questions to your account representative should give you the information you need:

- When is payment due?

- Do you provide editing services?

- Can I choose my typeface and cover?

- Do you provide an ISBN or do I need to get one?

- Can you send me a sample book so I can assess the quality?

- Do I have the opportunity to proof my books?

- How much does it cost per copy for me to order my book?

- Do I get a discount for large orders?

- Is my book printed on demand or with a traditional press?

- How much do I pay to have my books shipped to me?

- Do you replace defective books?

- Do you place my book on Amazon.com and other online sites?

- Do you register my book with the Library of Congress and Books in Print?

The most important question of all: Do I retain the copyright? This is key. Never use a service that strips your copyright from you. Other than this last question, there are no right or wrong answers. All points are open to negotiation and subject to the specifics of your book and your platform.

The Best and Worst of Print-on-Demand

Print-on-demand (POD) is the technology that allows some companies to print copies of your book when orders are placed, rather than you having to print huge quantities in advance and crossing your fingers in hopes that someone will buy them. But, as with other elements of self-publishing, there are pros and cons.

If you choose self-publishing, you will also have to choose between a traditional printer or print-on-demand. This holds true whether you are going it alone or using a service. Some of the services you find will still use a traditional press (or give you the option), but most use print-on-demand. Even though you are paying them for the privilege of

---

publishing, print-on-demand is a way for these companies to control both costs and inventory.

While print-on-demand books used to be very poorly produced, in the past decade technology has improved to the point that only an expert can tell if a book came off a traditional press or was produced by print-on-demand. The bad part about this is those experts tend to be store and library book buyers, most of whom still shudder at the thought of stocking a print-on-demand title. This is due to the seemingly never-ending issues regarding the quality of the writing, editing, and cover design.

The best thing about print-on-demand, though, is it takes the guesswork out of your print runs and allows you maximum control over your inventory. In traditional printing, you might choose to print three thousand copies of your book. Then you either have stacks and stacks (and stacks) of books in your basement, or you are paying a small-press warehouser, wholesaler, or distributor a monthly fee to store them for you.

Time is also a factor. It can take five to seven weeks to complete a traditional print run, versus five to seven days for print-on-demand. Yes, the cost per book is higher, sometimes significantly so, but in some cases the cost is negligible if compared with not having any books for a big event, or figuring the long-term cost of warehousing.

The last thing to consider when pondering the self-publishing question is: If you self-publish, and if your book only sells a few hundred copies, then traditional publishers will look at you as an author whose books do not sell. Fair or not, this is Reality rearing its ugly head.

 HOT TIP!

If your ultimate goal is to be an A-list author, self-publishing can be a noose around your neck.

SELF-PUBLISHING AS A MEANS TO AN END

Many new authors think that self-publishing their book is a good way to attract a large publisher, but that is rarely the case. Yes, there have been significant successes with some self-publishers who have gone on to achieve huge advances (and even bigger sales) from a traditional publisher, but those cases are few and far between. *What Color Is Your Parachute?*, *The Celestine Prophecy*, and the *Rich Dad, Poor Dad* series are great examples. But the authors of these books worked their behinds off. They sold books out of the trunks of their cars, in parking lots, and at school and church events, and it took them years to achieve the success they have today.

Plus, the authors all had strong platforms. It's not enough just to be in print anymore. Self-publishing and print-on-demand have ensured that anyone can be in print—and self-publishing doesn't change the fact that you have to have national visibility to make sales.

Remember that the average self-published book sells fewer than two hundred copies over the lifetime of the book. If you plan to use your self-published book as a launching pad to a traditional publisher, you must ask yourself if you have what it takes to be a relentless advocate for your book. Will you actually take time to sell books at several events every week? Can you do your own PR? Just as industry book buyers hesitate to stock a self-published book, for the same reasons book publicists are reluctant to take a book like this on.

Can it happen? Yes, it can, and we're going to tell you about two of our formerly self-published clients.

HOT TIP!

A self-published book that goes on to earn a major publishing contract is the rare exception to the rule.

Case Study 1: *You'll Never Nanny in This Town Again*

You might remember our client, Suzanne Hansen, from her excellent query letter in chapter 9. Suzanne is the author of the previously self-published book, *You'll Never Nanny in This Town Again*, and sold five thousand books out of the back of her car. As a former nanny to some of Hollywood's most powerful moguls, she also created a wonderful website and then hired a service to send individual queries to editors of major publishing firms. Her impressive sales, combined with witty writing, her website, and the celebrity insider nature of the book caused more than forty editors to respond. If you haven't figured it out by now, forty is an absolutely amazing number.

As we mentioned, the book sold to Crown Publishing Group/Random House for a six-figure advance. It also landed on *The New York Times* and the *Los Angeles Times* best-seller lists. It has been optioned multiple times for film and television, but as of this writing has not yet been produced.

Suzanne took part of her advance and hired a top PR firm. They got her a number of national television appearances (and she was even paid for some of them). Now she is positioned as an expert in the world of celebrity nannies.

Crown asked that Suzanne stop selling her self-published book, of course, and brought in a ghostwriter to rewrite the manuscript and add new material. The book is now in both hardcover and trade paperback and has earned out its advance. This author is in the royalty phase of earnings and can look forward to a nice check several times a year.

But remember, this only happened because of the great website, the impressive number of sales in a short period of time, the interesting subject matter, the targeted public relations campaign, and the engaging nature of the author. All combined to make this book very salable.

Case Study 2: *Notes Left Behind*

Like children, every book evolves a little differently. The self-published book *Notes Left Behind* began as a journal written by Keith and Brooke Desserich. Their older daughter, Elena, five years old, had been diagnosed with pediatric brain cancer and they wanted to keep a memory of this journey for their younger daughter, Gracie, who was then three.

As family and friends across the country wanted updates, Keith and Brooke turned their journal into an online blog. Word spread and the Desserichs began receiving hundreds of letters and e-mails of support from strangers across the globe.

By the end of the journey, when Elena passed, Keith and Brooke had written more than seven hundred pages. Because of the incredible support they had received, the Desserichs decided to self-publish a book that they could pass down to Gracie. They also became fully enmeshed in and passionate about finding a cure for the disease that took Elena, so they started a foundation, The Cure Starts Now (www.thecurestartsnow.org).

What they learned was that the most common kinds of cancer are colon and breast cancer, but the cure for all cancers will most likely be found when they find the cure for pediatric brain cancer, which at this time is 100 percent fatal. They believe, as does an entire community of doctors, that the bulk of cancer research, and the funding for it, is being spent in the wrong places.

But what is most compelling is that after Elena passed away, her family began to find little love notes from her tucked away between books and other out-of-the-way places in their home. Elena knew her time with her family was ending and she left them hundreds of reminders of how much she loved them.

The Desserichs edited their manuscript down to 286 pages and went to Pen & Publish, a self-publishing service in Bloomington, Indiana, who did a great job with the book. Due to the support of the people who read their blog, *Notes Left Behind* began to sell very well on their website, Amazon.com and www.bn.com. A Barnes & Noble rep noticed the steady sales and ordered 3,500 copies for their stores.

If that wasn't enough, producers at *Good Morning America* heard about Elena's story, the book, and the foundation, and did a segment. As a result of the airing, the book went into a second printing and dropped into the top one hundred in sales on www.bn.com.

As you can imagine, all of this attention was beginning to become a little overwhelming, so they sought the advice of book publicist Justin Loeber at Mouth Public Relations. About this same time, Sterling Publishing, the book publishing division of Barnes & Noble, made the Desserichs an offer for the book, which now had eight thousand copies in print. Realizing they needed an agent, they asked their publicist for a referral and he suggested Martin Literary Management.

In the end, Keith asked us to write a letter telling him why we wanted to represent the book. Based on the letter, he signed with us. We took the book to auction and it sold to Wm. Morrow, an imprint of HarperCollins. Here's a short version of the letter I wrote him:

Dear Keith:

I understand the difficulty of your choice regarding the representation of your book and ancillary opportunities. However, I shouldn't have to convince you I'm the right advocate, your heart should tell you that.

I studied your website, found your story moving and compelling, and want to be of assistance. And, I will strategize with you about various scenarios that might be the best plan for you and your family.

As a show of sincere interest, I read the entire manuscript so I could better evaluate how to help you. I am willing to bet few of the other six agents you contacted have taken the weekend before Christmas to do the same. Words are meaningless; actions show one's true intent. How many read the book?

I am an advocate for your cause, as well as many others, and have demonstrated that in the kinds of books I represent: *Front of the Class* for those with Tourette syndrome, *Reclaiming the Sky* for the families of 9/11, and *If I Did It* on behalf of the Goldman family and the Ron Goldman Foundation for Justice in memory of their son and brother, Ron Goldman, who was murdered by O.J. Simpson.

I have my own personal interest in helping find a cure for brain cancer. My cousin, Max Paul, from Cincinnati, is an example of my own family's commitment to cure. And, as I explained in our phone conversation, Dawn Steele, a close friend, passed away from a glioblastoma, and I was instrumental in getting her into a protocol in Texas that extended her life more than a year.

You'll note that many of the testimonials on my website call me "tenacious." I believe my tenacity is exhibited by my actions and not by my promises.

I wish you well in finding the strength to come to the decision that is in Elena's legacy's best interest. And whether that decision leads you to me, or another, I know my integrity and good intention, at the end of the day, serves my clients' needs well.

Please let me know what you decide to do.

Merry Christmas to you, Brooke and Gracie.

All of this happened very quickly, basically less than a month from the first airing of the *Good Morning America* segment to the sale to HarperCollins. To facilitate the sale, we asked Jeffrey Zaslow, co-author of the best-selling book *The Last Lecture*, which was the story of Carnegie Mellon professor Dr. Randy Pausch's inspiring last lecture, for a cover blurb. Dr. Pausch died of pancreatic cancer, as did Sharlene's mother. Plus, her son and Jeffrey are both graduates of Carnegie Mellon, so there were a lot of connections here. Here's what Jeffrey kindly sent:

> "Elena has left behind a story of resilience, hope, and most of all, love. We can't help but take her into our hearts, and carry the best of her into our own lives."
>
> —*Jeffrey Zaslow, co-author,* The Last Lecture

Additionally, we have placed the book with Lucy Stille, a film agent at Paradigm, who has had extensive interest, including from the production company of an A-list actor. She also has a special interest because her husband was fatally stricken by brain cancer at the age of sixty-two.

As of this writing we have sold over a dozen foreign sales markets and publisher HarperCollins is planning an initial print run of 250,000 copies.

You can see that it took a lot of team effort to make all this happen. Plus, please note that every person involved in this project carefully and thoughtfully researched the next person before coming aboard. The result is that we all have a deep connection to each other, to Elena, and to the Desserich family.

THE FINAL DECISION

Can this happen for your self-published book? Maybe. We've given you the pros and cons, and the criteria for national interest. Only you can decide if your book—and you—can thrive in a self-publishing environment. Remember that in self-publishing, getting the book produced is easy; the issue will be in letting people know that your book is there while working at it without the "badge" of the publisher's name to assure the market that your book has been thoroughly vetted and evaluated.

CHAPTER 15

DISCIPLINE IS YOUR FRIEND: FOLLOW THIS SCHEDULE TO FINISH YOUR BOOK

It goes without saying that writing is an intensely personal endeavor. It makes perfect sense that writers each have their own particular narrative style, so long as the writing process is functional, the necessary pages are being completed—and deadlines are being met. But writing seminars everywhere are filled with fledgling authors who are mired in frustration. Testimonies at these same seminars often concern the struggle to maintain a steady page count. Even experienced writers occasionally find themselves stuck for the right words.

Pressure from life's uncountable stressors can diminish your capacity to reach your daily page or word count, in spite of your talent and determination. A blank page, a blinking cursor, even a silently waiting dictation recorder can be daunting enough to put you into the freeze mode. When you look closely at the problem, it is evident that the amount of time you spend frozen is equal to the amount of distraction in your life. It is difficult to overstate the power wielded by the force of distraction when it comes to fragmenting creative thought.

You must have noticed that there is a virtual cancer of distraction eating at the minds of all who live within reach of commercial media. Even if your personal life is in lovely condition, you are continually being robbed of the necessary time to organize your thoughts and write them down. In this milieu, you propose to write a book?

THE ETERNAL STRUGGLE

Almost all authors struggle at some point in their writing career. And like most editors, Lisa Kaufman, marketing director and senior editor at PublicAffairs, has had to walk her share of authors through trouble spots. Her process will be helpful to you.

"First I'll ask to read what the author has gotten down on paper," says Kaufman. "Often that will give me an idea of what the author is struggling with: Is it a technical problem, or a personal one? Is the author struggling with writing or with life? Is he trying too hard to do something that doesn't need doing? Missing the forest of the narrative for the trees of perfect prose? Has she actually stumbled into a different thesis or sort of book than she set out to write, and doesn't recognize it? Too often authors are too proud to deliver drafts when they are struggling, but that's what an editor is for! My job is to have a vision of the finished book, and to guide the author how to get there if he or she loses his/her way."

Kaufman added that she sometimes meets with the author in person or by phone so they can talk through the problem, then she tries to give perspective, direction, and ideas. "I try to break down the task into small bites and specific assignments," she says. "I may also call the author's agent to get insight on what is going on with them psychologically or personally, and strategize on how best to help."

Michael Fragnito, Vice President and Editorial Director of Sterling Publishing, has a unique perspective. "I encourage my editors to be in touch with authors three months in advance of the due date. I believe we generally use a combination of back patting and threats in order to try to get an author to finish. In my experience, if the author is a professional writer, the delays have more to do with other obligations than an inability to finish."

The point here is that you have plenty of company if you are struggling to get (and keep) the pages flowing. Know that you, dear Struggling Writer, are not alone. You just need a method, a clear and simple procedure by which you can turn on the creative spigot and begin the step-by-step process of laying out your book. And never fear, that method is here for you.

THE TWO (2) PAGE RULE: FOLLOW THIS SCHEDULE TO YOUR FINISHED BOOK

So why insert the (2) up there? Why not just call it the Two Page Rule? Answer: to emphasize, via repetition, that you can actually complete your book in a measured way by writing only two (2) pages per writing session. In that way you will accomplish your goal at a reasonable pace—your pace—one that respects the fact that if you are like everyone else, the forces of chaos are forever conspiring to prevent you from writing at all.

The Two (2) Page Rule allows you to accomplish your goal of completing a market-ready book proposal or manuscript, and it works because the person who is utilizing its power (you) provides the fundamental element: determination. With the Two (2) Page Rule you only need to bring a small but steady output of energy to each work session.

The power of the Two (2) Page Rule lies in constant repetition, in your *unceasing determination* to achieve the goal of getting your book published and connected with a readership. It is no different than resolving to do small amounts of physical exercise every day.

 HOT TIP!

It is vital that you write on a regular scheduled basis, utilizing every available block of potential writing time.

Every Reasonable Opportunity

Writers cursed with tendencies toward procrastination are already well aware of the danger in any scheduled writing program, i.e., five sessions a week easily becomes four, three, maybe none at all for a week or so, until hey, didn't you say something about writing a book?

Before we engage any further in this method for structuring your writing output, let's take on the task of selecting a schedule that fits with the rest of your life's obligations. This works much better than setting yourself up to fail with a schedule you cannot actually keep. It is ideal to write every day when it is feasible, but sometimes life simply says no to that. When that happens it should not stop you; instead, it should simply motivate you to alter your plan of attack.

When you are estimating your optimum writing schedule, be honest with yourself and conservative in your estimate of the amount of time you can spare away from everything else to work on your book. If you cannot be a full-time writer at this point, focus on the time you *can* spend writing, rather than all the time that you cannot. Good ideas don't disappear. If your inspiration is genuine you will get your book written—just later, rather than sooner. It is better to adapt to the situation by scaling back your writing sessions to four a week, two a week, even one a week. The key here is *scheduled* repetition. Writers who write "when I can" often lose the struggle against all of the times when they can't.

If you can spare Saturday afternoons from two to four, then those two hours are your writing time, every single week, without fail. You would no more miss that scheduled writing session than jealous lovers will miss a chance to be with their objects of desire. As long as you set your schedule to a pace that realistically fits into the rest of your life, you will eventually accomplish your goal. And most people can find at least two hours a week if they try.

Feel free to copy this next Hot Tip and stick it on your wall.

What Is "Available Writing Time"?

Simple question: How much time can you make in your daily life to work on your book? The answer is as personal as your writing life itself and boils down to how much determination you actually have to see this thing through. If you have enough determination, then your book is going to happen and you are already on the road to its completion.

Still, every writer also has to consider the social component that factors into an estimation of available writing time. It begins with the question of how much time your significant other thinks that you can spare. The same question spreads to your other primary relationships, the rest of your family. Got any friends? How will they feel about your sudden lack of availability? If you are employed, how much time would your boss estimate that you have for writing a book?

Finding the Time

With rare exceptions granted to untalented famous people, a writer who makes the leap to successful authorship is someone who confronts the cold realization that they have no time to write their book by finding the time to write it anyway.

Making the Time

A writer who does not care for the thought of failure will respond by giving up activities that are not essential to life's fundamental responsibilities. Move meetings around. Pack household chores together. Maximize commute time. Economize movement and effort. As if by magic, holes will appear in your schedule. Bubbles of newfound quiet time arrive—spaces where you can do the writing that will reach out to your readers with your advice, your method, your story.

Stealing the Time

Writers who would rather eat a bowl of pea gravel for breakfast than see their dreams of authorship fade away but don't have time to write a book will steal the time to write it anyway. Whether it's the security guard who works on his memoir, *Rent-A-Life*, while he waves cars past his guard hut or a busy parent writing during their kid's soccer game. It could be anyone. The writer may be someone who does not care about the consequences of ignoring responsibilities while he completes his book. Or the writer may be someone who is plagued by a compulsive disorder and absolutely has to write. But here's the thing: The writer may be so creatively inspired and in such a state of enthusiasm for seeing creative visions become reality that priorities fall out of sync with the demands of everyday life.

"Writers write," the saying goes. The difficulty is that not only do writers write, they write whether they are supposed to or not.

Therefore, no matter where you fall on the scale of determination or compulsion, your preplanned writing schedule is a safety net against falling away from your goal. It also keeps you from pursuing your book too hard with respect to your other obligations. The progress of your writing using the humble Two (2) Page Rule may feel gradual, especially if you can only spare a single writing session each week, but rest assured that this approach will move you toward your finished book without throwing your life out of balance. Slow and steady, your page count will grow. Remember that you are going for distance, not speed. Your race is all about the finish line.

Step One: Setting Your Schedule

Once you have addressed the crucial question of how much time you can realistically afford to invest on a regular basis, set your days and times. There is no wrong number here, so long as the number of sessions per week and hours per session are goals you can realistically achieve.

Step Two: Mark Your Calendar

It is essential to have a formal reminder system to keep you on track once you are underway. Hang a calendar near your desk, or anyplace where you will always see it. Or program a tickler into your cell phone or PDA to remind you. You know what sort of reminder method will work best for you. It is vital that you allow it to keep you reminded about upcoming writing sessions.

The issue behind your schedule is one of consistency. It will not work to keep your writing schedule tucked into the back of your mind, to write "whenever" you get an opportunity. Your formal writing schedule will function as your compass on this journey, so put it right where you can't escape it. Every time you check your calendar to see whether you are free to attend a certain event or make an appointment, you should also get a jolting reminder about your next scheduled writing session.

Let Guilt Work for You

Consider the manner in which guilt has plagued you for one reason or another throughout your life. This is payback time; now you can consciously employ the power of guilt to help you show up as scheduled. For example, if you use a paper calendar, hang it next to the window that you stare out of when you're procrastinating. Get extreme about it. You're serious about completing this book, so hang the damn schedule next to the TV! Put it on the bathroom wall where it will be at eye level when you have a seat. Put a copy in the kitchen on top of the container holding the chocolate cake. In fact, put several copies in the kitchen. The power that your schedule bestows by dividing the flow of time into manageable segments is nearly magical in its scope. Daunting accomplishments can be achieved by filling those segments with consistent activity, focusing on each one in its turn.

You should be able to write a minimum of two hours a week. This is an amount of time virtually anyone can find. Of course you will do all of that, and perhaps much more if you are able. Speaking now for the whole gang down here in the Rewrite Department (we're next to the boiler room; turn left at the swinging light bulb), we agree that the writer who cannot find two hours a week for their book is not likely to make it to chapter 15 of this one, anyway. So at this point we can all feel free to talk about them and they'll never know.

Step Three: Now Activate the Two (2) Page Rule

The simplicity of this principal almost contradicts its creative power. Here's the secret: Complete two pages at every writing session—*No Matter What*. Two full pages.

This is the bedrock of your work procedure. It means that, at the very least, you are committing two hours a week to writing your book. You are more fortunate if you can spare two hours a day or as many as you can fill, but even the minimum of a single two-hour session every week will yield a steady flow of pages for you. Show up for every one of your scheduled writing sessions and complete two pages before you quit. Even a fierce case of writer's block goes away when you know you only have to write two pages.

Whether you have already begun to write your book or you are just now beginning the research for a project that you intend to write later, your goal remains the same: *two pages of completed writing for every session.*

This method primes your pump in a way that keeps your creative output flowing. After all, any good book is an extensive piece of intellectual architecture. Your optimum response to the challenge is to break your complex project down into bite-sized pieces by holding to this minimum goal in each session—and by maintaining your commitment to the finished book. You will demonstrate that commitment every time you have a chance to write. The proof will be in at least two pages of anything that applies directly to your book (correspondence doesn't count). And if you happen to have five pages in you that day, or even ten or fifteen, or push it full throttle and imagine that some whirlwind of inspiration sweeps you into its orbit and squeezes twenty pages from your aching fingers, well, good on you. Sometimes you catch a wave. But still, two pages, right? Every time.

Here are some examples of a legitimate two-page output. You can:

- write two pages of research notes
- write two pages of practice dialogue
- write two pages of character description
- write two pages of outline material for your book
- write two pages of your book proposal, moving through each element
- write two pages of your sample chapters
- write two pages of your contact list (it sometimes helps to use this content-neutral research work as a break from the greater intensity of the creative process of the actual writing)

HOT TIP!

Any writing based on your goal of completing your book is good. It will not only move you forward, your page count will continue to accumulate with a steady momentum.

Research Notes

When you begin your book in earnest, you will move from generalized reading on a topic that interests you to the methodical gathering and collating of your book's database. At this point, most writers find it so easy to put out two pages in a single session that they wind up doing a lot more. (Remember, there's no maximum.) If there was ever a point in working with the Two (2) Page Rule that you push yourself for more output, it is likely to be here. The process of researching carries its own momentum, and once you begin to find and copy down the vital pieces of information that will define your book's position, the pages quickly build over a writing session of two hours because your notes are taken from other sources. You are not yet in the stage of concerning yourself with your narrative voice. These pages are still just for you as you assemble your vital tool kit. When this tool is ready, it will consist of *a complete and balanced overview* of your subject. The importance of accuracy in your presentation is shared with every writer of nonfiction, no matter the category or topic. In the end, it all comes down to your database.

The memoir form is less dependent upon publicly available factoids, but there can still be a fair amount of research in a self-based book. A memoir generally requires its author to conduct private research through the obtaining of letters and documents from surviving relatives and friends, perhaps interviewing them, and always securing their permission to quote them or to use their documents or their interview responses. (Get it in writing!)

Practice Dialogue

No two people speak in exactly the same way, unless they are roughly the same age and from the same family or the same neighborhood. This means that any dialogue your book may employ is consciously written to sound like that character's way of speaking. Many nonfiction writers find it easy to gloss over the importance of good dialogue, considering it to be in the domain of novelists. This is a mistake, because with the exception of those nonfiction books that are function-based, you are still going to be quoting certain people or reconstructing certain conversations. Unless those quotes are already written and you are merely transcribing them, you will find that your dialogue reads best when it sounds as if somebody actually said it.

Employ Self-Talk

Self-talk is a technique that works for many writers, and it is simple to do. Write down a line or two, then stop to read it out loud. You want to listen for clarity first of all, then for authenticity of sound. Read it several times over, and revise as needed until it sounds perfect. Then write the new version down.

It's easy to report a conversation that you have personally witnessed by saying nearly the same thing the actual person said at the time without realizing you are actually using words or phrases that are your own. The best way to avoid this unconscious paraphrasing is to match the spoken sound of each line of dialogue to the attributes of the character who is speaking them. More telling than a character's regional accent are the vocabulary traits that express their personal level of intelligence and education. Don't choose their words for them; allow each character's personal traits to choose their words for you.

If you are dramatizing or re-enacting a historical scene, this will give your written dialogue the same crisp and readable feel you would expect from a good novel. In the memoir or the personal witness forms, this process will also prompt you to recall whatever scenes you personally overheard in terms of the specific words that were actually spoken, instead of the way you would express those thoughts yourself.

Character Descriptions

Spend some time on your book's character descriptions. Never make the mistake of thinking that your book has no "characters" because it is not a work of fiction. Even if your book is instructional and you think it has no characters in it, you are the character. Your narrative voice is the personality of your book. You, as narrator, are the leading character, and you must ask yourself the same questions about your image on the page as you would ask about a real or invented character. This is not the same thing as your platform. This is about the way you present yourself in the writing of your words; about the way you inhabit the piece of literary space that is your book. It will have a major effect on the way that you *sound* to the reader's literary ear.

If your book uses historical or composite characters and there are dramatic scenes to be played out, then the more you have already decided and written down about the details of any given character's life, the easier it will be to render that character in a unique and compelling way. You can make it your goal to write two pages of character description in any given writing session, but you are likely to find that you write more than that. Once you turn on your imagination regarding the details of a character's background and personality, the words and ideas will flow. You will experience that sensation of being picked up and swept along by a creative wave.

Your Outline

When you have researched your topic, tended to your platform, given voice and description to any characters who may be in your book—including you—this brings you to the next important tool for your writer's kit. You will also find that it is easy to get your two pages and more when you are working on your outline. Begin by sketching out the general structure of your book over a couple of pages, then flesh it out by adding the layers of detail.

The question of how much outline to employ is a bit touchy, with a range of responses from writers. In general, the best answer to the question is "as much as you need." As much of the big picture that you can plan out in advance, and as much detail about how that picture stacks up, will sustain your momentum once you get into the middle of your book.

HOT TIP!

If the outline works for you, it is correctly done. You will know it works if your page count stays up.

The Full Permission Aspect

Fears of every stripe can be placed in a submission hold by the Full Permission aspect of the Two (2) Page Rule. There is usable power in this tool. The Full Permission aspect functions like a verbal magic wand that charms the word flow right out of you. Here is how it works:

The regular output of a fixed minimum of Two (2) pages is the essence of this method and it cannot work without your commitment to that modest goal. However, you can help the desire along, because the Full Permission aspect of the Two (2) Page Rule is this: You have *full permission* to write the worst stream of effluvia ever to spring from either end of a queasy seal.

Understand, this means that no matter what you write, as long as it genuinely consists of two pages of text for your book, you are in good shape and you are working along with the process.

HOT TIP!

This process will immediately (or very soon) jump-start your flow of usable manuscript pages.

Therefore, no matter what you write, it simply cannot fail to work. You are officially authorized to write the most egregious accumulation of pointless verbiage ever put to a page. Why shouldn't you? There is not a single soul in the world who ever has to see it. Alone in the privacy of your writing place, you can safely do the equivalent of smearing finger paint across the page, and it would not be inappropriate in any way.

Moreover, the Full Permission aspect of the Two (2) Page Rule is so absolute in its power that you are actively encouraged to write *anything* that your sense of good judgment tells you that you *should not write.* Put those shocking, unspeakable words onto the page right away! If you blush or feel a rush of self-consciousness at the moment you consider writing down any given thought or phrase, *be sure to write it down without stopping to question yourself about it.* The power of this particular tool lies in the fact that you do this writing in private and suffer no risk of judgment from others. This is a process of priming the pump. It is your business and yours alone.

Why ask anyone to write down thoughts that they would not be comfortable with allowing others to read? It is exactly the same thing as the deep stretching exercises that skilled runners do before they start off on a marathon. You stretch and experience your own parameters without help, guidance, suggestions, judgment, interference, or reactions. You feel for yourself exactly where those borders of acceptability lie within you. In this way you can define the difference between what you think and feel, as opposed to what you feel obliged to think and feel. The end result is authenticity. There, you find your genuine voice.

THE BOOK PROPOSAL STAGE

Here's where the payoff begins. If you have done your research, planned out your book's structure, described your "players" in detail as you will portray them, and completed your outline, then you have prepared yourself for this stage so well that you will find that the material pours out of you. It will not be as hard to make time to write as it will be to stop writing and go back to everything else that you have waiting.

Follow the book proposal format provided in chapter 5, and move through each element of the proposal in turn. If you feel stymied or blocked by any part of the proposal, turn to an easier section and do your two pages there, then come back and chip away on the harder stuff. Your page count will continue to roll forward.

Sample Chapters

If you love writing, this is the part that you will most enjoy. It is where you can finally set your narrative voice free and get your message across.

If you don't like writing and just want to have a book out in your name, this is the part where you hire somebody who is really good to do the writing for you. Even though the role of a writer's platform is more important than ever these days, the whole enchilada comes down to the writing. Oh them words. Do the words pull the reader along from page to page?

Occasionally one of the books we sell will need either a co-author or a ghostwriter. There are a lot of people who have good books to write, but not the skill to write them. We all have strengths and weaknesses and just because someone helps you bring your story to life on the page does not mean it is any less your story. We work with several freelancers, authors, and ghostwriters who are tried and true, and match them up with authors who need assistance. You can learn more about the people we work with on our website (www.martinliterarymanagement.com). Keep in mind, though, that if you need help with your sample chapter on the proposal level, most professional writers cannot write on spec because they earn their living that way. You must either commit your energy or your resources.

 HOT TIP!

Choose a collaborator with great care. There are many forms of writing. Just because you know an ad copywriter or a newspaper reporter does not mean they are qualified to help you write a nonfiction book.

It's impossible to come up with any specific number of pages that a sample chapter should contain. The consistent answer is that you must write enough to thoroughly demonstrate your narrative voice. Write enough that you don't come across as someone who will have difficulty in getting an entire book out. Write enough that your love of the game (or the hired writer's love of the game) shows plainly on the pages. But avoid padding the chapter with more than the topic needs. Trim the fat.

PROMOTIONAL CORRESPONDENCE

Promotional correspondence is a very important part of your book and proposal. This is the correspondence that you must generate to attract other professionals in your field for the purpose of writing the foreword or sending back a book blurb or a testimonial for you. These are key because it shows that other experts recognize you as one of their own, giving a double shot of credibility to both you and your book.

Plus, this list is designed to help you spread the word to people you know who may buy a book or attend a book signing. Your personal address list of Potential Readers is gold in your pocket.

The bad news is that correspondence does not apply to the Two (2) Page Rule because your daily quota is all about making sure you have something to correspond about in the first place.

Secondly, the more that you love the creative wordplay of writing, the less you will feel like going through the process of accumulating and verifying a trustworthy list of meaningful contacts regarding your book. Boy oh boy, this is almost as much fun as mucking out a horse stall. No, you cannot get away with buying a list from one of those contact list services, because there is no way of verifying that the information is current until you buy it, and there is no way that it can be as effectively tailored to the specific needs of your book as the custom contact list that you are going to construct.

Time for the Good News

Your homework here will pay you back many times over. This unglamorous chore also brings you a stellar opportunity in that many of your competitors will loathe it as much or more than you do. Because these writers are not building their correspondence lists like they mean it, they will unintentionally volunteer their place in the crowded field to any writer who wants to out-work them. This means you.

Your contacts are worth the time and effort you spend in accumulating them. Here are effective ways for you to cultivate contacts pertaining to your book's topic. (This method will work with any kind of nonfiction book.)

To begin, create four categories of how to make contact. Label them:

1. In Person
2. Phone
3. E-Mail
4. Postal Mail or Messenger

Then, list any person or group who pertains to your book (and everybody you already know) in one of those four columns, considering how you choose to communicate with that particular person about your book.

Column #1: In Person

The field of your subject will have its luminaries whether they are famous to the general public or not, and they may be of assistance to you if you present a request to them in a clear and simple fashion. You should make these requests in person when it is possible to do so because your physical presence emphasizes the importance of what you are seeking. Practicality keeps most in-person visits to a local basis, so the people or organizations that belong on this list are those near enough to you that you can reasonably approach them for help.

There is an unlimited supply of insensitivity and arrogance in the business world, but there will always be those who surprise you with generosity of spirit. They are scattered here and there, and you can't identify them until you approach them and make your request. They are the ones you seek.

Offer them something you can easily make available: a place of honor in the Acknowledgements section of your book, or even a reference on the back cover. In return, you seek such things as their verbal endorsement, a photo together, points of advice on your topic, confirmation of any relevant fact or idea, technical insight, or professional affirmation.

Also, ask yourself if this person is a compelling candidate to write a foreword to your book. How about a front cover quote? The particulars will change with every writer, but in each case the essential question is, what do you need from them? With your researcher's cap firmly in place, boldly approach anyone whom you can personally reach. It never hurts to ask, when you do so with respect—especially if the request is small.

HOT TIP!

The savvy writer will also be gracious if rejected. Keep in mind that this is a business of rejection and that winners forge ahead anyway.

Column #2: By Phone

More people are making their phone numbers hard to find these days in favor of encouraging electronic contact, but for those whose numbers you already have or that you can obtain, a telephone call can be employed in lieu of a personal visit. Perhaps your targeted individual is too far away, or maybe she is just unavailable to you. All right then, but you can often get such "unavailable" people to take a phone call.

If you can get this person to speak with you, it will be important for you to have a brief description of your intended book ready to include in a written follow-up to your conversation. That way, you can allow your phone conversation to have a light tone, wherein you let your target individual know you are writing this book and there is a role you would like for this person to play. After you reveal what you want (a quote, an endorsement, etc.) and get the hoped-for agreement from that party, get off of the phone as quickly as you tactfully can. Send a follow-up letter that reiterates your conversation.

Consider that most people are operating under a mountain of their own concerns and be prepared to understand that no matter how good your book is going to be, some people are simply too preoccupied to help you. It only feels like it's about you. If you will truly swallow and digest that thought, you will save yourself countless episodes of unnecessary anxiety.

Column #3: E-Mail

With any form of e-mail communication regarding your book, always open with a salutation that uses the recipient's name, and tailor your comments specifically to that individual in some way. It is enough to make a simple reference to past work or to whatever causes you to be interested in that individual, but do not allow the small size of this task to fool you regarding its importance.

We are all overloaded with e-mail spam and its many variations. You can bet that your recipient hates it as much as you do. Therefore, the apparent ease of sending out bulk e-mail is a temptation that every savvy writer will avoid. Laziness here will entrap many writers who dread the uncomfortable clerical task of individualizing their correspondence. But they can never know the number of opportunities that will be lost because of impersonal correspondence. Make it a point to let each addressee know you are reaching out specifically to that person and see the difference that it makes when you start out on the right foot.

HOT TIP!

Many of your competitors will not do this.

Column #4: Postal Mail or Messenger

The fact that e-mail communication has replaced much of the need for postal mail can also present you with a good opportunity to stand out from the crowd. Provided that your recipient is willing to accept hard copies of your work or your promotional materials, the physical presentation of written material can impart a certain gravitas to your work, especially when the package includes impressive visual elements. You must consider your specific recipient and evaluate whether a hard copy presentation is your best choice in this instance.

Or you can step it up with the use of a personal messenger, but this is a costly way to go and you risk having the gesture interpreted by the recipient as a display of self-importance. Use this method only if time is of the essence to your recipient, in which case it can be a sign of your determination. And if you go this route, do your research to confirm that your recipient will be there to receive the package, so your efforts for a "Ta-dah!" moment are not wasted.

STARTING EACH TWO (2) HOUR SESSION

Here is the final important addition to your writer's toolkit: the *Secret of Sustained Momentum*.

After all, the more your life is packed with nonwriting activities, the more you will find yourself arriving for your writing sessions in the wrong state of mind. This is neither a sign to quit nor a signal to start drinking early that day. It is merely another obstacle on your obstacle-strewn pathway, and we have long since established that you are not going to let obstacles stop you.

The Daily Read

Begin each writing session by rereading the past session's work. There will be at least two pages to go over, maybe more. Think of a long-jumper taking a run at the pit before launching into the air. This reread is your running start. It brings you up to speed with the tone and feel of the material at that stage, focuses your creative energy, and serves to drown out the distractions that you brought in with you.

When you finish your daily read, you will find yourself back into your creative groove. If you do not, the solution is simple. Read it again, slower this time. It is possible for your brain to be stuck in overdrive, and this routine reasserts your conscious control over your speeding thoughts by deliberately slowing you down and tuning you back into harmony with the two pages you are rereading as you prepare to generate two more.

You may be inclined to skim over the material and then look for a way to quit for the day. The solution to that is to reread the work and take another run at it, but the larger truth is that you have to be willing to make the effort. Something has to turn you around at the same moment that your natural laziness is attempting to rationalize skipping your writing session. When that happens, it will be a quiet moment, something that may be too fleeting for an outside observer to spot, but you will stay on point via your own power of determination to do a job that you will be able to hold up with pride.

The sheer power of this form of discipline will come from the final, secret ingredient in the success that you create with the Two (2) Page Rule. That ingredient will be the invisible force that silently holds you in your chair and keeps your eyes on the task at hand. Nobody but you witnesses this important event when it occurs, but if you are willing to take this small step toward making discipline your friend, then no one else will need to hear about your strength of determination anyway. The quality of your results will communicate that message to anyone who reads your work.

CHAPTER 16

A TARGETED PUBLIC RELATIONS CAMPAIGN: YOUR TICKET TO THE TOP

Public relations, or the act or bringing the public's attention to your book, is a key component in making your book a success. While it is true that your publisher should take some responsibility for that, the reality is that not all have the time, staff, funding, or resources to do so. Even best-selling authors must put forth a strong effort to attract media and generate press, and if these authors are making the effort, then your effort must be greater still.

Before we get into the specifics, now would be a good time to review chapter 3 and shore up any holes in your platform. Much of what you will be doing now is an extension of all the things you began when you built your platform, so a quick review will allow you to more quickly expand your horizons and move your book forward.

THE BOOK TRAILER

A book trailer is a video commercial for your book, and for you as the author. Book trailers are relatively new as a marketing phenomenon, and although they represent yet another demand upon an author's time and money, they have quickly become *de rigueur* for writers who are intent upon finding a readership.

You can make one yourself if you have good hardware, software, and solid computer skills, or have a friend who can make one for you.

Otherwise you must turn to the nearest book trailer production business, which you can locate with a quick Web search.

If you are with a major publisher, it is possible that they will do this for you, but most authors have to take care of this themselves. To get a few ideas about how to do your trailer, visit the websites of authors whose work interests you and click on their book trailers. Most nonfiction authors today have one, and we have several on our website (www. martinliterarymanagement.com) that you can watch. As you will see, you can use very simple production techniques, with voice-over narration or scrolling text to deliver the teaser while images evoke your story. A book trailer may be very realistic, like a small movie, or it may be completely abstract and use visual suggestion to tease the imagination.

If you are a public persona, you should include photos or video of you on stage or in action. Your book trailer is like any other commercial, whether or not your name and reputation will draw a significant amount of readers. Its sole purpose is to grab the viewers' attention and hold it long enough to deliver a teaser that leaves them wanting more. You must give them a reason to click the "buy now" button.

WORKING WITH PUBLICISTS ... OR NOT

A book publicist is simply a public relations expert who specializes in authors and books. Some larger publishers have in-house publicists who work with authors—and who also solicit book reviews and video, radio, newspaper, and magazine interviews. But because each in-house publicist has an overwhelming workload, chances are that if you are assigned a publicist at all, what she will actually accomplish for you is very little. If you are with a small publisher who does not have either an in-house publicist or the means to hire an independent publicist for you, you might as well throw all your books over the edge of a cliff, because they are not going to sell unless you have an exceptionally heavy speaking schedule with potential for huge back-of-the-room sales. Somebody has to get the word out that you have a book in print. So then the question becomes: Should you hire an independent publicist, or try to go it alone?

Keep in mind that the book industry is not like *Field of Dreams*; just because you build it, people will not necessarily come. Without a public relations plan of attack for you and your book, the only people who will buy it are your immediate family and some of your friends. And they will all expect you to give them one of the few free copies that you get from your publisher. The general public typically does not understand that an author actually has to *buy* most of his books from the publisher.

The strength in a publicist—and in a public relations campaign—is in the depth of the contacts. Public relations is a "who you know" business, so if you have no previous experience in attracting PR or in doing interviews, if you have no contacts in the media, if you don't know the ins and outs of writing a press release, when to follow up on the release, when to call a member of the media, when to e-mail, and when to sit back and bite your fingernails, then you need the services of an expert book publicist.

The key word here is "book." If you know a corporate or entertainment publicist, that's great. They can definitely help you with a few things. But a publicist who is not entrenched in the world of books will not know, for example, the specific interests of the *USA Today* book reviewers, or the lead time needed to garner a review in *Kirkus Reviews*, or the genre of books being featured this spring in *ForeWord*.

Additionally, many publicists also help their authors to craft attention-getting sound bites and coach them in the art of doing interviews. Besides helping you know what to say and how to say it, media training helps you know what to wear on camera and off, how to walk into an interview, how to sit for the best camera angle, and the protocols you must follow before and after an interview.

Like many publicists, Lynn Goldberg, CEO of Goldberg McDuffie Communications, often prepares author questions and answers (Q&As)

for the press kit. "These serve two purposes," she says. "They help solicit interest from targeted media outlets and prepare authors for interviews. We also advise authors on timely talking points and provide them with information about each media interview scheduled."

If an author requires more preparation, Goldberg connects him to one of several media trainers who regularly work with authors. "We often recommend media training for first-time authors," she says, "so they are well prepared to answer questions in a very short time."

Other publicists, like Jill Danzig, president of Danzig Communications, prefer to prepare their authors themselves. "Media training is imperative, and I almost always do this myself," says Danzig. "Even the most articulate authors can tighten their messages so that none of the precious interview time is wasted."

HOT TIP!

Media training should give you the skills to come across as comfortable and well versed, no matter what question you are asked. Use this training to learn about the interview process and how to present yourself at your best, but don't let it turn you into a stiff, automated clone. The more training that you have, the more natural you should appear in an interview—not the other way around!

According to Justin Loeber, president of Mouth Public Relations, if you do decide to work with a publicist, there are a few things you can do that will help them help you. "Give the publicist all the information he or she asks for in a timely manner. Information such as a list of who [the author] knows in the media, other people who can come on camera to support the author's claims, sample DVDs or print clips of their previous interviews all help," he says, "as can lending a helping hand in creating a tip sheet and questions."

INTERVIEWS: HOW NOT TO SHOOT YOURSELF IN THE FOOT

According to many book publicists, the number one thing that authors do to hurt their career and book is to give poor interviews. In that vein of thought, publicist Gene Taft of GT/PR has some good advice for new authors regarding interviews.

"Make a point to be easy to work with. You need the producers much more than they need you, and you can easily be replaced," he says. "And do not expect the interviewer to have read your book."

Jane Wesman of Jane Wesman Public Relations, Inc. agrees, adding that most authors don't recognize the complexity of the publicity process. "More books than ever are being published and the competition for media attention is intense," she says. "Authors need to understand that if they want to get the best media coverage possible and achieve their goals, they need a strategic campaign."

HOT TIP!

This is your tap on the shoulder, reminding you to prepare your Media Self.

Sound Bites: The Key to a Memorable Interview

Sound bites are short, well-crafted sentences that clearly define you and your book, and make the media (and potential readers) sit up and take notice. In an ideal world, you are already practicing sound bites for your book. In this ideal world, you are also already camera and microphone ready. But the reality is that you *may not* have begun yet.

So what are you waiting for? The time to start is now! Poet Dylan Thomas lamented that God did not give us the power to see ourselves as others see us. But then someone developed video technology, and whoops, today's writers have the ability to see how well they are doing

---

in their promotional work (or how well they are not doing) before an interview actually takes place. In some professions, it might be a pointless exercise in vanity to show a great concern for one's own image, but for today's nonfiction author there is no reason and no excuse not to have at least half a dozen audio and video sound bites polished up and ready to deliver to the camera for any publicity opportunity.

Whether you are working with a publicist or not, it is good to be ready with sound bites for your book well before your publication date. In this instance, being "ready" with sound bites means that:

- You are prepared to type your way through an online book club chat
- You can speak clearly and cogently for a radio interview
- You are confident, presentable, and coherent in a video appearance
- You can get your point across in a print interview without confusing your interviewer

In the process you must come off as intelligent, but not so over the top that no one understands you. You must also be witty and likable, because readers do not want to buy books from the stereotypical morose, musing, caustic writer who makes others feel inferior.

This is so important that Marika Flatt, founder of PR by the Book, echoes other publicists: "Not giving a good, thorough interview and being labeled a bad guest is the number one thing an author can do to hurt their career," she says.

Developing the Perfect Sound Bite

Your ability to put carefully crafted publicity bites to good use will be the result of rehearsals at home. There, in front of a mirror—and then a camera—you will practice precisely how to describe your book to a stranger, using phrases that are clear and compelling. The practice will allow you to go beyond merely describing your book, to succinctly describing *the value that your book offers.*

For example, we sold *A Craving for Crab* by author Christine Quinn, who describes her book as "a love note to all things crab," and "the definitive guide for crab lovers."

Both of those very short sound bites are not only memorable and distinctive; they accurately sum up the contents of her cookbook.

You also need to have a few sentences ready that tell something about you, which will make an audience want to know more. This is your best course of action, because no matter how famous you may or may not be, you will always be the primary proponent of your book—ahead of your publisher, editor, agent, or even your publicity experts. This one cannot be delegated.

Watch and Learn

It is also helpful before you begin your interview process to take time to watch some interviews on television, and listen to some talk radio. But rather than sit back and enjoy the show, watch and listen carefully, and take notes. What is it about a particular interview that makes you sit up and listen? What about the host or guest do you find engaging, or distracting? What mannerisms are endearing? What vocal sounds do you find annoying?

By watching and listening with an educated eye and ear, you can both learn from the pros and also head off a few potential disasters in your own upcoming interviews.

Mock Interviews

Before you actually do an interview, you'll want to do several "mock" interviews. These are practice sessions that are set up as close to real interview sessions as possible. For instance, if you will be interviewed in a radio studio, set up a desk or table so you can sit across from, or at a right angle to, a friend who has agreed to pose as the radio host. Then give him a list of questions you think the host might ask during the interview. Keep in mind what you learned from your watching and listening sessions, and record the pretend interview. Then listen back to it with a critical ear. Practice honing your answers, then do it all over again. And again and again.

HOT TIP!

Mock interviews will help you polish your sound bites *and* give you confidence.

By the time you have your first real interview, you should have pitched your book to an imaginary audience countless times. The mental preparation from these mock sessions will allow you to speak with clarity and authority, and you will easily be able to sum up your book for a stranger in a way that will pique his interest.

The Camera Factor

Certain public figures and celebrities can fumble, or come across as befuddled, in front of the camera and get away with it by looking cute. You cannot, unless you are writing humorous pop-culture material, and even then you have to be very careful how you go about it. That's why you must also do mock video interviews in much the same manner as you did for radio.

There is immeasurable value in mock video interviews for any writer who is not comfortable or highly experienced before the camera. Today's writers of nonfiction can make good use of the digital explosion that has placed the powers of the Hollywood film director into our collective hands. Every publicity opportunity you get will bring you more readers, if you present yourself, your story, and your ideas in a compelling fashion. And what better place to do the necessary practice than in the comfort of your own living room?

Many people have access to a videocamera of some kind, or can get their hands on one with little effort. As a savvy writer, take full advantage of the fact that everyone has the power to brush up his public presence with ease and at low expense. The visual quality of your rehearsal video is irrelevant. It makes no difference whether you are working in front of a cell phone or the finest HD camera. What matters is your performance: how you look, how you sound, and whether you speak with clarity. For your purposes, anything that can record and playback will work. So grab the nearest videocamera and go shoot video of yourself already.

On camera, give the same basic description of your book several times in a row, then watch the playbacks and look for the best take. Do it over and over, until you look relaxed, your eye movements are calm, your voice is steady, and your thoughts are clear. Do it until you know just what you want to say and how you want to say it. That does not mean you have to memorize a script. There is nothing wrong with off-the-cuff speech, but your spontaneous remarks will have much more impact when their ideas and phrases have been coded into your brain through repetition, and polished by self-observation.

Rehearsal Is Better for You Than Vitamins

The public's attention span may flutter like a butterfly on speed, so it is the practice you put in ahead of time that will prepare you to capitalize on those brief flickers of attention when they come your way. Do not cheat yourself out of this. You only need to hold onto the public's attention for a few moments to get your message across. The skill and polish that you bring to those moments can capture your viewer's attention and win you another reader, instead of dissolving into the background static of the viewer's mind, where it is quickly forgotten.

Even if you go the route of self-publication and savor the freedom of the unchained writer, you still have to invest serious amounts of energy into ensuring that readers can find you.

Today's nonfiction authors simply do not have the option of social reticence. Every major publisher knows from long experience that books sell better when their authors get out and publicize them.

HOT TIP!

J.D. Salinger's reclusive image may have become a trademark for him, but ordinary mortals may not claim privileges such as those enjoyed by Mr. Salinger. We must all, every one of us, do everything we can to be as media friendly as possible.

THE INTERVIEW INFORMATION SHEET

Hopefully you will soon be doing plenty of interviews. But authors—and other celebrities as well—become confused about the minute details of specific interviews all the time. If you have a publicist, she will help you keep it all straight. But if you don't, keeping the information together in a notebook with each interview on a separate sheet of paper will help you manage it all. The following is some helpful information that you need to get concerning your interview when it is first booked. Either be certain that you have it yourself or ask your publicist to get it for you.

- Media type: radio, newspaper, etc.

- Media name: WSM-AM 650 radio or *People* magazine, etc.

- Method: live, taped, or live to tape— a taped program that tapes as if it was live, meaning no stopping or do-overs

- Via: phone, e-mail, or in person

- Phone number to call: if your interview is over the phone, the number will often be different than the number you call the schedule the interview

- Location: in-studio, reporter's office, your home, etc.

- Interview day and date: include the day of the week to avoid confusion in case you write down the wrong date

- Interview time: include the time zone you are in and also the time zone the interviewer is in (don't forget daylight savings) to avoid confusion

- Length of interview: this helps you know how much information you have time to give, and which sound bites to use

- Emergency contact and number: who should you call if the reporter doesn't show, if you can't get through on the radio call in line, or if you can't find your way to the studio?

- Air date or publication date: establish the time of day for broadcast interviews

- Interview contact: this is often a different person than who will be doing the actual interview, so be sure to include the contact's name, phone, and e-mail

- Online URL: for accessing the interview on the Internet—and giving your friends, family, and fans a place to find it

- Interviewer's name and title: lets you know if the person is a host or a correspondent, and what level of importance he has in the show

- Directions to the interview: don't get lost or be late

- Comments: anything else that will help you through the process

- Follow-up: the date and method you sent a thank-you card to your interviewer and contact person

Several times before the interview takes place, review the information on your interview sheet; also take some quiet time to think about what you will say and how you will say it. You *will* feel the positive difference that your preparation makes.

Tricks of the Interviewing Trade

If you've had experience doing media interviews, the following may be familiar, but it's a good refresher. If you're new to interviews, the information below will help you maximize every interview opportunity.

- **Never do an interview unless there is product already in stores waiting for readers to buy.** You will only get one shot, for example, at doing the morning show at your local ABC affiliate, and it doesn't help anyone to go on the air if your book will not be out for another two months. By the time your book hits the shelves viewers will not remember either you or your book. The only exception to this is an interview that won't run until your book is published.

- **Some media often request exclusivity.** So if you do a radio interview on local talk radio station WXYZ, then the other talk radio station will not be interested. WXYZ may also make exclusivity a condition of their interview with you. The time period of the exclusivity might be a day, or it might be thirty days.

- **Be sure you know how long the interview is scheduled for.** That knowledge will help you discuss enough talking points and sound bites during the interview without either overstaying your welcome or running out of things to say.

- **Never interrupt the person who is interviewing you.** Instead, really listen to the questions you are asked … and then answer them.

- **Know that you will inconvenience a great many people if you cancel the interview at the last minute.** You might even lose the interview opportunity entirely. Same thing applies if you are late.

- **It is inappropriate to contact a media venue that has already decided not to interview you or review your book.** That was a business decision, and who are you to tell them what their business is? There are other media outlets out there; go contact them.

- **At the end of every print interview, be sure to ask if there is anything the reporter is unclear about or wanted to cover that wasn't discussed.** Then be sure she has your card in case she needs to ask questions later. Also, *always* double-check that a print reporter has the correct title of your book and the correct spelling of your name.

THE DIFFERENT KINDS OF MEDIA

You've heard us mention several different kinds of media, and each of them can be helpful to you. The main two media categories are print and broadcast. Print encompasses magazines, newspapers, and newsletters, while broadcast incorporates radio and television. There is a third category that straddles both print and broadcast: the Internet, which includes blogs, plus all of the above.

The Basics of Print

We'll start with print, which is generally easier to do from an interview standpoint because you don't have to worry too much about how you look or how you sound. As a rule, print media has a relatively long shelf life. That's good, because the longer a copy of a print publication languishes on the table in your doctor's office, the more people who have a chance to read about you. Magazines, in particular, can be found years after their publication date.

The trouble with print is that it is easy for those who are inexperienced in doing interviews to say too much, and to be too candid. That's why it is important to hone your talking points.

Newspapers

Your hometown newspaper is a good place to start. Most papers are willing to tell their readers about a new author in their midst. But the larger the paper, the harder it will be to make this happen. Newspaper review space for books is shrinking daily and many newspapers no longer review books at all. To get any coverage you will have to tie your book's topic into a current event that is being covered in the news, or a large event that is happening in your area.

Generally, you can schedule a newspaper interview a month ahead of time, but a review copy of the book should be given to a newspaper's book reviewer as much as six months in advance of publication.

Magazines

Magazines often have a very long lead time, sometimes as much as a year. It is very difficult to get information on a new book published in a magazine unless you begin as soon as you know you have a publication date. Some magazines, especially those narrowly targeted to specific topics such as *Working Mother* or *Western Horseman*, have shorter lead times, but all of them have an annual editorial calendar they must follow.

Let's say you have a parenting book coming out in June that discusses the pros and cons of breastfeeding after returning to work. If the June theme for the magazine is summer office wardrobes, vacations, and projects for tweens, even though you contact the magazine's editor in advance, the editor might not be interested because your book does not fit into their editorial calendar,

Magazines, however, can give national exposure to a group of people specifically interested in your topic, so keep trying.

Newsletters

Newsletter articles are typically shorter than magazine articles and often are the "in-house" publication of an association or other group.

Their subject matter and viewpoints are narrow, but if you fit into their areas of focus, you can reach another group of people who may be interested in your book.

Many newsletters are only published quarterly, so again, getting information to the editor as soon as you can is imperative.

Blogs and Other Internet Print

The advantage of the Internet is that it is a fairly immediate form of disseminating information to the public. While many of the larger sites do have editorial calendars and fill their space quite far in advance, it is often easier to get Internet coverage than it is in traditional print.

There are several things to keep in mind here. Believe it or not, there are still some people out there who are not connected to the World Wide Web. These people tend to be very young or very old, those who live in rural areas, and those at the lower end of the economic scale. So, a book targeted to seniors with information on navigating our nation's health care system might not generate a lot of sales based on an Internet article, unless you make the senior's children and caregivers the intended audience.

Millions of people have blogs, some of which are quite popular with lots of exposure to readers. It can raise the visibility and sales of your book if you agree to be a "guest blogger" on a large, reputable site in your topic area. Or maybe a top blogger will interview you. You should also set up a blog yourself within your book's topic range.

A warning: There are quite a few Internet sites that, quite plainly, are run by people who do not know how to write. That's why it is very important to check out each site thoroughly before soliciting an interview or agreeing to one. You are the company you keep; if an article appears on the Internet with typos and incorrect information about you or your book, the poorly done page and its goofy information may be accessible forevermore, even if the Web host takes it down or corrects it.

The Huge Impact of Broadcast Media

While print media is important, it is through the wide reaches of broadcast media that you can truly reach the masses. National television and talk radio reach millions of people, and if you've done your homework, this is the arena in which you can get a slam-dunk and really start to move some books.

Getting Booked on Television

Securing a television interview can be a vicious circle. Many talent coordinators don't want to book a guest unless they have seen a tape of a previous interview. There are good reasons for this. Television time can be expensive to create as well as to air; if you mess up a taping you can cost the show money they might not have. And if the show is live, you can embarrass not only yourself, but the show's hosts as well. But there are a few ways around this.

Start small. Go to a high school, college, or community station and offer to do a segment about getting your book published, the process of writing, or some other related subject—if they will give you a copy of the interview when it is finished. This is the exception to the rule of not doing an interview before your book is published, because you are not discussing your book here. Instead, you are discussing writing and the book business in general. You can do this anytime after you have practiced a few mock interviews on the subject you will be discussing. How's next week looking for you?

Then, find a local show that has guests and offer the same thing. TV bookers are notorious for insisting on a "take-home" for their viewers. What action can viewers take as a result of watching your segment? Maybe you are speaking locally or teaching a class or talking to high school or college students about books. Maybe you are reading to senior citizens. There has to be a compelling reason for a talent coordinator to book you, so be creative and make your own opportunity. If the booker at the local network affiliate wants to see footage, hand her the segment you just did at the college.

When the local affiliate segment is done, ask for a copy of the interview. Then work your way up to a regionally syndicated show, and so on. By the time your book is published, you will have a ready arsenal for the national shows.

HOT TIP!

Start small and use each completed interview to attract larger media to you and your book.

Lead times for television are not as long as for print media, but you should allow at least thirty days for local television and twice that for larger outlets.

Talk Radio

There is a marked difference in the response you will get from a talk radio audience and a television audience. Television often plays against a background of other distractions while people tend to tune into a talk radio show specifically because they want to listen to that particular show. They are often isolated in their car or at work and make an ideal audience for a persuasive author with a compelling book.

The other thing about radio is that you have only your voice with which to attract listeners. With television there is the element of body language, hand gestures, and facial expressions that combine to make you likable and make viewers want to buy your book. With print media, usually there is an accompanying photo of you or your book. But in radio, your voice is your only tool. So, listen to your practice tapes carefully. Do you enunciate your words clearly? Do you speak too fast or too slowly? Does your voice inspire confidence? Those things become all important when it comes to radio.

Modern technology is such that many radio interviews can be done over the phone. These phone interviews are convenient because you do not have to get dressed up or leave the comfort of your own home. But that is also the problem. The setting may be casual, but the interview is not. Make sure you notify family and friends of the time you will be doing the interview so they do not interrupt you. Turn off all radios, televisions, fans, and appliances that might make noise. Put the dog outside if he tends to bark.

Be sure to do the interview from a landline and not your cell phone. Cell phone reception is iffy and it also tends to break up. Plus, for the purposes of a radio interview, the quality of the reception is not nearly as good as a landline.

It is best to do the interview standing up, as this will improve the quality of your voice. Be sure to have a glass of water handy and a few bullet points written or typed in large type so you can find and read them quickly.

As with print and television, your best bet with radio is to start locally, or with high school, college, or community radio. The audiences are smaller, so it won't be a career-ender if you make a flub. Then move to larger and larger outlets. Be sure also to give your radio buddies a month to schedule your interview.

Internet Radio and Television

As with print, the Internet also offers a host of opportunities for radio and television interviews. The same rules and cautions apply. We can't stress enough that anything that is posted to the Internet could be there forever. So be absolutely sure it is something you want to do. If you can't list three compelling benefits to you for doing an Internet radio or television show, then don't do it. That said, there are some very good ones. Just be sure you do your due diligence and check every opportunity out thoroughly.

Readings and Book Signings

Readings and book signings should be a staple of any author's plan for selling books. While there is a distinct difference between the two, the plan for set-up and execution is much the same.

At a traditional book signing, an author simply signs books at a table that is set up in a bookstore. A reading involves a short presentation by the author about the book, his compulsion for writing it, and some of the back story, and then a reading of several pages. The reading is usually followed by a traditional book signing.

Many bookstores do not do book signings, thinking that a reading is more likely to bring book lovers into the store. Eagle Harbor Book Company on Bainbridge Island, Washington, is such a store. We asked their events coordinator, Mary Gleysteen, to walk us through a typical reading at their store.

First, she points out that many new authors do not realize the lead time a store needs to host a reading or signing. Gleysteen says they generally need the industry average of three to four months. The number of books that they order will vary, but averages around twenty-five.

"We try to order enough books to create an eye-catching display in advance of the reading," she says. "We order as many books as we think we can sell at the event, with enough to last us for a month or two afterwards, so it varies with each author, with their sales history and our experience in the store. The number varies widely, obviously many more for well-known authors whose books sell well at our store."

Again, this is typical of most bookstores. If you are a new author, do not expect to sell hundreds of copies right off the bat.

Even if you have a publicist, it is traditionally the author's responsibility to solicit and coordinate their own book signing events. We asked Mary Gleysteen what authors can do to help her make the reading the best event possible.

"It's great to have an advance reading copy of the book and JPEGs of the author and book jacket and other press materials that we can use for our publicity efforts, including print and e-mail newsletters, website, calendars, fliers, window displays, and press releases," Gleysteen says.

"We love it when authors help with publicity by inviting their friends, sending e-mails to their neighbors, church groups, hairdressers, kids' PTA, etc., posting the event on their websites, and contacting local media offering interviews," she says.

Gleysteen adds that while a store will send out press releases every week to their media list, that media reps often like to hear from the author personally. She also suggests that an author call a few days in advance of the event to confirm with the bookstore's event coordinator that, yes, he will actually show up on time for the reading or signing.

The authors should also make his events as interesting and entertaining as possible. "The idea is to draw people in and make them want to read the book," Gleysteen says. "We've had great events with authors who have incorporated things like music, dance, actors, or writing contests and other forms of audience participation into their presentations."

Another idea is to have a "plant" in the audience to break the ice if things go slowly during the question and answer session, or to bring the topic back around if another audience member pulls you off track.

"Try to connect with each member of the audience and the staff," says Gleysteen. "If you make a good impression with the bookstore staff, it is more likely that they will make an effort to promote your book."

It is also helpful if the author is able to keep to the agreed schedule for presentation, question and answer session, and book signing.

"In small stores," she says. "Oftentimes the people who put away the chairs and tidy up the store at the end of an evening event are the same people who have to open bright and early the next day. If there's a great conversation going and staff isn't able to invite you and the customers to linger beyond closing hours, make arrangements to adjourn to a local coffee shop, restaurant, or bar."

FRONT OF THE CLASS: A CASE STUDY

We've mentioned the book *Front of the Class: How Tourette Syndrome Made Me the Teacher I Never Had* by Brad Cohen with Lisa Wysocky, which we represented (see chapter 9). This book is like "the little engine that could," except it took a concentrated public relations effort for it to achieve far more than any of us ever thought possible.

The book was one of a small handful published by a tiny publisher, VanderWyk & Burnham, in 2005. It is the story of a man, Brad Cohen, who has Tourette syndrome and went on to become a Teacher of the Year. As a child, Cohen was ridiculed, beaten, mocked, and shunned. Children, teachers, and even family members found it difficult to be around him. Even today, Brad is sometimes ejected from movie theaters and restaurants. Much more than a book on growing up with Tourette's, *Front of the Class* shows how everyone can make a difference in this world.

"When I read the book I knew immediately that I wanted to be a part of it," says Kate Siegel Bandos, founder and chief publicist at KSB Promotions and the book's publicist. "As we mapped out our PR plans, we dreamed big. We were thrilled that others found the book as moving as we did."

The highlights of the results of Bandos's efforts are:

- A four-page excerpt in *People* magazine

- A spot on *Inside Edition*, which was a direct result of the *People* story. The show went to Atlanta and filmed Brad in his classroom. This piece has run several times since its initial airing.

- A guest segment on *The Oprah Winfrey Show*. The show topic was "Beating the Odds" and has aired several times. Bandos and her team pitched Oprah's people numerous times with many different hooks. It wasn't until almost nine months after the book's publication date that Brad walked onto Oprah's set.

- Numerous reviews and articles, including *ForeWord* magazine, *Instructor* magazine, *The Atlanta Journal-Constitution*, *Atlanta Jewish Times*, *San Diego Jewish Times*, and the front page of his local weekly: *East Cobber*. There were also numerous radio interviews from *American Voices* with Senator Bill Bradley and KMOX in St. Louis, to WTMA in Charleston, and KPTK in Seattle.

- The book also won two impressive awards: IPPY (Independent Publisher) Best Education Book of the Year, and *ForeWord* magazine's Gold Award for Best Education Book.

"Then came word that the book had been sold for a Hallmark Hall of Fame made-for-TV movie and that trade paperback and foreign rights were sold," said Bandos. "Seeing the TV movie, which aired in December of 2008 on CBS, was amazing."

Bandos added that Brad, and Lisa Wysocky, his co-author, contributed to that success by:

- always responding immediately to any query sent them
- being willing to do anything they could to help promote the book
- sending leads to media that Bandos might not have thought to contact
- giving interviews that impressed the media and the public
- supplying Bandos with new ideas and angles she could use in pitches

The movie version of *Front of the Class* has since been nominated for a Faith and Freedom Award by Movieguide.

Obviously, *Front of the Class* benefited from a group effort. Kate Bandos and her team left no stone unturned, the publisher was motivated, Brad and Lisa worked very hard to help spread the word in a professional manner, and we kept abreast of new opportunities for the book. When we were certain the movie deal was going to go through, we knew it was time to sell the trade paperback and foreign rights.

Your story and your book can have the same happy ending. But, as you have seen, it takes a lot of work and a little bit of luck. You now know everything that has to be done to make your book a success. All you have to do is do it.

CHAPTER 17

THE NONFICTION WRITER'S LIFE AND YOU: WHAT'S NEXT?

WHAT DO YOU WANT FROM YOUR WRITING?

Let's step away from your current project for a moment and look at the overall picture of your potential life as a writer. It doesn't matter if that picture includes you as a full-time writer with a consistent income or someone who lives by another profession and writes on a part-time basis. In either case, there is a writer's life for those who attempt to live it. There are also ways to self-test and figure out your ideal pathway, and this is the perfect time to honestly answer the following question in the privacy of your own mind. It will cost less than a therapist's time and may get you to the same place.

The question is: What do you want from your writing? This is no casual question. There is genuine power in the answer. Insecurities are permitted—though not encouraged—but they are absolutely not allowed to take the wheel and drive.

What *do* you want from your writing? It is imperative that the most responsible version of yourself be kept in charge while you formulate your answer. That's because, just like so many of life's irritating little mysteries, the question of what you want from your writing is more complicated than it seems at first. If it really were a simple issue of living off of your mind, your language, and your typing skills, the competitive nature of today's book industry would pale in comparison to the rush of new authors and their book proposals. So, what holds back so many prospective authors from further jamming this overcrowded space?

The answer is that they may feel the desire but do not feel the need. We all come to this table knowing that motivation is the universal fuel of success. Those other would-be competitors simply have other concerns or distractions that prevent them from getting around to writing—or they don't see why anyone should put that much effort into it. We who remain to cast our shadows in the world of books know from personal experience that there is a shared social value available to every author of a newly published book, and while it may hold some passing appeal, let us agree that it hardly qualifies as the motivation to undertake nonfiction in the long form. The hours are too long and the pay too small.

Your own personal involvement and motivation begins with your private hopes for the effects your book will have on your life. There is no guilt involved in this judgment; its purpose is not to find fault with your ambitions, but to understand them. The professional end of the answer may have to do with building an audience for public speaking ventures, classroom or seminar work, or for any other professional consideration.

The personal side of the question taps into a deeper vein of individual issues. It does not matter what they are so much as it matters that they are there. Perhaps you visualize that having a book in the bookstores, maybe even right there in the window where people can see it, will help you overcome personal shyness and social inhibition (in spite of the way these forces helped free up time for writing). Perhaps you seek to justify your advanced education, or compensate for not having one. The issue of motivation also cannot help but be attached to longstanding points of joy and pain that make up your unique experience of what it is to be alive.

Because a person takes up writing does not mean he is of a mind to tackle such introspective goals. There will be writers who are uncomfortable thinking about the question of what it is they want from their writing. When you answer the question of what you want to get out of your writing, you begin to see a more complete picture. You are rewarded by the ability to align your writing energies in the most productive way and get the most out of them.

That means, specifically, that you *consistently* turn out your desired page count (no matter how slowly you pace it) and, more importantly, that you *consistently* write from a deeper level than mere description. You accomplish that by keeping the common human elements between your readership and the subject at the forefront of your work. Since you can never come to know your entire readership, you can deal with them by proxy in the form of your Internal Reader.

YOUR INTERNAL READER

Your Internal Reader is not an editor; it is comprised of that mass of readers whom your book strives to find. Your imaginary Internal Reader can be estimated both logically and intuitively as a representative of the best readers who will see your words. Your Reader must exist as an image of someone whose opinion matters, someone you hope to entertain well enough that they will completely read and reflect upon your work.

The apparent contradiction of finding your Internal Reader within masses of individuals resolves when you consider that no matter how diverse your readership is, there are common elements among all your readers. These elements are things that cause each of them to resonate with ideas or verbal images that you have wrestled onto the page.

It is now time to clear the room of insecurity by clarifying your image of your specific Reader. To do this, ignore physical description and market terminology; instead imagine that your personal Reader is someone you like, and someone who likes your work.

Flush all the nags and drill sergeant types out of this room. Tell them to go down the hall and apply for the "Internal Editor" position, which we will encounter next. Check your Reader for any trace of the crabby old teacher who made you feel foolish in front of the class. Twist her arm up high behind her back and force-walk her out the service exit.

Any authority figure who has ever cast aspersion onto your writing is also banished. Cleanse your mental room of all negative figures, of those who are repeating insults and draining your confidence. The goal is to avoid allowing even the smallest presence of a sneering comment, dismissive memory, or personal image to play in the back of your mind. They will give defensive or reactive tones to your narrative that you do not need. They are word static. Instead, reserve the space for a genuine friend: your Internal Reader.

Your Reader is the one person it is safe to address within your mind while you sketch out your ideas and shape the words. Your process of consciously creating this Reader will affect the way that you compose every sentence. Therefore, even when you are making a point that requires references to very dark things or which requires you to describe actions of some foul sort, you are telling these things to someone whose thoughts, feelings, and reactions matter to you: your Reader.

MOTIVATION

Motivation applies to the driving force behind the creation of your finished work. Surface motivations (money, fame, fun) do not count. Without the surface lures as distractions, a much clearer look is available to reveal what drives the writing of your book. This question is asked of you with all due respect to the pain that the answers may reveal. Old hurts or resentments or the trauma of betrayal: any or all of them can appear when you dare to take a peek into the motive. Part of the reason some of your ideas are so powerful is that they gain power by resonating with specific issues within yourself. They also resonate with similar issues or forces within your audience.

When you zero in on the best stuff, your natural anxiety at the novelty of that state may make you want to jump onto the phone to talk to somebody or to rush to the nearest movie screen for escape. You may crave chocolate.

These indicators are as good as a compass needle in showing that you are onto something. They guide your next steps in the writing life by keeping you connected to the emotions and ideas that move your story.

HOT TIP!

Your degree of motivation will be revealed in the frequency of your work sessions and the honesty of your voice.

WRITERS WRITE

This troubling phrase has been around for decades, at least, possibly for much longer. They may have had something like it in Sanskrit. It is a whiplash of simple truth: "Writers write." We approach it with offerings of beautiful excuses, lips trembling with sadness and pain while we explain our inability get any writing done. But we are writers nevertheless, are we not? We must be. "We are if we say we are!" we cry. Aren't we?

And yet there sits the old adage like a giant jade Buddha, perpetually serene, unmoved. "Writers write," it almost smiles.

Yes, writers write, and so does the competition. Competition? You want to talk about competition? What can be done about such people? Put them in prison cells, they will scratch on the stone walls with rocks.

WHEN YOU NEED TO SET YOUR WRITING ASIDE

Writers are out there—right at this very instant—and they are writing away. You can almost hear the clicking of the keyboards, the scratches of the pencils and pens across a page. Of course nobody understands how difficult it is for you or how hard you try. If you are like the vast mass of humanity, then you have already known plenty of difficulty in your life. Some of your travails were visited upon you like bad weather. Some were things that you visited upon yourself.

It makes no difference. The lingering question will always be the same for those who are convinced they have some serious writing to do: Are you prepared to power through whatever resistance to your writing life the rest of your life presents?

If you are not able to do that, then the solution is to consciously and deliberately set your writing aside on a temporary basis (you may even want to give it a specific time estimate) and then go deal with whatever problems are holding you back. There is no shame in finding yourself too overwhelmed by daily life to get a decent page count going. The only real shame is in having something worthy to say but failing to get the rest of your life in order so that you can take the time to say it.

It may be at this juncture where you discover that you are not all that passionate about writing in the first place. You may be good or you may be brilliant at any number of other things, but perhaps not this. Where's the shame in that? If it turns out that you are not a writer, peace be unto you and thank you kindly for reading this book.

However—if you are a writer, then the moment that you encounter a situation that requires you to set your writing aside, you will automatically begin to arrange your life so that you can return to your writing within a reasonably short length of time. It is helpful when others encourage you, but the fact is that you are going to do it whether you get any support or not. You will do it because you are a writer, and writers write. The question, then, is who can stop you? Note that the question is *not* "who is going to present an obstacle?" Everything is an obstacle. It is about priorities. Who is going to stop you? Nobody can stop you from writing except you.

Even though the circumstances of your life may temporarily overwhelm you, there is not a soul in the world who can stop you from organizing that same life with all due speed, so that you can get back to the process of putting it down on the page. This book began with a simple question: "How badly do you want it?" The question was directed at whatever your writing project may be, but consider what happens when you apply the same words to the living of the writer's life. How badly do you want it?

THE QUITTING FACTOR

Anyone who aspires to live the writer's life must eventually face a monstrous truth: *There are people out there who will actually do this, whether I do it or not.*

It hurts, but it is true. Every writer who succeeds at reaching an audience will have already faced the same choice that faces you: whether to quit or push through to the finish. Not a single quitter will be among the folks at the finish line. There are still readers out there ready to read your book, or someone else's. The tough economic times, the other media distractions, the distractions in your life—they will all still be there. They are only excuses not to finish the journey. Only those who persevere, only the ones who truly need to write will be there to see the end. Are you one of them?

WHAT YOUR BOOK CAN DO FOR YOU

You will have to gauge whether your book can provide you with a livelihood. Consider the short term, the long term, whether it's a breakaway hit or the beginning of a series, or whether you can benefit through ancillary income from book-related appearances. The answer may not be evident right away, so don't rush into anything.

If you have another line of work that you don't plan to leave in the near future, then the question becomes one of whether or not this book can increase your professional standing in a way that will produce secondary opportunities in your field. If you are teaching at the university level, can this book keep you employed, or line you up for tenure? If you are employed in the corporate sector, can this book raise your professional viability—whether or not its topic has anything to do with your job function?

A good portion of these answers lies in how much time, energy, and expense you will invest in promoting your book and seeing to it that as many people as possible are aware that it exists. The authority of a major publisher's name does little for a book if nobody knows it's there. Such forlorn tomes are the ones that wind up selling three for a dollar at garage sales, or propping up the short leg on dorm room furniture.

The Internet has made it attractive to the intrepid writer to kick back and trust in (insert one: God; Fate; Karma; The Cosmos; the law of probability; random chance) to see that the light of their brilliance summons the reading public. You could gamble that you will somehow catch a wave of public fancy and get your fifteen seconds of fame. Why not? Such things happen, and could happen to you.

Then again, it's always one out of millions, and will again be one out of millions tomorrow. No one has ever shown reliable skill at predicting such strikes of fortune. The formula for success changes in every instance according to forces so subtle as to make consequences appear random.

In the book world, though, many of the forces that are at play are often in full view and subject to the determination of those authors who have decided to do it like they mean it.

From the vantage point of those who work within the publishing world, it appears that authors who have a comprehensive idea of how their books fit into their lives or career goals are the ones who derive the most satisfaction from the publishing event and its aftermath. This does not guarantee success but it puts you firmly on the road to it.

FINDING THE REALITY OF YOUR WRITER'S LIFE

The question of how to find the reality of your writer's life brings us full circle to the opening question: *What do you want from your writing?* What do you genuinely want from this book that you are creating? Will your writing validate you in the eyes of others, or of some specific other? Is that it? It is not an unworthy goal; what matters is that you have a clear and conscious picture of what it is you want from your writing—both from the force of the work itself and from its impact upon a readership.

Aside from issues of market visibility, ask yourself whether you want your writing to cause people to be more interested in you—or do you prefer to remain anonymous? If the public does take an interest in you, will that be something you can enjoy, or will it be a source of worrisome interaction with strangers? The answers to these questions pertain directly to the writer's life and to you because they allow you a taste of the future, to cast ahead and see if it feels like home.

Visualize the answer in specifics. Don't settle for easy generalizations; the answer to this question is more than the feeling that if you do a certain thing, life will improve.

Do you see yourself as a writer—as a published author—to the point that you can imagine enjoying the company of other authors at a book event? An integral part of the writer's life is to attend every reasonable book promotion opportunity you can. This is especially true if you are the sort of writer who is not inhibited about speaking in public. You don't need to be the Toastmaster General, but the savvy writer will never forget that no matter your topic, you may find yourself needing to make intelligent conversation with a particle physicist, an ancient historian, a political outcast, or a newly sort-of-sober celebrity. Is this something you are prepared to do with some measure of grace? All of it counts toward giving your book the best chance it can possibly have to breathe life in the world and to find a significant readership.

The primary test as to whether or not you are doing it like you mean it when it comes to living the writer's life is that eternal, infernal question: Are you writing? The damn thing never goes away. Well, are you?

Writers write.

HOT TIP!

Many of your competitors will choke at this point.

MANAGING YOUR INTERNAL EDITOR

"Writer's block" is that familiar catchall phrase for "I'm not writing." It is a condition that takes truckloads of blame for what can truthfully be explained best as laziness or fear.

Overcoming Writer's Laziness

Laziness is a perfectly understandable reaction when it comes to writing in the long form. After all, the sustained level of concentration required for the job is not something everyone can achieve. There are times when someone who feels compelled to write a book will falter once the true nature of the work becomes clear. However, unless laziness in general is an ingrained habit—which would make the choice to write a book puzzling—then such laziness as may be focused upon your writing process is a message from the deep and primal part of your brain reminding you that you don't feel like it.

So who is holding the gun to your head? Quit. Sure, why not? Plenty of people quit. Except that this doesn't describe you, of course, and we feel confident of that when it comes to you. How can we know such an intimate thing about you? Easy: We have already noted that people who take a lot of "incompletes" in life dropped out of reading this book a long time before they would have made it to this page, so we can gossip about them all we want.

Every Writer's Fear

Fear may be the greatest obstacle to the creative writing process, and although nonfiction is structured more rigidly than fiction, a good non-fiction book will require as much creativity as a novel. Fear is the great destroyer rattling the gates of every intention to write. Fear is what remains when your Internal Editor expands its role from merely keeping an eye over your shoulder and nudging you away from unfortunate choices, and instead progresses to challenging every concept, every thought, every turn of phrase that you try to deploy. It sounds something like this:

"You're not going to write *that*, are you?"

Which is about all it takes to sink the blade to the handle. You know. We all know.

One way to combat this fear is to employ the Full Permission aspect of the Two (2) Page Rule (see chapter 15). That will get the words flowing.

THE BEST RESULT FOR YOUR BOOK—AND FOR YOU

Well, well—look at you, all dressed up for success. You have pounded all of the negative indicators into submission with your sustained creative will. You have reduced the odds caused by the sheer numbers of your competition down to harmless threats. You have dispatched those threats with style, snatching up success the way a Zen master plucks a fly from the air.

Summing up: This time the moment really is all about you, kid! So smile like a winner, because nobody gets to this place by accident.

Now, while we go on to consider what the best result for your book might be, let's once again dismiss the first-level items that can be fairly assumed: a shot on *Oprah*, a fabulous *New York Times* review, a burst of public interest, a sharp spike in sales.

Really? You'd like those things? Quick, somebody write that down.

Remember that your book has a purpose beyond its function in the marketplace. Why was your book written the way it was? Consider the book as a tool, and visualize what it is supposed to do once it is in a reader's hands. That image and the reality it represents are the end results of this long process. It is why you rolled that boulder up the mountain. Your particular goal may be as simple as the desire to entertain with a compelling story, or the book may be written to teach or instruct others in something. And just as you use the idea of your Internal Reader to help focus your narrative during the writing of the book, you can now employ your image of your Reader in the role of a customer who is discovering your book.

Consciously ask the question and form an answer clear enough that you could put it into words that a stranger would understand—what effect is your book having upon that person when he opens it and begins to read?

This keeps the image clear in your mind during and after the launch of your book. It is how you take on a state of preparedness for any promotional opportunity. Even if you should find yourself speaking in any sort of situation that you did not see coming, you will still be able to be your ideal self, that is, speaking clearly to your Reader from within the writer's life.

Then, no matter what you say, you will automatically frame it toward this imaginary Reader in representing your general readership. This is how you keep your message in focus and convey the maximum clarity of communication at any promotional opportunity that you encounter, even when it is completely spontaneous. It plays directly into the ongoing process of living the writer's life. Here is where you piece together your answer to the question of what's next for you as a writer.

MOVING FORWARD: DETERMINING YOUR NEXT STEP

While the immediate purpose of any promotion is to sell that particular book, each one of your promotional opportunities for your book helps to build the overall conditions that can service your desire to continue writing. There is one question that only you can answer, and only after you have been through the experience once already: *Is the experience of authoring and promoting a book something you want to repeat?* If so, this is the way.

Since writers write, one can only live the writer's life by continuing to write. If and when you continue writing, the writing itself will focus your energy. During times when you must be away from your writing to tend to life's demands, it will always make sense to keep your goals for your book and for your writing life right up there at the top of your conscious priority list. If you find yourself daydreaming a book idea while you are stuck in traffic, this is a very good sign that your next writing project is already taking form within you. In that way you will create this writer's life by living as close to the writer's life that you are able.

Some say fake it until you make it. We say do it like you mean it. The best secrets are simple. This one is a variation on an often-heard phrase: *"Write. Rinse. Repeat."*

Write your Two (2) Page Rule minimum at each writing session; *rinse* life's distractions whenever necessary by rereading and reworking the passage leading up to your current position; and *repeat* this process every time you write, whenever that may be. The *write* portion is the last thing that you do each time. You begin your session with the *rinse* process by clearing the day from your mind while you are rereading and rewording the last session's work. If you can jump right into the writing process without going over the product of your last session, then skip the rinse and go right to work. Still, Two (2) Pages every time, rock bottom. If you cannot find two hours a week to work on a book then you are too busy to engage in the project.

If you are writing at least those two hours, then you must produce two pages of usable work every time. Anytime that you cannot produce two pages in two hours, you are not writing. If you are not writing, you are not a writer. If you are not a writer, no problem! Why do this to yourself? No one can be a writer just by claiming to be one. You can only be a writer if you actually write.

Every rationale for not writing comes back to that same infuriating truth. Writers write.

Take all the breaks that you need. Life calls. Life is always calling. Do what you need to do. Then reorder your life so that you can return to writing once again.

That's it then. Your journey to this point has been long, but since you willed yourself into the position to be among the few who get this far, the chances are good that the journey for you is longer still—and that you will make that journey as a writer, an author.

So hit the showers. There, of course, you will commence with your writing, your rinsing, and of course your repeating, on a session-by-session basis until your Internal Reader is satisfied. As long as you are doing that, you are living the writer's life. You deserve it as much as you want it.

RESOURCES

BUILDING YOUR PLATFORM

- *The Author's Guide to Building an Online Platform: Leveraging the Internet to Sell More Books* by Stephanie Chandler (Quill Driver Books, 2008)

- *Get Known Before the Book Deal: Use Your Personal Strengths to Grow an Author Platform* by Christina Katz (Writer's Digest Books, 2008)

FINDING AN AGENT

- *How to Be a Literary Agent: An Introductory Guide to Literary Representation* by Richard Mariotti and Bruce Fife (Piccadilly Books, 2008)

- *How to Be Your Own Literary Agent: An Insider's Guide to Getting Your Book Published* by Richard Curtis (Houghton Mifflin, 2003)

- *How to Get a Literary Agent* by Michael Larsen (Sourcebooks, Inc., 2006)

- *Jeff Herman's Guide to Book Publishers, Editors & Literary Agents* by Jeff Herman (Three Dog Press, annual)

- *Writer's Market* edited by Robert Lee Brewer (Writer's Digest Books, annual)

FREELANCE WRITING

- *The ASJA Guide to Freelance Writing: A Professional Guide to the Business, for Nonfiction Writers of All Experience Levels* edited by Timothy Harper (St. Martin's Griffin, 2003)

- *Getting Started as a Freelance Writer* by Robert W. Bly (Sentient Publications, 2008)

- *Make a Real Living as a Freelance Writer: How to Win Top Writing Assignments* by Jenna Glatzer (Nomad Press, 2004)

GENERAL INFORMATION FOR NONFICTION WRITERS

- *265 Troubleshooting Strategies for Writing Nonfiction* by Barbara Fine Clouse (McGraw-Hill, 2005)

- *The Art of Nonfiction: A Guide for Writers and Readers* by Ayn Rand (Plume, 2001)

- *Becoming a Writer* by Dorothea Brande (Mariner Books, 1981)

- *Damn! Why Didn't I Write That?: How Ordinary People Are Raking in $100,000.00 or More Writing Nonfiction Books & How You Can Too!* by Mark McCutcheon (Quill Driver Books, 2006)

- *Fact and Artifact: Writing Nonfiction* by Lynn Z. Bloom (Prentice Hall, 1993)

- *Follow the Story: How to Write Successful Nonfiction* by James B. Stewart (Simon & Schuster, 1998)

- *How to Write a Nonfiction Book in 60 Days* by Paul Lima (Five Rivers Chapmanry, 2009)

- *How to Write It: A Complete Guide to Everything You'll Ever Write* by Sandra E. Lamb (Ten Speed Press, 2006)

- *Keep It Real: Everything You Need to Know About Researching and Writing Creative Nonfiction* edited by Lee Gutkind (W.W. Norton & Co., 2008)

- *Line by Line: How to Improve Your Own Writing* by Claire Kehrwald Cook (Houghton Mifflin, 1985)

- *Mastering the Business of Writing* by Richard Curtis (Allworth Press, 1996)

- *The Observation Deck: A Tool Kit for Writers* by Naomi Epel (Chronicle Books, 1998)

- *On Writing Well* by William Zinsser (HarperCollins, 2006)

- *Stein on Writing: A Master Editor of Some of the Most Successful Writers of Our Century Shares His Craft, Techniques, and Strategies* by Sol Stein (St. Martin's Griffin, 2000)

- *Tell It Slant: Writing and Shaping Creative Nonfiction* by Brenda Miller and Suzanne Paola (McGraw-Hill, 2004)

- *The Writer's Block: 786 Ideas to Jump-Start Your Imagination* by Jason Rekulak (Running Press, 2001)

- *A Writer's Guide to Nonfiction* by Elizabeth Lyon (Perigee Trade, 2003)

- *Writing Creative Nonfiction: Fiction Techniques for Crafting Great Nonfiction* by Theodore A. Rees Cheney (Ten Speed Press, 2001)

- *Writing Nonfiction: Turning Thoughts Into Books* by Dan Poynter (Para Publishing, 2000)

- *Writing the Nonfiction Book* by Eva Shaw (Loveland Press, 1999)

PUBLIC RELATIONS

- *The Complete Guide to Book Publicity* by Jodee Blanco (Allworth Press, 2004)

- *Plug Your Book! Online Book Marketing for Authors, Book Publicity Through Social Networking* by Steve Weber (Weber Books, 2007)

- *Publicize Your Book: An Insider's Guide to Getting Your Book the Attention It Deserves* by Jacqueline Deval (Perigree Trade, 2008)

- *Red Hot Internet Publicity: An Insider's Guide to Promoting Your Book on the Internet* by Penny C. Sansevieri (Morgan James Publishing, 2007)

- *The Savvy Author's Guide to Book Publicity* by Lissa Warren (Carroll & Graf, 2004)

SELF-PUBLISHING RESOURCES

- AuthorHouse: www.authorhouse.com
- BookSurge: www.booksurge.com
- CreateSpace: www.createspace.com
- iUniverse: www.iuniverse.com

- Lightning Source: www.lightningsource.com

- Lulu: www.lulu.com

- Pen & Publish: www.penandpublish.com

- Xlibris: www2.xlibris.com

SELLING YOUR NONFICTION BOOK

- *The Art of Creative Nonfiction: Writing and Selling the Literature of Reality* by Lee Gutkind (Wiley, 1997)

- *The Complete Idiot's Guide to Getting Published* by Sheree Bykofsky and Jennifer Basye Sander (Alpha, 2006)

- *How to Get Happily Published* by Judith Appelbaum (Collins, 1998)

- *How to Publish Your Nonfiction Book: A Complete Guide to Making the Right Publisher Say Yes* by Rudy Shur (Square One Publishers, 2001)

- *How to Sell, Then Write Your Nonfiction Book* by Blythe Camenson (McGraw-Hill, 2002)

- *How to Write & Sell Your First Nonfiction Book* by Oscar Collier with Frances Spatz Leighton (St. Martin's Press, 1994)

- *The Shortest Distance Between You and a Published Book* by Susan Page (Broadway Books, 1997)

WEBSITES OF INTEREST

- About Freelance Writing: www.aboutfreelancewriting.com
Resources to help writers hone their skills, plus listings to find paying writing gigs

- Agent Query: www.agentquery.com

  Learn about and find agents

- Book Industry Study Group (BISG): www.bisg.org

  In-depth information about the supply and manufacturing sides of the book world

- firstwriter.com: www.firstwriter.com

  Writer resources and information for authors

- FundsforWriters: www.fundsforwriters.com

  A site and newsletter with writer tips and information on writing jobs, grants, publishers, etc.

- The Learning Annex: www.learningannex.com

  For possible teaching opportunities

- MediaBistro.com: www.mediabistro.com

  Daily news and commentary on the book business

- Preditors & Editors: www.anotherealm.com/prededitors

  Links to and comments about agents and editors

- Publishers Marketplace: www.publishersmarketplace.com

  Search listings for industry insiders, including agents and editors

- QueryTracker.net: www.querytracker.net

  Searchable online database of agents

- Writer's Digest: www.writersdigest.com

  Wonderful writer's resource including a list of 101 best sites for writers

WRITING ACADEMIC NONFICTION

- *Getting It Published: A Guide for Scholars and Anyone Else Serious About Serious Books* by William Germano (University of Chicago Press, 2008)

- *Handbook for Academic Authors* by Beth Luey (Cambridge University Press, 2002)

- *How to Write a Lot: A Practical Guide to Productive Academic Writing* by Paul Silvia (American Psychological Association, 2007)

- *Thinking Like Your Editor: How to Write Great Serious Nonfiction—and Get It Published* by Susan Rabiner and Alfred Fortunato (W.W. Norton & Co., 2003)

WRITING ASSOCIATIONS

- American Book Producers Association (ABPA) www.abpaonline.org

- American Booksellers Association (ABA) www.bookweb.org

- American Library Association (ALA) www.ala.org

- The Association of American Publishers (AAP) www.publishers.org

- Association of American University Presses (AAUP) www.aaupnet.org

- The Association of Authors' Representatives, Inc. (AAR) www.aar-online.org

- Canadian Booksellers Association (CBA)
  www.cbabook.org

- Christian Booksellers Association (CBA) also The Association
  for Christian Retail
  www.cbaonline.org

- Council of Literary Magazines and Presses (CLMP)
  www.clmp.org

- Evangelical Christian Publishers Association (ECPA)
  www.ecpa.org

- Independent Book Publishers Association (IBPA)
  www.ibpa-online.org

- Publishers Association of the West (PubWest)
  www.pubwest.org

WRITING EVENTS

- BookExpo America (BEA): www.bookexpoamerica.com
  The largest book trade show in the United States

- The Center for the Book: http://loc.gov/loc/cfbook/bookfair.html
  A Library of Congress site listing most of the book fairs and festivals in the country

WRITING MEMOIRS

- *Courage & Craft: Writing Your Life Into Story* by Barbara Abercrombie (New World Library, 2007)

- *Old Friend From Far Away: The Practice of Writing Memoir* by Natalie Goldberg (Free Press, 2008)

- *Shimmering Images: A Handy Little Guide to Writing Memoir* by Lisa Dale Norton (St. Martin's Griffin, 2008)

- *Writing the Memoir: From Truth to Art* by Judith Barrington (The Eighth Mountain Press, 2002)

- *Your Life as Story* by Tristine Rainer (Tarcher, 1998)

WRITING NONFICTION BOOK PROPOSALS

- *Author 101: Bestselling Book Proposals* by Rick Frishman and Robyn Freedman Spizman (Adams Media, 2005)

- *Book Proposals That Sell: 21 Secrets to Speed Your Success* by W. Terry Whalin (Write Now!, 2005)

- *The Fast-Track Course on How to Write a Nonfiction Book Proposal* by Stephen Blake Mettee (Quill Driver Books, 2008)

- *Nonfiction Book Proposals Anybody Can Write* by Elizabeth Lyon (Perigee Trade, 2002)

- *Write the Perfect Book Proposal: 10 That Sold and Why* by Jeff Herman and Deborah Levine Herman (Wiley, 2001)

WRITING NONFICTION: OTHER CATEGORIES

- *The Elements of Narrative Nonfiction: How to Write and Sell the Novel of True Events* by Peter Rubie (Quill Driver Books, 2008)

- *Telling the Story: How to Write and Sell Narrative Nonfiction* by Peter Rubie (Collins, 2003)

- *Travel Writing: See the World. Sell the Story.* by L. Peat O'Neil (Writer's Digest Books, 2005)

- *Writing Successful Self-Help & How-To Books* by Jean Marie Stine (Wiley, 1997)

WRITING QUERIES

- *How to Write Attention-Grabbing Query & Cover Letters* by John Wood (Writer's Digest Books, 2000)

- *The Writer's Digest Guide to Query Letters* by Wendy Burt-Thomas (Writer's Digest Books, 2008)

INDEX

PUBLISH YOUR NONFICTION BOOK